"Jennifer has done one hellava job bringing teachers along in our understanding of teaching writing rhetorically instead of grammatically. *Writing Rhetorically* is rich with guiding examples, templates, and a rhetorical voice that is warm and encouraging, though respectfully unrelenting on the best practices for teaching writing. This pedagogy not only helps student agency (I love this) but buttresses their authority and authenticity. Three things traditional approaches flatten and try to root out, wittingly or unwittingly."

—Vershawn Ashanti Young, co-author of *Other People's English*.

"This well-written book is a must-read for ELA teachers, curriculum specialists and all others interested in helping students think and write more fully and deeply. It offers a thorough discussion of the critical aspects of rhetorical teaching, and is packed with examples teachers can easily use and adapt to their own class needs. In addition to being read by individual and groups of teachers, it would make an important addition to the reading lists of teacher preparation and professional development courses."

—Judith Langer, the Vincent O'Leary Distinguished Professor Emeritus at the University of Albany, SUNY, and the co-author of *Writing Instruction That Works*.

"This is a book I wish I had read at the start of my career. Jennifer shares practices and insights from her own teaching journey that help us feel as though we are part of a team, working together, helping students develop as writers. I have marked so many pages that my copy looks like an advertisement for sticky notes!"

—Deborah Dean, author of *Strategic Writing*, Second Edition.

"If you are convinced that another dimension exists where students are motivated to maximize the communication power of their writing, then this book is for you. It offers a wide array of vital insights for helping your students write reflectively in order to improve their lives and the world."

—Jeff Zwiers, author of *Next Steps with Academic Conversations*.

"Writing is a process of continuous decision making and problem solving. Writers decide what to say and how to say it. They arrange the writing environment, manage the writing process, orchestrate their thinking and behavior, and silently converse with their intended audience. To learn how to do all of these things effectively, students need skillful guidance and the opportunity to learn by doing. This book provides practical advice and suggestions for helping your students become independent, self-directed, and thoughtful writers. What a gift."

—Steve Graham, Regents and Warner Professor at Arizona State University ⁀-editor of *Best Practices in Writing Instruction*, Third Edition.

"While reading Fletcher's deftly written book, I constantly found myself not only reflecting on practices that I hadn't thought about in a while but using her plentiful examples to create new writing units and projects that were purposely designed to help my students use rhetorical thinking to be their best writing selves. I highly recommend it!"

—Matthew Kay, author of *Not Light, But Fire*.

"What if our students saw writing as the communicative dance that it is—as an opportunity for creativity, problem-solving, growth, and connection? That is the vision that Jennifer Fletcher pursues. This book comes from the heart of a teacher and the mind of a master. A must-read for any teacher of writing."

—Dave Stuart, Jr., author of *These 6 Things*.

"In this thoughtful and thought-provoking book, Jennifer Fletcher offers a clear theoretical framework and a rich array of strategies and activities to develop students' rhetorical agency, dispositions, and habits of mind, empowering them to become independent problem solvers who can transfer learning to new situations. This book will enhance and enrich the instructional repertoires of both secondary and college writing teachers."

—Carol Booth Olson, author of *The Reading/Writing Connection*
and *Helping English Learners to Write*.

"Jennifer Fletcher demystifies the teaching and learning of something that our contemporary context has made at once both frightening and necessary: rhetoric. This text takes teachers and students well-beyond what many have come to see as the process of writing for writing's sake and into the worlds and contexts of readers."

—Brandon Abdon, co-author of *Advanced Placement
English Language and Composition*.

"Jennifer Fletcher has helped answer the two most important questions that plague writing teachers: *why* do we teach the research paper? And *how* should I teach the research process? Every teacher who hopes to create independent writers should read this book."

—Tanya Baker, Director of National Programs for the National Writing Project.

"Jennifer Fletcher expresses faith in young people's ability to engage in productive struggle as they learn to craft thoughtful, passionate arguments. *Writing Rhetorically* will be a constant companion for writing teachers seeking to support students as they become informed, engaged, and openminded contributors to democratic discourse."

—Linda Friedrich, Director of Literacy, WestEd.

Writing Rhetorically

Writing Rhetorically

Fostering Responsive Thinkers and Communicators

Jennifer Fletcher
Foreword by Jim Burke

STENHOUSE PUBLISHERS
PORTSMOUTH, NEW HAMPSHIRE

Stenhouse Publishers
www.stenhouse.com

Credits

p. 38 Figure 2.10 Zaretta Hammond, *Culturally Responsive Teaching and the Brain*, Figure 1.1. Copyright © 2014 by Corwin. Reprinted by permission of SAGE Publications, Inc.

p. 49 CSU Expository Reading and Writing Curriculum, Chapter 2, page 28 activities: "Assignment Template Overview" from *The Expository Reading and Writing Curriculum* © California State University. Used with permission.

p. 55 Figure 3.1 From *Words, Words, Words: Teaching Vocabulary in Grades 4–12* by Janet Allen, copyright © 1998, reproduced with permission of Stenhouse Publishers. www.stenhouse.com

p. 85 Figure 4.1 (left) Photograph supplied by Deborah Dean. Used with permission.

p. 85 Figure 4.1 (center) Photograph supplied by April Baker-Bell. Used with permission.

p. 85 Figure 4.1 (right) Photograph supplied by Vershawn Ashanti Young. Used with permission.

p. 90 Chapter 4: "Who's a Nerd Anyway": From *The New York Times*. © 2007 The New York Times Company. All rights reserved. Used under license.

p. 93 Figure 4.5 Licensed By: Warner Bros. Entertainment Inc. All Rights Reserved.

p. 108 Figure 4.8 "Rhetorical Grammar" © 2014 California State University. Used with permission.

p. 111 Figure 4.11 Used with permission from the Modern Language Association of America (www.mla.org).

p. 138 Figure 5.11 Interior Art from *The Important Book* by Margaret Wise Brown. Illustrated by: Leonard Weisgard. Text copyright © 1949 By Margaret Wise Brown. Illustrations by Leonard Weisgard. Used by permission of HarperCollins Publishers.

p. 154 Figure 6.2 (bottom) *The Snow Leopard* by Peter Matthiessen © 1996 Penguin Random House. Used with permission.

p. 192 Figure 7.7a © TfL from the London Transport Museum collection

(Credits continue on p. viii)

Library of Congress Cataloging-in-Publication Data

Names: Fletcher, Jennifer, author.
Title: Writing rhetorically : fostering responsive thinkers and communicators / Jennifer Fletcher.
Description: Portsmouth, New Hampshire : Stenhouse Publishers, 2021. |
   Includes bibliographical references and index.
Identifiers: LCCN 2020055030 (print) | LCCN 2020055031 (ebook) |
   ISBN 9781625313881 (paperback) | ISBN 9781625313898 (ebook)
Subjects: LCSH: English language—Composition and exercises—Study and teaching (Middle school) |
   English language—Composition and exercises—Study and teaching (Secondary) |
   Composition (Language arts)—Study and teaching (Middle school) |
   Composition (Language arts)—Study and teaching (Secondary)
Classification: LCC LB1631 .F629 2021 (print) | LCC LB1631 (ebook) | DDC 808/.0420712—dc23
LC record available at https://lccn.loc.gov/2020055030
LC ebook record available at https://lccn.loc.gov/2020055031

Cover design, interior design, and typesetting by Progressive Publishing Services

Printed in the United States of America

This book is printed on paper certified by third-party standards for sustainably managed forestry.

26 25 24 23 22 21   4371   9 8 7 6 5 4 3 2 1

To Dryden and Ellerie, with all my love

CONTENTS

Foreword
Jim Burke

Every book makes a promise to its readers. How well it keeps that promise determines the book's value to us as readers and, in the case of a professional book, how likely we are to recommend it to other teachers. Jennifer Fletcher's *Writing Rhetorically* delivers on a very important promise: to help us become excellent writing teachers so that we can say about our students, as Jennifer does about her own, that "they carry away with them writing skills and knowledge that will enable them to go into any situation, analyze the situation, and produce a text that works for that situation, while internalizing the habits of mind that support effective and ethical communication."

She accomplishes these results by using the teaching techniques that she has developed over the years as not only a high school English teacher, but one of the leaders of California's Expository Reading and Writing Curriculum (ERWC), an ambitious program designed to prepare students for college-level reading and writing while still in high school. Finally, as Jennifer routinely speaks here of the importance of transferring knowledge from one domain to another, from past to present units of instruction, this book refers to but adds substantively to the ideas that she explored in her previous books, *Teaching Arguments* and *Teaching Literature Rhetorically*, both of which should be required reading for any teacher in middle and high school whose goal is to improve students' ability to read, write, and think rhetorically. In all her work, Jennifer Fletcher's primary goal is to develop in teachers a firm grasp of key rhetorical elements and strategies that we can teach to all our students after gaining a better grasp of them ourselves.

One of the questions we routinely ask of professional authors when we read their books is, *Yes, but what does that LOOK like to teach it?* Throughout *Writing Rhetorically*, Jennifer Fletcher takes ideas we have learned about—rhetorical sensitivity, teaching for transfer, metacognition—and shows us what it looks like to teach those concepts and skills in the context of meaningful units deliberately designed to both engage and instruct students. She does this by including in this book a rich array of sample assignments with corresponding student examples that allow us to see *what* she does and *how* she does it; she consistently follows through to explain *why* she does what she does. Whenever she examines an assignment or teaching technique through these examples, she addresses the fundamental importance of equity and access for all students, whether she is talking about middle and high school or college students. Central to her point throughout the book is the idea that all students can learn and do the many different types of rhetorical thinking she examines here.

If I were designing a course to prepare new teachers to teach academic reading and writing, something we all need to keep improving on no matter how long we have taught, I would make this book the centerpiece of that course. What Jennifer Fletcher shows us in each chapter is that reading and writing can and should be integrated in meaningful and sustainable ways by allowing students to investigate those topics important to them whenever possible. Through such inquiry-focused assignments, Fletcher meets students where they are as readers, writers, and thinkers—then guides them (and us!) so that when they enter college, they will be prepared for the demands of those classes whether they are in the English, Social Science, or any other department on campus.

This readiness for the demands of college-level work matters a great deal to me, as it obviously does to Jennifer. As someone who graduated in the bottom 20 percent of my high school class, who was the first in my family to attend college, I knew nothing of the academic literacies and rhetorical moves she teaches her students. What a difference it would have made for me to have Jennifer Fletcher as my teacher in high school or at the local community college where I was placed in a remedial English class and struggled so much that first year with the demands of the assignments I had to write. These days, I find her work and the ideas in this book even more useful and urgent in my own classroom. For I now teach in a "middle college" program on a two-year college campus attended by high school students, some of whom are not much more ready for the demands of college reading and writing than I was at their age. After attending my high school English class, my students run off to their different college classes. In such college classes as Psych 101 or Computer Science 110, my students are expected to make the moves discussed throughout this book. In my students' Psych 101 class, for example, they write papers that require them to classify, compare and contrast, or construct their own argument as to the merits of the theories they study. In Computer Science 110, which I assumed would require little writing from them, students must write a paper the first week in which they compare and contrast the human and computer interface, citing a range of sources whose arguments they must summarize and critique, before advancing and supporting their own.

Many English teachers feel a certain anxiety when they get into the weeds on more demanding and precise concepts and terms, such as those that arise in the study of rhetoric. As any great teacher does, Jennifer Fletcher anticipates these moments and helps teachers understand such key terms as *exigence*, stasis theory, and *kairos* with examples that enable us to immediately see how we can apply those ideas to our own class. I'll be honest, I was reading this manuscript in the month leading up to the new school year, a year still very much in the draft stage for me, as I am new to this program. There were moments when I would jump up to copy a page and make notes on it about how to apply its ideas to my class, only to jump up a moment later when the next page introduced yet other idea, like the doubting game and believing game, which I had not considered bringing into my class. On several occasions, I just stood by the copy machine in my office and read so I could copy and make notes without having to get up so often.

I know in the months ahead I will be a more effective teacher for having read this book. One last thing warrants mention, for it further distinguishes this book and contributes to the pleasure of reading it: Jennifer Fletcher's wit and voice. As she takes you on her own journey from novice to expert teacher, she weaves in poignant and endearing stories about the lessons she learned through "birthday cake fails" and her early days as a serious ballet dancer. But, as with any rhetorically effective writing, she uses these details to make her argument—that we can learn and, through feedback, grow as people or, in the context of her book, as writers and teachers of writing.

A teacher, a writer, a thinker, and a leader within our field, Jennifer Fletcher has become, for me and so many others, both a mentor and a model. In *Writing Rhetorically*, she shows us how to keep the promise we made to ourselves and our students when we began teaching, and when we begin every new year—to give our students the literacy skills they'll need not only to survive in this world, but to thrive.

Acknowledgments

So many people to thank—and for so much! My ERWC family continues to be the heart of this work. My involvement with California State University's Expository Reading and Writing Curriculum (ERWC) has been the most transformative learning experience of my career. These are the folks who taught me what it means to take a rhetorical approach to texts. They make me a better teacher and inspire me to be a better human. Deepest gratitude and much love to Meline Akashian, Adele Arellano, Lisa Benham, Molly Berger, Debra Boggs, Nancy Brynelson, Roberta Ching, Zee Cline, Virginia Crisco, John Edlund, Kim Flachmann, Tony Fong, Nelson Graff, Shirley Hargis, Dutch Henry, Carol Jago, Glen McClish, Mariam Ogle, Anne Porterfield, Debra Robinson, Chris Street, and Norm Unrau. And extra thanks to John and Nancy and to the California State University for permission to include the ERWC Assignment Template Overview and activities from the curriculum in this book.

Deepest appreciation, as well, to my students and colleagues at California State University, Monterey Bay: I learn from you every day. Thank you, Nanda Warren, for allowing me to include your excellent lesson on paraphrase and synthesis in this book.

Megan Kortlandt: You are a brilliant writing teacher. This is a better book because you took the time to read each chapter with such meticulous care. Your feedback was an extraordinary gift.

My teacher role models, Tamara Rodriguez-Kam and Silva Shamassian: You are a continuous source of inspiration.

I am likewise grateful for the new and continued learning I've experienced as a member of the Advisory Board for the WRITE (Writing Research to Improve Teaching and Evaluation) Center for Secondary Students under the directorship of Carol Booth Olson.

Jennifer Benge: Once again, your artwork is everything. What a joy to work with you!

It is hard for me to heave my heart into my mouth, so, Bill Varner, let me just say thank you for all you've done to bring this book to life. I so admire and respect your knowledge of writing and writers. The whole Stenhouse team—Dan Tobin, Shannon St. Peter, Leah Coombs, Jay Kilburn, Faye LaCasse, Jill Backman, Nate Butler, Lisa Sullivan, and Carly Daubach—is superb.

And my family: Dan and Dorothy Kimble; Henry, Coreen, Caitlyn, and Steven Cardenas; and the center of my world, my husband, Ken, and our amazing teenagers, Dryden and Ellerie. Thank you for your support and encouragement. I love you more than words can say.

Understanding Writing as Communication and Problem Solving

I wouldn't be a very good swimming instructor. That signature look of terror and betrayal on a person's face as they struggle to stay afloat would be my undoing. My first impulse would probably be to pull them out of the water, wrap them in a towel, and give them a cookie. I don't like seeing people struggle. "It's OK," I'd probably say. "Just use this kick board. Or the noodle. That looks like fun."

So it's been no small feat for me to finally reach a point in my work as a writing teacher where I don't rush in to solve my students' problems for them. Writing can cause painful feelings of being in-over-our-head and out-of-our-element that don't necessarily go away once we've "learned" to write. I hear this anxiety in my students' voices when they ask me questions about their writing:

"How do I start?"

"What do I say now?"

"Should I just write one paragraph on each source?"

"Is this right?"

"What's my thesis?"

For many years, I'd do my best to answer these questions. I wanted to help. And I had answers (or at least opinions), so I generously dispensed my advice to students, and their writing often improved.

But I noticed that my high school students continued to ask me these same kinds of questions, grade after grade, year after year. And when I started teaching first-year college writing classes, I noticed that students were still asking these questions. They weren't yet practicing rhetorical problem solving—the ability to analyze a communication task and to make their own choices about content and form based on the contingencies of particular rhetorical situations. They were depending on me to tell them what to do and how to do it.

Cultivating Independent Learners Through Rhetorical Thinking

In contrast, students who have learned to think rhetorically about writing can tackle new tasks without extensive scaffolding. They have their own strategies and processes for responding to unfamiliar literacy demands. They can change how they write in response to diverse audiences, purposes, and occasions. Rhetorical problem solvers are independent learners. In *Culturally Responsive Teaching and the Brain*, Zaretta Hammond describes "independent learners" as students who can "size up any task, map out a strategy for completing it and then execute the plan" (2015, 122). These capacities are the goal of equitable writing instruction.

We sometimes teach writing in ways that increase students' dependence on us and delay their growth as problem solvers. To grow as a problem solver, you need extended experience troubleshooting problems. But we often don't let students practice solving rhetorical problems. We tell them their audience (usually us). We choose their genre for them. We give them their purpose. And then we make all the stylistic and organizational choices for them by handing them a paragraph template and list of rules to follow. No wonder, then, that so many new college students want their instructors to just tell them what to do.

This book offers a different approach. When we teach writing rhetorically, we honor and nurture students' rhetorical agency. Instead of telling students what to write, we help them approach writing as communication and problem solving—and we understand that this is challenging intellectual work students will ultimately have to do for themselves.

That doesn't mean that we leave students to sink or swim. Throughout this book, you'll find strategies for engaging and supporting students in the productive struggle that leads to growth and independence.

From Novice to Expert: Writing (and Teaching) Rhetorically

Writing rhetorically, explains composition professor E. Shelley Reid, means paying "attention to the needs of the author and the needs of the reader rather than the needs of the teacher—or the rules in the textbook" (2011, 4). When we write this way, we make moment-by-moment decisions based on our message, audience, purpose, and occasion as we struggle with "the live, negotiated process of writing for real people" (Reid 2011, 4). And, boy, do we struggle.

I always try to remember that my students are progressing on a continuum from novice to expert, and that there are special steps I can take to make sure those learners in the novice range feel fully supported. What novices do as novices is not wrong. It's expected. For example, the National Research Council describes novices as being "more likely [than experts] to approach problems by searching for correct formulas and pat answers that fit their everyday intuitions" (2000, 49). This is certainly what I did as a novice teacher, which is why I took a prescriptive approach to writing instruction. I hadn't yet learned to see the big patterns and ideas in my field, so a set of rules and formulas was a satisfying starting place.

Like those Facebook fails of birthday cakes gone wrong, some of my early attempts to teach writing were well-intentioned mistakes. My biggest concern as a new teacher were all those zeros in my grade book. Many of my sophomores and juniors were in danger of failing my classes, so I tried to find ways to make sure everyone had at least *something* to turn in on the days essays were due. My solution was to do much of the work for my students. I wrote their introductions for them. I wrote their conclusions for them. I wrote their topic sentences. I even picked a selection of quotations for them to use as support. And, of course, I told them their essays should be exactly five paragraphs long. Here's one of my old overhead transparencies for an interpretive essay on the short story "The Monkey's Paw" by W. W. Jacobs.

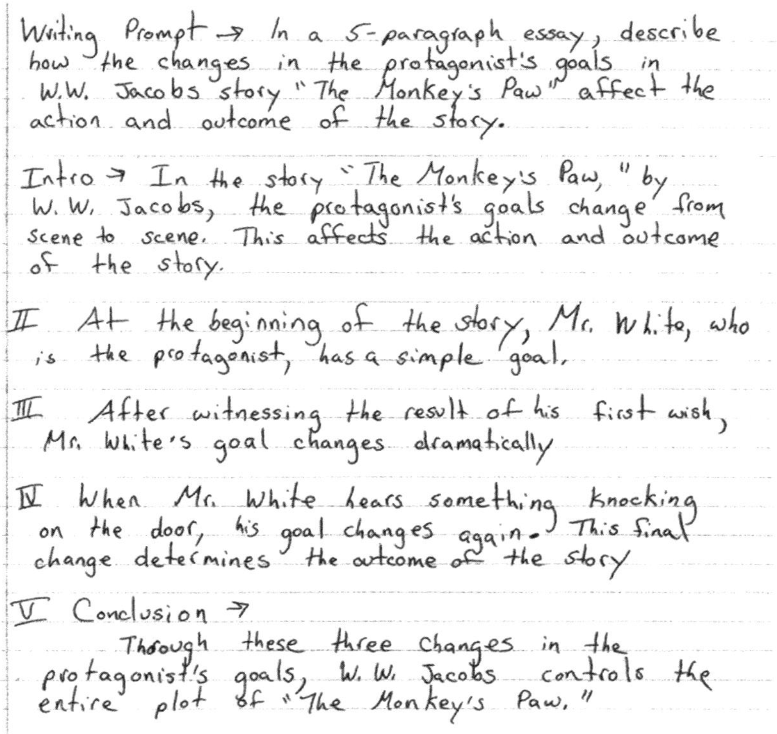

Writing Prompt → In a 5-paragraph essay, describe how the changes in the protagonist's goals in W.W. Jacobs story "The Monkey's Paw" affect the action and outcome of the story.

Intro → In the story "The Monkey's Paw," by W. W. Jacobs, the protagonist's goals change from scene to scene. This affects the action and outcome of the story.

II At the beginning of the story, Mr. White, who is the protagonist, has a simple goal.

III After witnessing the result of his first wish, Mr. White's goal changes dramatically

IV When Mr. White hears something knocking on the door, his goal changes again. This final change determines the outcome of the story

V Conclusion →
    Through these three changes in the protagonist's goals, W. W. Jacobs controls the entire plot of "The Monkey's Paw."

FIGURE I.1

"Just do what I tell you to do, and you'll be fine."

I thought I was providing scaffolding and modeling, but I wasn't allowing students to make any substantive decisions for themselves. The take-away message was that academic writing is a matter of conformity, not creativity and communication. I was teaching for compliance, not teaching for transfer and agency.

I had to learn to trust my students to make their own choices—and their own mistakes. This is the path to expertise, the only way novice writers (and teachers) grow beyond their reliance on rules and formulas. Our students deserve to have teachers who support their full intellectual development, with all its messy growing pains.

> Rhetorician Linda Flower explains that rhetorical problem solving entails a variety of cognitive strategies for "exploring the rhetorical problem, for generating ideas, for adapting to the reader, and for understanding and monitoring one's own writing process" (1989, 13).

The Challenge

I need to be honest here: What I'm asking you to do may actually make your students' writing seem worse for a while. When we give students step-by-step instructions, paragraph formulas, and sentence templates to follow, their writing instantly looks better. Students who were struggling to write anything before are suddenly producing cohesive academic prose. That feels like a win.

But this is kit writing, not rhetorical problem solving. It's like those packaged sets for building bird houses you can buy in craft stores. While some assembly is required, the creative design work has already been done for you. John Warner, author of the popular book *Why They Can't Write: Killing the Five Paragraph Essay and Other Necessities*, says students are underprepared for college writing classes because they've learned to produce "imitations rather than the genuine article" (2018, 7). Formulas replicate the surface features of academic writing but don't allow writers to engage in real composing.

"To write," says Warner, "is to make choices, word by word, sentence by sentence, paragraph by paragraph" (2018, 5). Students don't get better at making choices if all the choices are made for them. We need to move novices past mimicking the forms of academic writing without fully experiencing the intellectual processes that produce those forms in authentic contexts.

Empowering Students to Solve Problems and Make Decisions

A rhetorical mindset helps students see themselves as independent writers who are capable of figuring out how to write well in new situations. This is now a common scenario in my teaching life: A student says, "I don't know how to do this." And then I say, "I bet you'll figure it out."

I've had to learn I'm not being mean when I say this. If I give students a nudge toward independence and then sit back and wait, chances are they try something that works. I don't abandon them—I'm their teacher, after all—but I do give them room to think, write, and experiment. I'm there as a sounding board as soon as they have an idea to test. Once students get comfortable with this kind of struggle, I find that letting them work through their own problem-solving process is actually less frustrating for us both than me trying to tell them exactly what to do. When I'm in charge—and it's my model they're trying to replicate—there's a chance they can get it wrong. But when we're facing a new rhetorical situation together as colleagues and colearners, then whatever works—works. We might both be surprised by the eventual solution.

Developing a repertoire of troubleshooting strategies is more important than ever. A 2015 report published by the Association of American Colleges and Universities (AAC&U) identifies communication and problem solving as employers' top priorities for college students. The survey of business and nonprofit leaders on which the report is based found the following:

> Nearly all employers (91 percent) agree that for career success, "a candidate's demonstrated capacity to think critically, communicate clearly, and solve complex problems is more important than his or her undergraduate major."

> Nearly all employers (96 percent) agree that "all college students should have experiences that teach them how to solve problems with people whose views are different from their own." (Hart Research Associates 2015)

Consider your own approach to writing. When you write, what kinds of decisions do you need to make? How do you know how to make these decisions? And how do you know when something's not working? Now think about your students. How do they know what to do? What's their process for making—and evaluating—writing decisions?

Metacognitive awareness helps writers break free from an over-reliance on rules or teacher directions. As Flower notes, "understanding and monitoring one's own writing process" (1989, 13) is a key aspect of rhetorical problem solving.

> Teaching for rhetorical agency calls for an approach to writing that honors student choice.

Teaching for Transfer

The goal of a rhetorical approach is transfer of learning. Transfer of learning is the use of past learning in new situations. Because situations vary widely, making appropriate use of prior knowledge and skills often calls for significant adjustments. Teaching writing for transfer thus helps students think differentially about literacy tasks and contexts. That is, students have to assume that reading and writing in one setting could be different from reading and writing in another setting. As John T. Gage notes, "no two pieces of writing arise from the same situations or need to satisfy the same conditions" (2001, 6).

This is why rhetorical thinking is key to transfer of learning. In a rhetorical approach, one size does not fit all.

Teaching for transfer also requires long-term thinking. It doesn't work to take short-cuts on the road to transfer. Transfer happens as a result of deep, internalized, principled learning. It's driven as much by learners' beliefs and attitudes as their knowledge and skills. Many formulas and templates intended to accelerate students' proficiency in academic writing do little to develop the deeper understandings and dispositions needed for effective communication and productive problem solving. This worries me.

Short-term thinking doesn't help us solve complex problems—like a global pandemic or the threat climate change poses to the world's food supply. Of course we want to help students pass their classes and do well on high-stakes tests. But we don't want to be shortsighted in meeting short-term goals. Some strategies used to help students succeed on school-based tasks can become obstacles to success down the road. This is especially true of strategies that interfere with students' ability to think rhetorically or make their own decisions.

Students' beliefs and attitudes often endure long after they have forgotten the formula for slope or the definition of iambic pentameter. We need to consider the learning most likely to stick.

Considering the Principles Behind Our Writing (and Teaching) Practices

In my early teen years, I took ballet classes five days a week at a little studio in a strip mall in Orange, California. My teacher, a stern woman with a commanding presence, had performed with the American Ballet Theater in the days when the dance world was still orbiting around George Balanchine's star. She used to enthrall us with stories of dancing on the raked stages of Europe, a feat that seemed almost impossible to me since I could barely manage my pointe shoes on level ground.

While I never danced at an elite level, ballet has been something I've carried with me throughout my life. It's still a part of me. Never mind that I haven't been able to do a double pirouette since 1992. Dance changed the way I see the world and myself.

What has stuck with me all these years later isn't the technical knowledge. It is the joy in a certain quality of movement, the experience of embodied art, and the satisfaction of working hard enough to make progress. These are foundational principles I've retained from all those ballet classes that I now apply to other areas of my life, especially my writing. Dance taught me to work for the criticism, not the praise. The real prize is the expert feedback that helps you grow.

When we teach writing, we need to consider the learning students will carry with them into their future lives. Teaching writing for transfer entails paying special attention to the foundational principles fostered by our instructional approach, including learners' beliefs about what constitutes ethical and effective writing. When we understand the underlying principles of an approach, we can adapt its methods to new contexts and purposes. This is what the research on transfer tells us (Haskell 2001).

This book asks several questions about the principles behind our practices:

- What kinds of communication habits are we fostering by our instructional approach?

- What mindsets are we fostering?

- How does the way we teach writing—and especially argument writing—impact our students' capacity for collaboration, ability to solve problems, and way of being in the world?

We need to look beyond shortcuts to "proficiency" to the transferable learning that will still be valuable in years to come.

Developing Theoretical Knowledge

Students need a conscious awareness of their operating system—their own "theory of writing" (Yancey, Robertson, and Taczak 2014, 4)—if they're going to effectively repurpose their learning in new settings.

If you ask, "Why did you do that?" and students answer, "Because you told me to," chances are they're not yet thinking rhetorically about their communication choices. Writing instruction that puts the burden of making rhetorical decisions on the students helps them to develop theoretical knowledge—what I think of as "writer's brain," that constant (and sometimes obsessive) sifting of options that goes on in a writer's head during acts of composition.

Instead of giving students directions to follow (e.g., "Please organize your ideas into paragraphs"), we can ask them questions that trigger writerly thinking (e.g., "What are the main purpose and focus of this section?"). Instead of teaching students the features of "good" writing, we can help them *to learn how to learn* the conventions of writing in new situations they will encounter" (2007, 15) (emphasis added) as Anne Beaufort recommends in *College Writing and Beyond*. Students who can think critically about writers' choices have a framework for adapting to new writing situations.

I don't want my students to just remember what I taught them. I want them to discover and develop their own set of guiding beliefs—a theory of written communication they can take with them wherever they go, a theory that will help them figure out how to communicate in forms that haven't been invented yet and in contexts that don't exist now.

Professional Knowledge for the Teaching of Writing

In 2016, the National Council of Teachers of English (NCTE) published a position statement on the professional knowledge needed for the teaching of writing that makes clear the central importance of rhetoric and transfer to our work as writing teachers.

NCTE offers a list of several core concepts and aspects of writing that teachers need to understand in order to provide high-quality writing opportunities for all students. These include the following:

- The wide range of purposes for which people write and the different kinds of texts and processes that arise from those purposes;
- Strategies and forms for writing for public participation in a democratic society;
- How people make creative and literary texts, aesthetic genres, for the purposes of entertainment, pleasure, or exploration;
- The ways digital environments have added new modalities while constantly creating new publics, audiences, purposes, and invitations to compose;
- Appropriate genres for varied academic disciplines and the purposes and relationships that create those forms;
- Ways of organizing and transforming school curricula in order to provide students with adequate education in varied purposes for writing;
- How to set up a course that asks students to write for varied purposes and audiences. (See the Position Statement for the full list.)

These are the teacher understandings that foster rhetorical thinking and transfer of learning in students. The Position Statement makes the goal of transfer explicit, adding that "the teaching of writing should also be geared toward making sense in a life outside of school" (NCTE 2016 *Position Statement on Professional Knowledge for the Teaching of Writing*).

What This Book Offers

Throughout the chapters that follow, you'll find explicit support for helping your students develop rhetorical writing skills and practices that can be adapted and applied across contexts. These include the following:

- Inquiry, invention, and rhetorical thinking (Chapters 1 and 3)
- Writing for transfer (Chapter 2)
- Paraphrase, summary, synthesis, and citation (Chapter 4)
- Research skills and processes (Chapter 5)
- Evidence-based reasoning (Chapter 6)
- Rhetorical decision making (Chapter 7)
- Revision and conferring (Chapter 8)

You'll find tips for teaching for transfer throughout this book, too, including ways to frame instruction that help students see the larger relevance of what they're learning. My goal is to show you what it looks like to actually do this work with students—to dig into real texts and tasks with novice writers and support them in making their own informed decisions.

Why This Matters

Teaching writing as communication and problem solving is a vastly different enterprise—with vastly different social implications—from teaching students to follow rules and formulas. It's the difference between honoring students' autonomy and enforcing their compliance. When we teach writing rhetorically, we support students in becoming independent problem solvers who are well prepared to take rhetorical action: to discover their own questions, design their own inquiry process, develop their own positions and purposes, and contribute to conversations that matter to them.

CHAPTER ONE

Taking the Rhetorical Approach

When it is effective, writing is rhetorical, i.e., it takes into account the values, ideologies, interests, needs, and commitments of the people, the audiences, for whom it is intended.

**—NATIONAL COUNCIL OF TEACHERS OF ENGLISH,
POSITION STATEMENT ON UNDERSTANDING AND TEACHING WRITING**

Let me tell you about Tim White. I first met Tim when I heard him speak on ocean fisheries at the Monterey Bay Aquarium. Tim is a scientist who studies sharks, great white sharks to be exact. Part of his research involves leaning over the side of a boat to tag great whites . . . by hand.

What follows is an excerpt from a research paper Tim coauthored (2017) on the interactions between shark behavior and the activities of fishermen that was published in *Biological Conservation*, a peer-reviewed academic journal.[1] See what you notice about this real-world example of science writing, especially the language I've marked in bold:

> Collectively these diverse forms of insight into how coastal sharks use space . . . **empowers us** to make much more informed decisions about how best to tailor marine management tools to meet conservation objectives.

- - - - - - - - - - - - - - - - - -

1. *Biological Conservation is an international journal in the discipline of conservation science that uses a double-blind review process. Its audience includes botanists, marine scientists, ecologists, biologists, and zoologists. See the "Author Information Pack" for the journal's full rhetorical context, at https://www.elsevier.com/journals/biological-conservation/0006-3207?generatepdf=true.*

> ... these results also make it **equally clear** that it would be **prudent** to develop diverse portfolios of conservation measures.

> **Our** capacity, for the first time, to summarize publicly accessible data on fishing activity along the perimeter of large MPAs ... provides **an exciting and sobering view** of the significance of the observed movements of grey reef sharks beyond MPA boundaries.

Besides getting up close with great whites, Tim's doing some other seemingly risky things: He's using the first-person pronoun ("we") and emotional language in a scientific research paper.[2] If his K12 education was typical, at some point he was probably told not to do these things. He was probably taught the "rules" of science writing:

- No "I believe" or "I think"
- No emotion or "fluff"
- No opinions
- No persuasion—just facts

But Tim's not following these rules. Why not? Because the way scientists communicate with each other in their own discourse communities does not necessarily match the conventions of academic writing being taught in many high schools.

What's more, scientists don't write only for other scientists. They also need to be able to communicate the importance of their research to nonspecialists. Here's White again, this time in an interview for the *Stanford News* (2017), a publication that reaches a broad audience, including potential donors. Notice the use of casual language:

> If marine monuments are axed we could also see oil drilling and deep-sea mining happening just a 20-minute boat ride away from our nation's healthiest coral reefs.

If this seems like a rather obvious point, let's consider the implications of telling students to avoid opinion or personal feeling in science writing. What exactly are we teaching students? And why are we teaching them this? What beliefs about writing are we cultivating through our instructional approach?

----

2. *The article also uses genre conventions common to scholarly papers, including an abstract, list of keywords, figures and tables with numerical data, dense sentences, Latinate vocabulary, numerous citations, and standard section headings (e.g., Introduction, Materials and Methods, Results, and Discussion).*

The Rhetorical Approach

The rhetorical approach is as much a mindset as it is a set of concepts and strategies. It's a mindset that says, *Here's a communication problem—now how I do solve that problem with the materials and resources I have on hand?* Rhetoric should not be just an extra unit we squeeze into our curriculum; it's a way of thinking.

What it means to take a rhetorical approach—to read and write rhetorically—is different from the treatment rhetoric sometimes gets in English classes, where rhetoric is seen as more of an enhancement to the literacy staples: a kind of postproduction filter that can make writing look better (Now add some pathos!) or a bonus level to ELA that only needs to be accessed by students in Advanced Placement courses. The kind of rhetorical thinking and rhetorical writing I'm talking about in this book is important for all students and all aspects of communication.

When I sat down to write this chapter, I didn't start with an acronym or a six-step process or a template or a list of what not to do. Instead, just as Tim White probably did, I started by thinking about my audience and what I can contribute to the conversation. What do teachers already know about rhetoric? What do they know about writing? What makes these topics timely and important right now? I pictured the educators I've worked with over the years in K12 and higher education, my former colleagues at Buena Park High School in Southern California, and the many teachers I've worked with through California State University's Expository Reading and Writing Curriculum. I thought of how many things have changed since I earned my Single Subject Credential in 1995. And I looked at my favorite professional resources—those by people like Sara K. Ahmed, Thomas Newkirk, Cornelius Minor, and Donalyn Miller—to remind myself what kinds of books are most valuable to busy teachers. Beginning with these considerations of audience, context, purpose, and genre is a key part of writing rhetorically.

Effective teaching begins with these same considerations. When we study the characteristics of workplace or scholarly writing in preparation for designing a lesson, we're teaching rhetorically. When we situate a text in its unique historical or cultural moment, we're teaching rhetorically. When we customize activities for an extra-lively sixth-period class or differentiate instruction for a striving writer, we're teaching rhetorically. Think of all the times you've handpicked books for particular students ("I thought of you when I read this novel!") or interrupted your lesson plans to reteach a difficult concept. We may not explicitly be teaching rhetoric, but when we do these things, we're practicing the alert responsiveness to the situational and social contingencies at the heart of rhetorical theory.

This chapter is about what it means to adopt a rhetorical approach to texts, to forgo formulas in favor of contingencies. It's about how the study and practice of rhetoric can prepare students for the varying literacy demands of school and life, and how teaching rhetorically can help teachers respond to the diverse communities of learners we serve. It's an ambitious approach; the ultimate goal is deep and transferrable learning.

What's Rhetoric?

In *The Elements of Reasoning*, revered rhetorician Edward P. J. Corbett and Rosa A. Eberly define rhetoric as "the elemental art of humans and their language—written and spoken, read and heard" (2000, 8). Rhetoric's fundamental concern is how to communicate effectively in diverse contexts. You may have seen a diagram of Aristotle's rhetorical situation before (Figure 1.1).

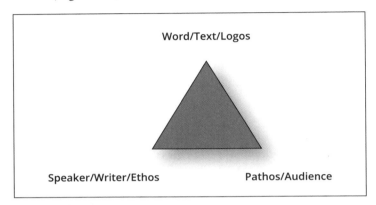

FIGURE 1.1
The rhetorical triangle

Aristotle, of course, didn't use graphic organizers. But the numerous representations of "the rhetorical triangle" on the Internet do get at a key idea in Aristotle's lectures: the skilled rhetorician has to keep tabs on all the connections among the meaning-making agents in an act of communication, including appeals to the speaker's or writer's image (ethos), the content and structure of a "text" (logos), and the audience's frame of mind (pathos). Framing and informing all these elements is the unique social context of individual texts, whether spoken or written.

Rhetoric is intended to affect the making of decisions. The presumption is that the audience will think, act, or feel differently if persuaded by rhetorical action. The effective practice of rhetoric is thus essential to civic participation, workplace collaboration, community activism, social advocacy, and any other form of collective decision making. This is why audience is so important. Rhetorical action seeks to reach real audiences, not just imagined or hypothetical audiences. Rhetors truly try to change the world.

Writing rhetorically, then, is about taking action to achieve real purposes. The National Council of Teachers of English (NCTE) position statement on Professional Knowledge for the Teaching of Writing highlights the importance of rhetorical knowledge:

> The different purposes and genres [of writing] both grow out of and create varied relationships between the writers and the readers, and existing relationships are reflected in degrees of formality in language, as well as assumptions about what knowledge and experience are already shared, and what needs to be explained. (NCTE 2016)

The Common Core State Standards (NGA and CCSSO 2010) also calls for adaptability and responsiveness in students' communication practices, recommending that students write "for *a range* of tasks, purposes, and audiences" (CCSS.ELA-LITERACY.W.9-10.10) while focusing on "what is *most significant* for a *specific* purpose and audience" (CCSS.ELA-LITERACY.W.9-10.5) (emphasis added).

The Framework for Success in Postsecondary Writing (2011)—a report by the Council of Writing Program Administrators (CWPA), the NCTE, and the National Writing Project (NWP)—similarly sees rhetorical knowledge as the basis of academic success. The *Framework* describes rhetorical knowledge as "the ability to analyze and act on understandings of audiences, purposes, and contexts in creating and comprehending texts" (1).

As these statements suggest, rhetoric is adaptive by design. Aristotle explains this built-in flexibility in his classic definition: "Rhetoric may be defined as the faculty of observing in any given case the available means of persuasion" (*Rhetoric* I.2). Learning to see what persuasive strategies are available in any given case helps students respond to the unique contexts of different academic conversations. They begin to understand that each conversation has new participants and guidelines—and that no single set of guidelines can cover all the contingencies they'll encounter.

We can tell students, as the Common Core does, that it's important for them to attend "to the norms and conventions of the discipline in which they are writing" (CCSS.ELA-LITERACY.W.11-12.1.D), but until they experience these situational shifts for themselves, it can be difficult for them to know what we're talking about. Indeed, we sometimes seem to work against this goal by adopting approaches that are more prescriptive and homogenizing than rhetorical. In the interest of supporting learning across content areas, for instance, teachers may agree to use all the same rubrics or the same structures for essays. Getting all teachers and students to be "on the same page" can seem like a good idea—and it certainly reduces the challenge students face in trying to understand different disciplinary ways of thinking and communicating.

But the problem with standardizing literacy practices across diverse rhetorical contexts is that this method doesn't prepare students to change how they read and write when the situation demands. What's more, training students to expect writing to follow the same standards regardless of context can result in serious misreadings of texts. A student might think a writer is doing something "wrong" if they don't follow the rules the student has been taught.

In their analysis of decades of writing research, Arthur N. Applebee and Judith A. Langer note that studies suggest that "what counts as 'good writing' is itself socially constructed and context specific" (2013, 6). The features that characterize effective writing vary widely across different disciplines and social contexts and continue to change in response to changing needs.

> Taking a rhetorical approach involves considering texts as rhetoric.

The Trouble with Prescriptivism

Understandably, the impulse to improve students' writing by teaching them formulas for generating academic prose often arises from grading frustration. Confronted with a stack of essays filled with wonky reasoning and incoherent syntax, we mutter to ourselves, "Why do they do this? Can't they see that this isn't a sentence? Why do they expect me to understand what they're saying if they don't understand what they're saying?" And so we start to compose our list of everything we *don't* want students to do the next time they write an essay for us: No more run-ons and fragments, no unsupported claims, no vague language, no digitalk. We do this because we hope to save ourselves the trouble of repeating all the same comments on the next round of essays. We also want to spend our time responding to the substance of our students' thinking, not untangling their prose. If we can just fix some of the common errors in style and structure, we reason, we can concentrate on higher-order competencies, like analytical reading skills.

In the context of our individual classrooms, this kind of contractual agreement between a teacher and students makes sense. If you, the student, will apply my feedback to your future drafts, then I, the teacher, agree to focus my comments on more important matters. The problem happens when situated feedback starts to take the shape of universal precepts in students' minds—either because our feedback is framed as a set of prescriptive writing rules or because we've launched a preemptive strike against grading frustration by giving students formulas in advance.

I've learned to ask myself a tough question: Is my instructional approach aimed at helping my students to read and write better or helping me to grade more easily? You can see how it might be the latter: I've written "example or evidence needed" for the 142nd time next to an unsupported claim in a research paper, and I think, "That's it! I'm not doing this anymore!"—and so the "Include at least one piece of evidence for every claim" rule is born.

I'll share with you some of the rules—and their rhetorical revisions—I've generated over the years (Figure 1.2).

As you can see from the list shown in Figure 1.2, much of my prescriptivism centered on the surface appearance of students' writing, unfortunately giving the impression that I cared more about form than content. Especially in my earliest teaching years and with my youngest students, I took the burden of inventing an organizational structure away from the writer. I had seen the kind of writing my students would produce without my help (I thought), so I fell into the habit of providing an outline that told students exactly what they needed to address in each section of their essay. Sometimes I even gave students whole introductions or conclusions that they could append to their own body paragraphs, and I often gave them skeletal frames of paragraphs that they then could complete according to their own topic or argument.

To be fair to myself, I was genuinely concerned about the number of zeros in my grade book. I thought more students would complete their assignments if I just provided more

PRESCRIPTIVE RULES	RHETORICAL GUIDELINES
Never use a "dead word."	Use precise language that is appropriate for your audience.
Introductions must identify the thesis or main idea of the writing.	Consider the rhetorical work your introduction performs, including the kind of reader-writer relationship it creates and the way it prepares your reader for what follows.
Include two parts commentary to every one part evidence in your body paragraphs.	Analyze your evidence carefully.
Include a con for every pro.	Respond to multiple perspectives.
Avoid emotional appeals.	Choose evidence and language that will put your audience in the "right" frame of mind to hear your argument.
Body paragraphs must have at least six sentences.	Know what you want each paragraph to say and do.
Include two direct quotations in each body paragraph.	Adequately support your claims.
Avoid using the first-person "I" in academic writing.	Evaluate the effectiveness of the persona you've created for your audience.
Be sure your essay is five paragraphs long.	Write an 800–1,000 word essay that is adequately supported and developed.

FIGURE 1.2

Prescriptive rules vs. rhetorical guidelines

"scaffolding." Unfortunately, my scaffolds were often far more literal than metaphorical. I wasn't just offering the modeling, cognitive support, and intellectual framing that would ultimately help my students achieve mastery and independence; I was building the essay for them. Worse, I was doing the thinking for them.

Taking a Rhetorical Approach to Argumentation

What's more, prescriptive thinking can sometimes produce rules that are almost impossible to follow. If we're told as teachers, for instance, that we *should* teach argumentation but *shouldn't* teach persuasion, we might be left scratching our heads, wondering where one begins and the other ends.[3] Similar injunctions to help students anticipate "the audience's knowledge level, concerns, values, and possible biases" (CCSS.ELA-LITERACY.W.11-12.1.B) but avoid the use of pathos can leave us nonplussed.

- - - - - - - - - - - - - - - - - -

3.   See John Duffy and Patrick Clauss's essay "Argument vs. Persuasion in the Common Core Writing Standards" (NCTE discussion forum) for a thoughtful critique of the specious distinction between these terms.

In contrast to narrow approaches to argumentation, rhetorician John Gage (2000) presents argumentation "as a process of inquiry into questions at issue that is best pursued if guided by principles but not governed by rules" (xv). Gage further sees argumentative writing as "a large enough category" (xv) to include an array of intellectual and literacy practices needed for postsecondary success. He explains: "Argumentative writing, for me, does not focus on one mode of developing ideas to the exclusion of another. The process of coming to conclusions may engage the writer in every possible kind of compositional pattern, depending on the nature of the issue and the writer's situation" (xv).

In fact, a prescriptive approach to argumentation can interfere with the engaged learning and problem solving John Bean (2001) describes as essential to the development of critical thinking skills. Predisposing students to see a pro for every con and a counterpoint for every point—regardless of the contingencies and particularities of individual texts and contexts—cuts short the intellectual struggle at the heart of impassioned inquiry. The student response to this is often disengagement. Bean explains:

> Once writing is imagined as "packaging," students find little use for it. Separated from the act of thinking and creating, writing becomes merely a skill that can be learned through grammar drills and through the production of pointless essays that students do not want to write and that teachers do not want to read. (16)

Prescriptive approaches can additionally make it harder for students to apply their learning to new tasks and contexts. Rhetorician Rebecca S. Nowacek (2011) says that "transfer [of learning] is best understood as an act of recontextualization" (8). However, if all contexts are treated the same—that is, if rules are presented as something we always or never do—how do writers know whether or not their prior knowledge is relevant in a new situation? How, for instance, can students tell if a research method they used in an English class transfers to a research project they're conducting in a history or science class?

Prescriptive approaches can also have a negative effect on students' attitudes. Rule-driven pedagogy can encourage high-achieving students to become cynical about academic discourse conventions because they see success as a matter of exploiting the arbitrary preferences of their teachers. I think of what my son's fifteen-year-old friend said about the secret to surviving high school: "You need to just do what they tell you to do, so you can get the 'A' and get out of there."

Other students who earnestly complied with the conventions prescribed by their teachers are deeply dismayed when they discover those rules don't apply in new situations ("But that's how I've always been told to do it!"). Both experiences can result in disengagement.

When we use a rhetorical approach to texts, we're trying to develop our students' conditional knowledge. Invoking shades of Aristotelian rhetoric, The National Research Council (NRC; 2012) says that conditionalized knowledge "includes a specification of the contexts in which it is useful" (43). The NRC moreover takes aim at "forms of curricula and instruction [that] do not help students conditionalize their knowledge" (43)—such as grammar books that list rules for proper usage without specifying when these rules apply.

Teaching Toward Expertise

A mark of expertise is knowing what to do when. In her classic study on the professional knowledge of nurses, Patricia Benner describes how inexperienced nurses lack "discretionary judgment" and must rely heavily on rules. "Since novices have no experience with the situation they face," Benner writes, "they must use these context-free rules to guide their task performance" (1982, 403). According to Benner, this overreliance on rules can result in less effective patient care since it doesn't account for exceptions or conditions of applicability. Seasoned professionals, on the other hand, demonstrate a keen ability to read the nuances of particular scenarios. A key difference between a rookie and a veteran, Benner says, is that "the expert operates from a deep understanding of the situation" (405). This is as true for writing as it is for nursing or teaching or any other practice.

Rule-governed behavior limits our ability to respond flexibly and appropriately to unique situations. One high school freshman told me, "I write how I'm told to write," when I asked him how he changes his writing style for different tasks or purposes. If we want to support our students in becoming expert learners—instead of plateauing in a perpetual state of rule dependency—then we need to give them opportunities to practice making their own decisions about what's needed and relevant in a specific context. Writing instruction should develop students' expertise.

Composition scholar Elizabeth Wardle unpacks the implications of prescriptive approaches in her discussion of teaching writing for transfer:

> If students are taught decontextualized skills or rigid formulas rather than general and flexible principles about writing, and if instructors in all classes do not explicitly discuss new and previous writing assignments, it stands to reason students will not see similarities between disparate writing situations or will apply rigid rules inappropriately. (2009, 770)

> While rules and established procedures continue to guide how experts do their work in many fields, experts have something that novices don't: discretionary judgment.

We need to help students grapple with diverse writing situations in ways that increase their independence and flexibility.

Teaching for Change

Educating students for adaptability presumes a future world that doesn't just maintain the status quo. Training students in rules and formulas only works if we think the world will never change. But, of course, the world does change. Think how many times we heard the words "unprecedented," "new normal," and "pivot" in 2020. Teaching for transfer means we take seriously the idea of lifelong learning because we believe the world of tomorrow will be different from the world of today, and we don't want our students to be left behind.

If we're teaching to the status quo, rather than teaching for change, we also run the risk of upholding practices that privilege the same students who have traditionally succeeded in high school and college. In an interview for the blog "Literacy Junkie," Cornelius Minor, lead staff developer at Teachers College Reading and Writing Project and author of *We Got This: Equity, Access, and the Quest to Be Who Our Students Need Us to Be* (2018), notes the inherent injustice of teaching to the status quo: "The biggest thing to know as an anti-oppressive educator is that the way things have always been done has gotten us where we are now, and that's not okay."

Rhetoric professor Vershawn Ashanti Young made a similar point about the importance of teaching for change in his Call for Proposals for the 2019 Convention of the Conference on College Composition and Communication (CCCC), the premier professional organization for scholars of writing studies. As program chair, Young invited colleagues to share "communication pedagogies that open possibilities, many of them yet unknown."

Young is one of the coauthors of *Other People's English: Code-Meshing, Code-Switching, and African American Literacy* (2018). He has also written teaching guides on helping students use code-meshing (i.e., blending standard and undervalued language codes) to create an authentic voice in academic speaking and writing. His code-meshing 2019 Call for Proposals—in it, he writes, "Ahm talkin bout buttressing the public good"—is a compelling demonstration of the power of rhetorical agility. It also stands as a critical reminder to teachers that academic language conventions aren't set in stone.

Admittedly, it can be challenging to be in perpetual learner mode. How often I wish the IT department at my institution would just pick one course management system and stick with it, so I could skip the endless training modules.

But I believe educating students for compliance carries even greater drawbacks: the job that never materializes or that turns out to be not at all what you expected or that undergoes radical changes midway through your career. Think of some of the resistant responses to change you've heard before:

"But we've always done it this way!"

"That's not what I signed up for."

"I'm too old to go back to school now."

"We just need to get things back to the way they used to be."

These aren't the reactions to change that lead to personal fulfillment and flourishing organizations and communities.

There are two student responses to unfamiliar tasks or content that are especially concerning to me: (1) "I don't know why I never learned this," and (2) "That's *not* how I learned this."

Both responses limit students' ability to adapt to new situations: the first, by attributing the unfamiliarity to a deficiency in the students' preparation, so that they feel they just aren't ready (and perhaps don't belong); and the second, by resisting any changes to the "rules" or methods the students previously mastered in their education.

This isn't just a problem in ELA classes. A professor in kinesiology I know described the challenges new students have when asked to design a physical therapy program for patients with particular needs and conditions. He shared that students often struggle with being told, "Here are your tools; you figure out what's needed," instead of being given step-by-step instructions for completing the assignment. All students need adaptive problem-solving skills and a spirit of resourcefulness. A rhetorical mindset helps learners tweak and troubleshoot their approach to meet the demands of new situations.

> Teaching for transfer is teaching for change.

Lessons Learned

Learning more about rhetoric and transfer of learning helped me rethink my prescriptive approach. While I still show students what academic brainwork looks like, I now do this kind of modeling as part of the inquiry process, so that by the time I'm assessing students' summative work, I'm reading their writing, not my own.

I've also grown more aware of the way my approach to writing instruction impacts my students' approach to reading. Transfer of learning naturally occurs between reading and writing. If I teach students to follow generic formulas in their own writing, I'm encouraging them to expect these formulas in the texts they read—an expectation sure to be frustrated by the many real-world texts that don't include two parts commentary to every one part evidence.

The take-away: Teaching for transfer prepares students to navigate change successfully; teaching formulas sets students up to be frustrated with change.

Classroom Activity: Writers Two Ways

To show students the kind of situational changes they'll be called on to navigate in their future lives, I share several examples of rhetorical style makeovers: instances in which writers make different language choices in response to different needs. Studying writers "two ways" makes clear the rhetorical adaptability that's the basis for transferrable literacy skills. The following activities also help students understand transfer as an act of transformation.

DEBORAH TANNEN TWO WAYS: TRADE BOOK VS. SCHOLARLY ARTICLE

Consider the following two passages by sociolinguist Deborah Tannen. The first excerpt is from a *New York Times* bestseller, and the second is from a scholarly article. Same writer, different contexts and purposes. Comparing and contrasting these two texts can help students see how Tannen adapts her style to suit the interests, values, and expectations of the particular audiences she's addressing.

Excerpt 1: from *You Just Don't Understand: Women and Men in Communication*:

> Granted, women have lower status than men in our society. But this is not necessarily why they prefer not to make outright demands. The explanation for a woman's indirectness could just as well be her seeking connection. If you get your way as a result of having demanded it, the payoff is satisfying in terms of status: You're one-up because others are doing as you told them. But if you get your way because others happened to want the same thing, or because they offered freely, the payoff is in rapport. You're neither one-up nor one-down but happily connected to others whose wants are the same as yours. Furthermore, if indirectness is understood by both parties, then there is nothing covert about it: That a request is being made is clear. Calling an indirect communication covert reflects the view of someone for whom the direct style seems "natural" and "logical"—a view more common among men.
>
> Indirectness itself does not reflect powerlessness. It is easy to think of situations where indirectness is the prerogative of those in power. For example, a wealthy couple who know that their servants will do their bidding need not give direct orders, but can simply state wishes: The woman of the house says, "It's chilly in here," and the servant sets about raising the temperature. The man of the house says, "It's dinner time," and the servant sees about having dinner served. Perhaps the ultimate indirectness is getting someone to do something without saying anything at all: The hostess rings a bell and the maid brings the next course; or a parent enters the room where children are misbehaving and stands with hands on hips, and the children immediately stop what they're doing. (1990, 225–226)

Try this: Have your students read this passage, and then ask them what they notice about Tannen's argument and rhetorical choices. What's her main point? Why does she say, "indirectness itself does not reflect powerlessness"? How does she support her claims? Students might note that Tannen offers descriptive anecdotes: for instance, a wealthy couple who compels their servants to do their bidding simply by ringing a bell or a parent who controls a child's behavior through an authoritative look and posture. Tannen doesn't explicitly refer to real people she's interviewed or observed, nor does she given any indication of the methods she used to gather this data—or even whether or not the examples she cites are research based. Rather, Tannen's anecdotes sound like speculations about what people *might* do based on patterns she's noticed.

This passage is further notable for its use of colloquialisms (e.g., being "one-up" or "one-down"), the second-person "you," a sentence starting with a conjunction ("But"), and unqualified generalizations (e.g., "Women have lower status than men in our society")—in other words, all the things we often tell students *not* to do in their academic writing. Tannen also doesn't use the kind of evidence, voice, or structure we typically ask high school students to use when they write a research paper. Why not?

To answer this question, students can examine another sample of Deborah Tannen's writing, this time from a peer-reviewed article published in the quarterly journal *TESOL Quarterly*. The article's title is the first clue that Tannen is writing for a different audience: "Researching Gender-Related Patterns in Classroom Discourse."

Excerpt 2:

> Ironically, although many researchers have found that men tend to interrupt women more than women interrupt men, James and Clarke (1993), surveying studies of interruption and gender, note that researchers who compared all-female to all-male conversations found a higher rate of interruption in the all-female conversations. However, these interruptions were typically supportive in nature, reinforcing the point made by the original speaker rather than wresting the floor.
>
> This brings us to further cautions that must be kept in mind whenever language is observed in action: One must take into account (a) the context in which a linguistic strategy is used, (b) the conversational style of the participants, and (c) the interaction of those styles. Furthermore, intentions and effects are not necessarily the same. For example, regardless of the speaker's intentions, the effect of an overlap can be obtrusive when used with a speaker who believes only one voice should be heard at a time—and consequently feels compelled to yield the floor—but constructive when used with a speaker who feels that two voices going at once is the sign of a lively, involved conversation—and consequently feels free to continue speaking over the overlap. (1996, 342)

Tannen's prose is still fairly accessible here (refreshingly so for an academic article), but she's clearly making different rhetorical choices from *You Just Don't Understand.* For instance, the third-person "one" has replaced the second-person "you," creating a more formal style. Even Tannen's use of the first-person "us" is more academic and precise than in the first passage because here she's directly addressing an insider audience; Tannen really does mean "*we* sociolinguists and teachers of English to speakers of other languages." Tannen's language is now more technical, her structure more methodical (e.g., using lettering to order key points). The use of passive voice (e.g., "language is observed") further depersonalizes her description of language study, and her generic references to "a speaker" instead of a detailed sketch of individuals (e.g., a wealthy couple, a disapproving parent) give the passage an objective, empirical quality. While there is still some casual diction in the passage (e.g., "two voices going at once"), Tannen's distinctive, personal voice is subdued here, and the reader has the sense that any competent sociolinguist could have conducted this research and produced the same results.

After comparing and contrasting the two passages, my students and I explore the following questions:

1. Which text is the research paper and which is the popular trade book?
2. Which one is written for a scholarly audience and which one is for people looking to improve their personal and professional relationships?
3. Which one is meant to inform and entertain and which one seeks to further the knowledge base in a specific academic field?
4. Which one could you find in a self-help section in a bookstore?
5. Which one would have an abstract?
6. Why does Tannen write in these different styles?

Here's how an eighth-grade girl from Monterey County responded to these questions:

1. "The second paper is the research paper, the first is the book."
2. "The second is for scholars, and the first is for people/couples improving their communication skills."
3. "The first is to inform, the second is to research."
4. "The first."
5. "The second."
6. "To appeal to and reach different audiences."

The conversation we have helps students to see that Tannen hasn't forgotten the rules of good academic writing in *You Just Don't Understand*. On the contrary, she's demonstrating her superb ability to do what the Common Core calls for all college- and career-ready students to do: "produce clear and coherent writing in which the development, organization, and style are *appropriate to task, purpose, and audience"* (CCSS.ELA-Literacy.CCRA.W.4) (emphasis added). Real-world writing means we're constantly changing how we write to suit the needs of particular rhetorical situations.

This can be a transformative idea to high school students who might at first be inclined to judge the excerpt from *You Just Don't Understand* as "bad writing," especially if they're used to more formulaic approaches like the five-paragraph essay. A few more examples of rhetorical style makeovers can drive this point home with high school students. When I discuss these examples with my classes, students say things like, "It doesn't even seem like the same writer." That "ah ha" moment leads to the realization that they, too, can develop this kind of versatility.

By the way, I've also had the experience where a student reads the two passages by Tannen and says they're exactly the same. That might be your starting place. If your students are new to rhetorical analysis, you'll probably need to offer extra support for reading and annotating these kind of passages (a "Think Aloud" works great). Students may need more help understanding the concepts of audience, purpose, context, and genre, too. (See Chapters 3, 7, and 8 for more on these concepts.)

One ninth grader I worked with, for instance, said both passages were written in the same "formal" genre with "the sole purpose to inform" and that the only difference between the two texts is what they're talking about.

When students only write what they're told to write, it's little wonder that they see all rhetorical situations as the same. Students need extended practice making their own choices in response to diverse rhetorical situations.

Developing Students' Rhetorical Sensitivity

For the following set of paired texts, ask students to describe how the writer's diction, syntax, structure, and tone change from the first excerpt to the second—and how these changes reflect the demands of each text's unique audience, purpose, and occasion.

LEON PANETTA TWO WAYS: NEWSPAPER COLUMN VS. LEGISLATION

Lawyer, walnut farmer, and former Central Intelligence Agency Director Leon Panetta was President Barack Obama's Secretary of Defense from 2011 to 2013. The first sample of Panetta's writing comes from a column published on September 9, 2001, in the *Monterey County Herald.*

Excerpt 1: from "The Price of 'Spin' Versus the 'Truth'" by Leon E. Panetta

> Huey Long—the infamous Louisiana politician of the Thirties—once promised a certain constituency in an election campaign that he would deliver a public works project to them if elected. When he failed to deliver the project after he was elected, he was asked why. His reply: "I lied!"

Long's admission was brutally frank. It was the kind of honesty that worked well for Long. Why is it so difficult to work for many of those in public office today?

The typical strategy is to tell people what consultants and pollsters say the public wants to hear and when the facts prove differently, to keep repeating the same words in the hope that repetition somehow will make it right. But there is a terrible price to be paid for this political "spin" game—the lost trust of the people.

Panetta's personal voice is strongly present throughout this column, as are the rhetorical strategies common to op-ed pieces: anecdote, dialogue, simple diction, short sentences, and forceful claims. It's an emotionally engaging piece with a human touch.

Now look at Excerpt 2, also written by Leon Panetta.

> H.R. 5973 (101st): Central Coast National Marine Sanctuary Act
>   Sponsor: Rep. Leon Panetta [D-CA17, 1993-1993]
>   Introduced: Oct 27, 1990
>   Referred to Committee: Oct 27, 1990
>   A BILL
> To designate the waters of the central coast of California as a national marine sanctuary.
> Be it enacted by the Senate and House of Representatives of the United States of America in Congress assembled,
>   SECTION 1. SHORT TITLE.
> This Act may be cited as the 'Central Coast National Marine Sanctuary Act'.
>   SEC. 2. CONGRESSIONAL FINDINGS.
> The Congress finds that—
> (1) the waters of the Central Coast have special national cultural, educational, research, and economic significance, because of their—
> (A) unique physical characteristics, including major permanent upwellings and current interactions located in the Californian transition zone between the Oregonian and Californian climatic provinces and its interrelationship with the Nipomo Dunes-Point Sal National Natural Landmark,
> (B) unique ecological and biological characteristics and productivity, including the presence of many endangered or threatened species of marine mammals, birds, and reptiles and a mixture of fish, mammal, shellfish, and plant species not found elsewhere in the Pacific Basin, and

(C) important economic values, including commercial and recreational fishing and tourism; [. . .]

The Bill concludes that "the designation and treatment of the waters of the Central Coast as a national marine sanctuary is necessary for the preservation and protection of this unique area of the national marine environment as an area of national significance." Nowhere does Panetta, native son of Monterey, make a personal appearance in this text, and indeed, it would be inappropriate and disruptive for him to do so. The ethos of the Bill is the voice of the United States Congress, and the rhetorical choices Panetta made in authoring this legislation are rigidly constrained by legal protocol and parliamentary procedure.

Panetta's versatility as a writer offers a powerful example of how different communicative functions call for different language forms.

Underlying the stylistic transformations achieved by Deborah Tannen and Leon Panetta is a deep understanding of how language functions in specific contexts. Both writers are keenly aware of their meaning-making options—that is, their "available means of persuasion"—in the rhetorical situations they face. If we want our students to develop this same expert knowledge and intellectual agility, we need to help them think and communicate rhetorically. Formulas and prescriptions don't lead to deep and transferrable learning. As the National Research Council dryly notes in *Education for Life and Work* (2012), "If the goal of instruction is to prepare students to accomplish tasks or solve problems exactly like the ones addressed during instruction, then deeper learning is not needed" (70).

See the activity directions and student sample that follow.

Developing Students' Rhetorical Sensitivity

SAME WRITER, DIFFERENT CHOICES

Directions to Students: Compare and contrast two different texts by the same writer. What do you notice? Start by recording your observations in a Venn Diagram. Then answer the questions that follow in your notes. Consider the writer's word choice, sentence structure, tone, and use of genre conventions in each text.

1. What do you notice about the choices this writer has made in each text? What are the similarities? What are the differences?

2. Why do you think the writer has made these choices?

3. What do these choices tell you about the writer's audiences and purposes?

4. What do they tell you about the genres the writer is writing in?

5. When have you had to change how you write to meet the needs of different situations?

Conclusion: Facilitating Rhetorical Decision Making

Facilitating rhetorical decision making is challenging work that calls for a delicate balance between support and freedom. Students want to make their own choices about their writing. They thrive when they act as self-directed learners who establish their own goals, pursue their own interests, and make their own mistakes. *And* they can feel frustrated and mystified if we repeatedly say, "It's up to you," when they ask us how to complete a task. Transparency and choice don't always make easy bedfellows.

I've learned that I can lighten the load for students, especially younger students, by narrowing the range of choices they have to make at one time. This keeps them moving forward in their growth as writers and thinkers without making them feel like we've abandoned them to find their way out of the woods alone.

I'll have more to say in later chapters about the specific kinds of choices students have to make when they write rhetorically, but for now, I want to note that we don't have to present students with the full smorgasbord of options on day one. Extensive practice and coaching in a few key aspects of rhetorical decision making—like how to choose the best resources of language or the best evidence—will go a long way toward shifting students' thinking about writing and writers.

The point is that, ultimately, we're preparing students for situations that don't come with teacher scaffolds or directions. We need to keep our eyes on that important future.

CHAPTER TWO

Teaching Writing for Transfer

Successful writing transfer occurs when a writer can transform rhetorical knowledge and rhetorical awareness into performance. Students facing a new and difficult rhetorical task draw on previous knowledge and strategies, and when they do that, they must transform or repurpose that prior knowledge, if only slightly.

—ELON STATEMENT ON WRITING TRANSFER

We do not teach for what is. We teach for what can be.

—CORNELIUS MINOR

While the other chapters in this book target rhetorical writing skills, this chapter offers extra support for instructional planning and delivery. If you've been reading about taking a rhetorical approach to writing instruction and thinking, *OK, how do I actually do this?*, then this chapter is for you. And if you've been hearing a lot about the importance of transfer of learning and want to know more, then this chapter is also for you.

First, I want to make a quick pitch for teaching for transfer. You'll find a planning guide at the end of this chapter that can help you create your own rhetorical writing curriculum, but for now I want to invite you to consider the why behind the how. After all, knowing the why is a big part of what makes transfer possible. And if you're going to repurpose anything from this book to make it fit your own school context, it's going to help to know the rationale behind the approach.

Here's my argument in a nutshell: If deep learning is the goal, then we need to teach writing for transfer, not compliance.

Understanding Transfer of Learning

Transfer of learning is the application of prior knowledge and skills to new tasks and contexts. It's the holy grail we seek as educators, the answer to the perennial questions of "When am I ever going to use this again?" and "Why do I need to know this?"

When I taught at Buena Park High School, I was dismayed by the number of repeat students I had who apparently forgot much of what I'd taught them before: those seniors, for instance, that I'd also taught as tenth graders who no longer used the note-taking or prewriting strategies they'd learned in my sophomore class. Such experiences are always humbling. I remember asking Marisela, an honors student I'd taught as a freshman, why she wasn't using in-text citations in the poetry analysis she was writing for my junior English class when she had mastered MLA style so beautifully two years before. "Oh, you wanted us to do that?" she said. "You didn't tell us."

I came to see that my students were waiting for me to tell them whether their prior learning was relevant or not. They weren't making the connections for themselves because they saw each new class as an idiosyncratic game with its own set of arbitrary rules—and the teacher as the sole and exclusive rule maker. Gerald Graff uses the term "the volleyball effect" (*Clueless in Academe* 2003, 27) to describe the way many students bounce superficially from course to course and teacher to teacher without internalizing the intellectual habits that would help them relate one learning experience to the next.

In our efforts to teach for transfer, there's a reason our reach often exceeds our grasp. It can be really difficult to repurpose prior learning in relevant ways. For students to use what they've previously learned in new situations, they need to be able to do the following:

- Compare and contrast contexts (including the people and places involved)
- Adjust their problem-solving skills and communication strategies as needed and appropriate

In other words, they need to know what to tweak, what to invent, and what to let go. They have to become, in rhetorician Rebecca S. Nowacek's words, "agents of integration" (2011, 3), master problem solvers who intentionally seek opportunities to connect their learning across different courses and content areas. All this takes sophisticated rhetorical knowledge and flexible rhetorical literacy skills.

I want to make an important distinction here: The kind of transfer I'm talking about in this book goes beyond just doing things like using the same vocabulary strategy in multiple classes. Educators sometimes talk about transferrable skills as if these are universal competencies that are relevant in any context or situation. We see this with writing models that claim to be all-purpose solutions to students' writing difficulties—one method to rule them all.

That approach to transfer doesn't do much to develop students' situational awareness or conditional knowledge. Repeatedly using the same skill is different from transforming that skill for new purposes.

Educational psychologist Robert E. Haskell (2001) defines transfer of learning as "our use of past learning when learning something new and the *application* of that learning to both similar and *new* situations" (xiii)—abilities Haskell sees as the basis of human compassion and reasoning (xiv, 64). Other scholars have described transfer of learning as a way to help students improve their work beyond a single class or content area (Nelson Graff 2010, 376) or to understand the limits of universality (Downs and Wardle 2007, 552–553). These definitions share the common idea that, for students to successfully transfer their learning from one assignment, class, discipline, or even institution to another, they must recognize— at some level—the similarities and differences between their past and present situations.

For instance, a college freshman who successfully wrote a literary analysis in her twelfth-grade English class will likely be able to transfer her knowledge of how to support claims with evidence to a similar assignment in her first-year composition course. A more challenging kind of transfer happens when this same student can then modify what she knows about evaluating literary evidence to suit the demands of a history paper. In these examples, the student's deep knowledge of *how* to analyze and compose texts is the key to transfer of learning.

> We teach for transfer by developing our students' ability to think rhetorically.

Transfer also happens when students have a deep knowledge of disciplinary concepts. A mathematics student who understands that a function is a way to describe a relationship between two things can metaphorically apply the principles of exponential and linear functions to nonmathematical relationships—like the way a bond between father and son increases in intensity over time or the way the steady loyalty of an old friend provides constant support (Figure 2.1a and Figure 2.1b). An apt ability to extract generalizations of this kind is the alchemy that turns science into poetry.

> In *Future Wise*, David N. Perkins says, "*Transfer* means that the learner acquires knowledge and skills in one setting and carries them over to other settings that may be very different [. . .]" (2014, 111) (original emphasis).

Transfer thus entails not just an ability to see similarities in different situations but also, as Elizabeth Wardle notes, an ability to "appropriately *transform and expand* knowledge so it works in a new situation" (2009, 770) (emphasis added).

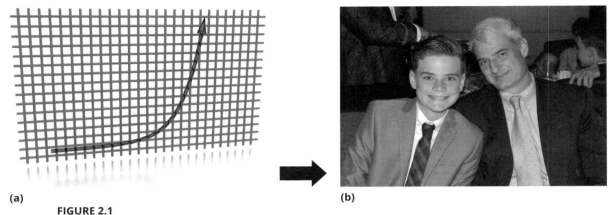

(a)

(b)

FIGURE 2.1

Applying exponential functions to father-son relationships is an example of transfer as transformation.

I want to invite you to take a step back and consider the intellectual agility required for our students to successfully negotiate all the different literacy sites and situations they'll encounter in the twenty-first-century world—and what kind of academic preparation they'll need to meet those challenges. It's a lot, right? As ELA teachers, we own a major piece of this real estate. We work with diverse and complex texts on a daily basis. Helping students read, write, and think across contexts is what we do.

The Goal of Transfer

We teach for transfer because we want to support students' growth from novice to expert writers. Depth, mastery, expertise, independence, self-direction—whatever we want to call it, there's a stage when learners shift from "fake it 'til you make it" to really owning their intellectual processes. This doesn't mean they work alone, but it does mean they're not overly reliant on someone else's instructions or authority. They can think on their feet and make their own choices. They know what to do when. That's when transfer happens.

But transfer, or to be more precise, teaching for transfer, is also a catalyst for deeper learning. In *Visible Literacy*, Doug Fisher, Nancy Frey, and John Hattie explain that transfer is "both a goal of learning and a mechanism for propelling learning" (Fisher, Frey, and Hattie 2016, 107). Teaching writing for transfer sets students on the path toward independence and supports them in becoming expert learners.

Keeping an eye on that developmental continuum is important. Much of writing instruction focuses on introducing students to skills and strategies. We teach things like RAFT (**R**ole, **A**udience, **F**ormat, **T**opic), or a six-step writing process, because we're apprenticing students in the practices of expert writers. But transfer is ultimately about the destination, not the starting point.

Knowledge Needed for Transfer of Learning

Several big ideas are emerging from the research on transfer of learning that have important implications for teachers. The most important is probably this: If we want students to apply their learning after they leave our classrooms, we have to explicitly teach for transfer.

That involves doing some things that we may not already be doing, such as developing students' procedural, conceptual, and conditional knowledge or providing "expansive framing." If *conditional knowledge* and *expansive framing* are relatively new terms to you, then we have that in common. The scholarship on teaching for transfer has sparked some of the newest learning I've experienced in my quarter century as a teacher. But it's also been some of the most important and exciting.

I'll talk about what it means to provide expansive framing a bit later in this chapter. For now, let's take a look at three interrelated types of knowledge that are especially important for transfer of learning (Figure 2.2):

1. Procedural knowledge: knowing *how* to do something

2. Conceptual knowledge: understanding the concepts, principles, and theories behind *why* we do something

3. Conditional knowledge: knowing *what* to do *when*

To make our prior learning work in new situations, we need to know how, why, and when to repurpose it. Of these three types of knowledge, we tend to do the best job helping students develop procedural knowledge. The other two can be more of a challenge.

But this is precisely the knowledge students need to break their dependence on rules and formulas. Let's look at each type more closely.

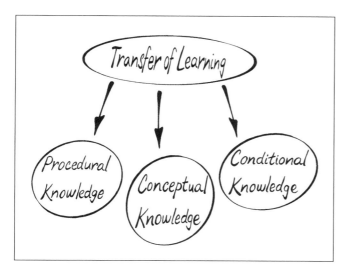

FIGURE 2.2
Knowledge needed for transfer
of learning

Developing Procedural Knowledge

We've done a pretty good job over the past fifty years teaching students about the writing process. Students tend to arrive on the job or a college campus already knowing quite a bit about prewriting, drafting, sharing, and revising. They understand that writing is a process with different stages of development.

What we perhaps haven't done as well is help students surface the procedural knowledge that guides other kinds of writing moves or tasks. Because the writing process is sometimes taught as a universal model, students can have difficulty articulating other things that they're doing as writers or how to modify the writing process to produce different kinds of texts. I think we also need to be honest about the way some of our writing scaffolds—especially overly prescriptive templates and formulas—have interfered with the development of students' procedural knowledge. The process that many students use (as my son has pointed out to me) is simply to wait for the teacher to tell them what to do.

The research on transfer tells us that students need conscious awareness of the processes they use for different academic tasks in order to strategically adapt those procedures to new contexts or classes. This could be as simple as modifying the prewriting strategies a student previously used to compose a poem to write a short story instead. Or it could be as complicated as drawing on the research methods learned in a social science class to design a community service project. Procedural knowledge is "the ability to apply conceptual knowledge to new problems by using the discipline's characteristic methods of thinking" (Bean, Chappell, and Gillam 2014, 4)—it is, as George Hillocks says, "how, when, and for what purpose to use procedures that are the province of that art" (1995, 124). In his review of experimental studies on writing pedagogy, Hillocks notes that "the treatments with the largest gains all focus on teaching procedural knowledge, knowledge of how to do things" (1995, 223).

In the activities that follow, I share ways to help students surface their procedural knowledge.

> Acronyms like SOAPS, RAFT, OSCAR, and so on, are procedural scaffolds; they help novice writers do things like analyze rhetorical situations and revise their writing. Experienced writers, on the other hand, have their own flexible processes for communicating across contexts.

HOW DO YOU KNOW AND WHAT DID YOU DO?

"How do you know?" and "What did you do?" are two of the most important questions we can ask students. The purpose of this next activity is to help students reflect on these questions. Students first read an article (in this example, the news article "How Well Do You Wash Your Hands?") and summarize the main idea of the article in a sentence or two. Then they reflect on their thinking process by describing how they identified the main idea and what they had to do to write the summary.

The examples that follow come from a class of fifth graders.

How Do You Know?

Directions to Students: Read "How Well Do You Wash Your Hands? New Machine Will Tell You." Then summarize the main idea of the article in a sentence or two.

Now reflect on your thinking process: How did you know that was the main idea? Write a short paragraph describing what you had to do to write the summary.

Here's what the students said:

"The main idea of this article is people should always take their time with washing their hands."

"After reading those paragraphs were all about hand washing. So I just looked at what the article mentioned the most. I know that the topic mentioned the most is always the main idea."

"The main idea was that people aren't washing their hands and the device would help to sanitize things better. I knew that was the main idea because that was the main problem and solution. I thought of all of the things in the article and then what was the most important."

"Two engineers had this idea of making a device that shows how well you wash your hands. Having read this article very well two times I rehearsed the shortened version in my head and wrote it."

Another student mentioned that she looked at the title for clues. Still another said he thought the first, second, or last sentence is the main idea. And one student said she reread the article to check her opinion.

The point of the reflection is to get students thinking about their own process, in their own words. What's important is the metacognition. If students are confused or need more help, you can ask them what they had to do to write whatever it is they've written. What choices did they make? How did they decide how to write their sentence or sentences? The goal of this kind of reflection is to move students toward greater independence as thinkers, readers, and writers.

And if they say, "I don't know what I did," that's helpful information, too. It means they don't yet have conscious control over their meaning-making choices, so developing that explicit procedural knowledge can be a helpful instructional goal. By the way, a lot of my first-year college students also struggle when asked these kinds of questions. They're not used to having to unpack their own thinking.

Metacognitive Prompts

When we teach for transfer, we make extra instructional space for the practice of reflecting on learning. We especially want to invite students to think about how they handled any roadblocks they encountered. The metacognitive prompts that follow move students toward being self-directed problem solvers.

- What language choices did you make? What organizational choices did you make?
- Why did you write it that way?
- How did you make those choices? What were your other options?
- What worked? What didn't? What might you do differently next time?
- What did you learn about your writing process?
- How did you deal with any difficulties or obstacles you encountered?

> See the discussion of descriptive outlining in Chapter 7 for additional ways to help your students think about what they are doing as writers.

Developing Conceptual Knowledge

If you have a deep understanding of rhetorical concepts and the principles of effective communication, you don't need an acronym or template to help you remember how to write.

Deep conceptual knowledge is needed to appropriately apply learning in new contexts. When it comes to written communication, the rhetorical concepts of audience, purpose, genre, and context have transformative power. A deep understanding of these concepts changes how students read and write. The Elon Statement on Writing Transfer (2013) recommends that teachers build students' conceptual knowledge by "constructing writing curricula and classes that focus on study of and practice with concepts that enable students to analyze expectations for writing and learning within specific contexts. These include rhetorically-based concepts (such as genre, purpose, and audience)."

I'll offer a close look at each of these concepts in subsequent chapters, but for now, it's probably helpful to keep in mind the role conceptual knowledge plays in learning and transfer. The National Research Council (NRC) reports that "organizing learning into a conceptual framework allows for greater 'transfer'; that is, it allows the student to apply what was learned in new situations and to learn related information more quickly" (2000, 17). The NRC likewise identifies deep conceptual knowledge as a distinguishing feature of expertise, noting that "experts' command of concepts shapes their understanding of new information: it allows them to see patterns, relationships, or discrepancies that are not apparent to novices" (2000, 16–17).

Here's what we can expect to happen: We introduce a complex concept such as genre to students, they write down a definition and examples, and we think, "OK, they get it." And then students start to work with that concept, and we realize they don't get it. Not yet. Building conceptual knowledge takes time and support. We can expect those surface understandings to differ significantly from the deep, internalized learning students achieve through extended practice analyzing and applying a concept.

THRESHOLD CONCEPTS FOR WRITING TRANSFER

I think it's also helpful to note a special category of concepts that researchers have described as "threshold concepts." These have been closely linked to transfer of learning. In the Editors' Preface to *Overcoming Barriers to Student Understanding: Threshold Concepts and Troublesome Knowledge*, Jan H. F. Meyer and Ray Land describe a threshold concept "as akin to a portal, opening up a new and previously inaccessible way of thinking about something" (2006, xv). Threshold concepts represent the transformative understandings needed for continued progression and participation in a field.

Think of a time in your educational journey when you first felt like you were starting to make that leap from novice to expert. This could be an experience you had as a student or a teacher, when, after an extended period of struggle and confusion, you finally felt like you were starting to connect the dots and see the big picture. Think of that moment when you no longer felt like an amateur "trying to fake it 'til you make it" and instead felt like an expert at home in a community of experts. That memory that you're recalling is a memory of a threshold crossing.

This idea of threshold concepts is important for moving students from an introductory or superficial understanding toward deeper learning because it explains why students might get stuck at the introductory stage. Some concepts really are more difficult to learn than others and will take extended time, effort, support, and practice to master. According to Meyer and Land (2006, xv), threshold concepts are generally

- transformative
- irreversible
- troublesome
- counterintuitive or destabilizing

To cross a learning threshold, we have to step outside of our comfort zone. Meyer and Land write that "such transformation entails a letting go of earlier, comfortable positions and encountering less familiar and sometimes disconcerting new territory" (2006, xv). Developing writers, for example, might find it a challenge to let go of the familiar pro/con essay structure as they shift from binary thinking to engaging and synthesizing multiple perspectives.

A rhetorical concept such as genre acts as a threshold concept when students' basic understanding of this concept (i.e., a genre is a fixed category of writing) conflicts with the deeper understanding needed to progress toward expertise and mastery (i.e., genres are flexible, socially situated forms that have evolved to accomplish particular communicative purposes).

In *Naming What We Know: Threshold Concepts of Writing Studies*, a group of thirty-three leading writing scholars identifies several concepts that are "critical for anyone who wants to help learners write more effectively, whatever their disciplines or professions may be" (Adler-Kassner and Wardle 2015, 5). These include the following ideas:

- Writing addresses, invokes, and/or creates audiences.
- Writing expresses and shares meaning to be reconstructed by the reader.
- Writing enacts and creates identities and ideologies. (2015, v–vi)

These transformative concepts from the field of writing studies might at first seem to be more than your students need to take on at this moment, but I'd like you to consider how these big ideas can help students think critically about written communication, especially if we turn these into student-friendly principles:

- Writing speaks to and shapes us as readers.
- Meaning is created by both readers and writers.
- Writing reflects and shapes who we are and what we believe.

Conceptual knowledge needed for writing transfer includes an understanding of the principles that guide effective communication in different contexts.

"It Depends": Developing Conditional Knowledge

Paying attention to changing conditions is essential for successfully negotiating the various twists, turns, and challenges we encounter in different situations. This is often what's missing from writing instruction. We say that writing is decision making, but students often don't know how to make the best choices in a particular situation. If you ask your students if they know when to use paraphrase instead of direct quotation or when it's OK to use contractions, they'll probably say that they don't. These aren't questions we typically ask student writers.

An understanding of rhetorical concepts such as genre, audience, and purpose helps students to conditionalize their knowledge of writing, that is, to understand "the contexts in which it is useful" (National Research Council 2000, 43). But conditional knowledge isn't needed just for effective communication. Conditional knowledge is important in all academic content areas and, indeed, in probably all areas of our lives (Figure 2.3).

FIGURE 2.3
Conditions impact our choices and actions.

Knowing when to apply a particular formula to solve a problem is an essential part of mathematical competence. In baseball, knowing whether to pitch a fast ball or a curve ball depends upon the type of hitter at the plate and the situation in the game (Figure 2.4). Drivers need to know how to adjust their speed and following distance in response to road conditions. And a nurse needs to know what kind of care is most relevant to a patient's condition.

FIGURE 2.4
Knowing what to do when is essential knowledge in baseball.

But students rarely hear their teachers talk about the conditions under which their writing advice is relevant. Teachers often say things like "use descriptive details" or "avoid contractions" as if doing this will always automatically improve our writing. As a result, students often internalize a fixed set of precepts about "good" writing. If you asked your students how to write a good speech, for example, here's what you might hear them say:

"Use big words."

"Start with a story."

"Use humor and emotion."

But when is using big words a good idea? What does a writer need to know about the audience, genre, and context before making this determination? These types of "context-free rules" (Benner 1982, 403) can interfere with students' performance in situations in which the rules do not apply.

John Warner, author of *Why They Can't Write* and *The Writer's Practice*, shares a similar observation from his own experience as a college writing instructor that speaks to the limited opportunities students have to develop conceptual and conditional knowledge: "When I ask students what they've been told about writing, they can list rule after rule. When I ask where these rules come from, why these rules are rules, they shrug" (2018, 4).

Knowing the contexts and purposes of writing "rules"—or better yet, writing choices and principles—empowers students to answer those "What should I do?" questions for themselves.

The NCTE position statement on Professional Knowledge for the Teaching of Writing notes that "even within more academic settings like college courses, the characteristics of good writing vary among disciplines . . ." (National Council of Teachers of English, 2016)

Experts have deep conditional knowledge. In *How People Learn: Brain, Mind, Experience, and School*, the National Research Council (NRC) explains that experts' knowledge "reflects contexts of applicability: that is, the knowledge is 'conditionalized' on a set of circumstances" (2000, 31). Experts, the NRC notes, are "good at retrieving the knowledge that is relevant to a particular task" (2000, 43).

Novices, on the other hand, might know how to do something but they don't yet have an understanding of the principles behind why they should do something or when they should do something different.

KNOWING WHAT TO DO WHEN

The purpose of this next activity is to help students conceptualize and conditionalize their writing knowledge.

Directions to Students: **How do you know what kinds of writing choices to make in different situations? What do you base your decisions on? In the table below, think through some of the options you have as a writer and how you know what to do when. Then identify the concepts, principles, or circumstances that guide your thinking in the space on the right.**

HOW DO YOU KNOW WHEN . . .	THIS DEPENDS ON . . . *(WHAT CONCEPTS, PRINCIPLES, OR CIRCUMSTANCES HELP YOU KNOW WHAT TO DO WHEN?)*
. . . to use a formal or casual style of writing?	
. . . to include citations for sources?	
. . . to paraphrase instead of quote directly?	
. . . to use MLA instead of APA or other style guide?	
. . . to refute someone else's claim?	
. . . to use a personal story to develop an argument?	
. . . to use active voice instead of passive voice?	
. . . to use contractions or slang?	
. . . to include a thesis in the introduction?	
. . . to use "I" in academic writing?	

You might want to adjust the list of options based on your students' writing knowledge, for instance, omitting the item on passive voice if this is an unfamiliar term. You could also start by making the activity a checklist and just asking students *if* they know how to figure out what to do in each case.

If we give students a set of writing instructions to follow (e.g., "Be sure to capitalize the pronoun 'I' and the first letter of a proper noun"), we need to help students also understand the conditions under which those instructions are relevant. It's important to follow conventions of capitalization in much academic and workplace writing, but not in digitalk or in some poetry and critical theory. We empower students when we help them understand the rationale for written language conventions—for instance, how capitalization draws attention to the status of a word or how using lowercase letters when capitalization is expected (e.g., "one day anyone died i guess" or bell hooks) can cause readers to reexamine their assumptions and priorities. Unpacking the social and rhetorical work performed by conventions prepares students to critically examine the relationship between language and power.

> If you use Graff and Birkenstein's (2014) popular sentence templates from *They Say, I Say*, you can challenge your students to conditionalize their knowledge of writers' moves. For instance, you can ask students, "How do you know when to agree and disagree simultaneously?" or "How do you know when to name your naysayers?" Invite students to consider the circumstances under which these might be effective moves.

The Importance of Expansive Framing

The messages we send students matter. If I tell students, "We're doing this because we have to do this," I'm telling them to focus on the short term and not to worry about the long term. And if I give students a formula instead of encouraging them to make their own choices about content and structure based on their assessment of the rhetorical situation, I'm training them in compliance rather than educating them for a changing world. How we frame instruction significantly affects our students' perception of the value of what they're learning and of their roles as learners.

Teaching for transfer requires the kind of expansive framing that will help students see the big picture while they focus on challenging tasks in the present moment. Students need to know that they are learning to write rhetorically so that they can be informed citizens, effective communicators and problem solvers, and caring community and family members. When we provide this framing, we tell students, "Where you've been, and where you are, and where you're going are all important and connected."

In "How Does Expansive Framing Promote Transfer?" educational researchers Randi A. Engle, Diane P. Lam, Xenia S. Meyer, and Sarah E. Nix (2012) discuss two types of instructional framing, or ways of setting up learning expectations: expansive framing and bounded framing. Whereas expansive framing encourages students to see multiple applications for learning, bounded framing ties learning to a single task, test, or class.

As teachers, we're providing instructional framing anytime we introduce a lesson, establish a learning goal, or assign a task. We can frame an activity as something students just have to do to earn points or as an aspect of lifelong intellectual and professional growth. Frames create focus (see Figure 2.5). They say, "Look here." Expansive framing encourages

 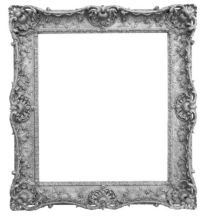 

FIGURE 2.5
Frames influence how we see things.

students to focus on the broad view of learning. Bounded framing, on the other hand, directs students' gaze to the task at hand.

Engle and her coauthors note additional differences between expansive and bounded framing in their article (see Figure 2.6).

> Expansive framing sets students up to be flexible and adaptive in new situations.

EXPANSIVE FRAMING	BOUNDED FRAMING
Extends learning to include the past and the future	Constrains learning solely to a short span of the present time
Extends learning to include different places	Constrains learning to a small part of the available physical space
Extends learning to include different people	Constrains learning to just a few people
Encourages students to use what they learn later	Discourages students from later using what they learn
Positions learners as active participants in a learning context where they serve as authors of their own ideas and respondents to the ideas of others	Positions learners on the periphery of a learning context, where, rather than sharing their own ideas, they are expected to report on their learning about the ideas of others, such as those presented by a text or a teacher
Encourages students to actively engage with the learning throughout their lives	Suggests the lesson is a one-time event

FIGURE 2.6
Expansive framing vs. bounded framing (See Appendix A for additional aspects of learning that can be framed.) *SOURCE: ADAPTED FROM RANDI A. ENGLE ET AL. (2012)*

I'd like to add two more distinctions that I've discovered for myself:

- Bounded framing maintains the status quo while expansive framing prepares students to be change agents.

- Bounded framing is about surviving while expansive framing is about thriving.

After considering these differences, see whether you think the following teacher comments sound like expansive or bounded framing:

"You have to know this for the test."

"This is what we have to do to meet the state standards."

"I don't like this either. It's boring. But it's required."

"Every senior has to complete a senior project to graduate."

Bounded, right? Most of us chafe at the sound of narrow mandates like these (even if we've said them ourselves). Bounded framing reinforces our authority as teachers and grade givers. It can also impede rhetorical thinking. That double impediment to agency and transfer is implicit in the NCTE's concerns with instruction that narrows students' experience with writing. In its position statement on Professional Knowledge for the Teaching of Writing, NCTE identifies two problematic practices: (1) writing "only to prove that they did something they were asked to do" and (2) learning only "a single type of writing" that they are led to believe "will suffice in all situations" (2016).

Try this: For each of the following teaching scenarios, consider how writing instruction might be framed for transfer. What is the bigger picture we want students to see? How can we expand students' view of the value of what they're learning? Beyond a specific task or class, when are students going to use these skills, knowledge, or dispositions again?

TEACHING SCENARIO	EXPANSIVE FRAMING: WHAT RATIONALE COULD WE PROVIDE FOR WHY THIS LEARNING IS VALUABLE IN MULTIPLE CONTEXTS?
A lesson in which students study the key features of a writing rubric in preparation for conducting holistic scoring of an essay	?
A lesson on different types of thesis statements common to school writing, such as the three-part thesis, the open thesis, or the integrated thesis	?
A lesson on common paragraph structures in academic writing (e.g., topic sentence, evidence, commentary, evidence, commentary, concluding sentence)	?

FIGURE 2.7
Providing expansive framing

Did you come up with some ideas? Perhaps introducing the rubric study as practice in assessing rhetorical constraints and audience expectations? Or presenting the work with thesis statements and paragraph structure as a way to understand genre conventions and mentor texts? (See Figure 2.7.) This kind of expansive framing can help students see that they're learning more than just how to do schoolwork; they're developing abilities that will help them effectively assess and respond to real-world rhetorical situations.

Figure 2.8 shows some of the transferable learning that can be mined from studying a rubric.

TEACHING SCENARIO	TRANSFERABLE LEARNING
A lesson in which students study the key features of a writing rubric in preparation for conducting holistic scoring of an essay	• Understanding audience expectations and genre conventions • Understanding the values of a discourse community • Understanding that these expectations, conventions, and values can change over time

FIGURE 2.8
Teaching for transfer

Or consider this scenario: Suppose the directions for a synthesis essay require students to use at least three sources. Are there some underlying principles that can justify this direction? Are there other considerations writers need to keep in mind when deciding how many sources to cite? Now think about this: Does this direction meet a teacher need or a student need? What's the motivation for this direction? How does it relate to real-world rhetorical situations? Can the direction be revised to provide expansive framing and develop conditional knowledge?

Sometimes the attempt to provide expansive framing leads us to reconsider our instructional focus. If we can *only* come up with bounded framing for an activity, we might want to replace that activity with a learning experience that develops more portable competencies and understandings.

Students can also frame their own learning for transfer. Try sharing the following comparisons with your class (see Figure 2.9). Then ask what they notice about the differences between the bounded and expansive questions.

BOUNDED FRAMING	EXPANSIVE FRAMING
What do I have to do to get an A?	What do I want to learn how to do or do better?
Is this going to be on the test?	Why do I need to learn this? How will it help me in school, work, and life?

FIGURE 2.9
Learning for transfer

If your students find that they tend to frame their own learning in narrow ways, invite them to imagine a broader context and purpose for the skills, knowledge, and habits of mind they are developing. Encourage them to expand their thinking about the uses of education.

Remember: Frames have an important influence on the abilities and dispositions students take with them into their postsecondary lives.

We can evaluate the transfer potential of instructional strategies by asking ourselves some honest questions:

> Students need to see academic work as personally meaningful. Framing writing instruction for transfer helps students engage the larger value and relevance of what they're learning.

- What habits of mind does this lesson develop?
- What are the underlying principles about inquiry, reasoning, and communication that students can extract from this lesson? Do my students know that they're learning these things? Are they developing the conditional knowledge that will help them adapt and apply this learning appropriately?
- What might this strategy look like repurposed for other tasks and contexts? What about this strategy can be transformed (not just reused)?

Framing writing instruction for transfer involves helping students see beyond the task at hand to the procedural, conceptual, and conditional knowledge they're developing as writers. Our instructional frames need to expand students' opportunities for applying their learning, not create barriers to their long-term success.

Framing Professional Development for Transfer

If you don't mind causing trouble at a faculty meeting, you might even push your administrators to frame your professional conversations to promote students' transfer of learning. Have you ever heard an administrator say, "Our goal is improving achievement data"? Yes? Next time you hear this kind of comment, you might ask *why* this particular kind of achievement is important. What exactly do we want to help students achieve? What is the larger goal worth pursuing?

The Challenge of Expansive Framing

To be perfectly candid, I sometimes still use bounded framing with my students. I understand why teachers might feel like we need to remind students that something will be on a test or is worth 20 percent of their grade or whatever stick or carrot we grab when we feel students aren't taking the work seriously. Classroom management issues are a big part of why teachers provide bounded framing. We see heads start to drop to desks or eyes wander to phones, and we feel like we need something immediate to bring students back to the task at hand. So, we go for the quick fix: "Remember: this will be on your final exam!"

Reality checks can be helpful. Sometimes students really do need those concrete, here-and-now answers to their "Why are we doing this?" questions. There's a practical as well as an aspirational side to education. But if we consistently teach for compliance instead of transfer, we have to wonder what mindsets we're cultivating and whose status quo we're supporting.

Bounded framing can also devalue our work as writing teachers. What we do has importance beyond a single class or grade. Helping students become better thinkers and communicators is so important, in fact, that we shouldn't need to lean on an accountability system to engage students. Our grade book shouldn't be the only thing keeping students from blowing us off.

This shift toward expansive framing—toward independence, transfer, and deep learning—can be a stretch for students and teachers. Teenagers often feel like they have their hands full just trying to master the surface-level stuff. A lot of them are pretty OK with earning their points and credits and letting tomorrow take care of itself. And it is developmentally appropriate for them to feel this way.

But, as teachers, we have the benefit of both hindsight and foresight. We remember what it's like to struggle with those critical life transitions, such as starting college or a new job, and we can look ahead to the challenges our students will encounter down the road. We also have access to a growing research base that tells us many students continue to face significant obstacles to college access and completion—obstacles that include some of our own well-intentioned instructional practices, as Applebee and Langer note in their systematic study of writing classrooms (2013, see pages 4–6).

I find I'm more careful now about how I set up activities and tasks. While I'll still remind students that the quick-write they just did is prewriting for the essay they'll compose later, I also explain the transfer value of quick-writes—that this is a flexible strategy for exploratory thinking. We're not just working on individual assignments; we're developing processes and frameworks for doing intellectual work.

From Faking It to Making It: Moving from Mimicry to Mastery

There's another idea from the scholarship on transfer and learning thresholds that I'd like to share with you: the idea of the mimicry stage, a liminal state in which learners mimic the surface features of expert task performance. The mimicry stage looks like me in a Zumba class. I can sort of follow the instructor's movements, but I'm really not working my muscles or aligning my body in the same way as someone who knows what they're doing.

In progressing from novice to expert, it's common for newcomers to deal with the challenges they're facing by imitating the experts around them. Meyer and Land say that during this stage "students present a partial, limited, or superficial understanding of the concept to be learned" (2006, xv). The researchers don't intend this as a negative description since such mimicry "might be a purposive coping strategy in the wrestle for understanding and clarity" (2006, xv).

This is an expected phase of development. Few of us make it in life without faking it first. What we don't want is for students to confuse faking it with making it. Too often, learning stalls out at the mimicry stage. Even worse, we sometimes teach toward mimicry instead of mastery by giving students reductive formulas to follow instead of authentic rhetorical problems to solve. Warner argues that much of today's writing instruction asks students to create "fakes designed to pass surface-level muster that are revealed as hollow facades when inspected more closely" (2018, 6). It doesn't do students any favors to teach toward mimicry; novices naturally start there. We don't need to make this happen for them.

> We help students move from novice to expert by teaching beyond the mimicry stage, not teaching toward it.

Writing instruction should instead support students in developing competencies needed for authentic written communication. You might consider the extent to which your own students are progressing beyond the mimicry stage by noting how frequently they make the novice moves shown in the table.

COPING STRATEGIES USED BY NOVICES (SEE BENNER 1982 OR MEYER AND LAND 2006)
• Seek and follow rules and formulas
• Substitute an easier task for a more complex task
• Rush to finish a task
• Use a checklist to determine when a task is complete
• Rely on acronyms to remember procedures
• Bluff their way through a task
• Cheat or plagiarize
• Ask for step-by-step directions

There are no shortcuts on the road to transfer. *Naming What We Know* offers an important caution: "This type of [deep] learning is messy, time consuming, and unpredictable. It does not lend itself to shortcuts or checklists or competency tests" (Adler-Kassner and Wardle 2015, 9).

> The National Research Council says that "adaptive experts are able to approach new situations flexibly and to learn throughout their lifetimes" (2000, 48).

Fostering Students' Independence

A colleague of mine who works in our campus writing center describes a common occurrence: A new student walks into the writing center, hands a tutor their assignment directions, and says,

"I don't know what the professor wants this to be about." If the professor won't tell them exactly what to do, maybe the tutor will.

Writing instruction that stalls out at the introductory stage increases students' dependence on teachers. By prepping students to produce "an *imitation* of writing" (Warner 2018, 5) (emphasis in original) for high-stakes assessments, schools give them "little experience with making choices in the context of writing" (Warner 2018, 5)—the essential skill that moves novices from mimicry to mastery.

Zaretta Hammond's important book *Culturally Responsive Teaching and the Brain: Promoting Authentic Engagement and Rigor Among Culturally and Linguistically Diverse Students* offers an additional way to understand student autonomy: as a matter of educational equity. Hammond describes our charge as educators in relation to the learning continuum: "As children enter school, we expect that they are dependent learners. One of our key jobs in the early school years is to help students to become independent learners" (Hammond 2015, 13).

Figure 2.10 lists the characteristics of dependent and independent learners that Hammond discusses in her book.

THE DEPENDENT LEARNER	THE INDEPENDENT LEARNER
Is dependent on the teacher to carry most of the cognitive load of a task always	Relies on the teacher to carry some of the cognitive load temporarily
Is unsure of how to tackle a new task	Utilizes strategies and processes for tackling a new task
Cannot complete a task without scaffolds	Regularly attempts new tasks without scaffolds
Will sit passively if stuck and wait until the teacher intervenes	Has cognitive strategies for getting unstuck
Doesn't retain information well or "doesn't get it"	Has learned how to retrieve information from long-term memory

FIGURE 2.10
Characteristics of dependent and independent learners

While some form of dependence is the starting place for all learners, Hammond notes that not all students have the same opportunities to develop as independent learners—to exercise choice, act on their own initiative, and engage in problem solving. She cites research that shows culturally and linguistically diverse students more frequently experience school in ways that work against their autonomy. Hammond argues that failing to offer all students opportunities for rigor "sets students up to leave high school with outdated skills and shallow knowledge" (2015, 14). Such students, Hammond notes, "are able to regurgitate facts and concepts but have difficulty applying this knowledge in new and practical ways" (2015, 14). For these students, instruction has unjustly stalled at the novice level.

> Framing instruction for transfer of learning is important. We're preparing students for an unpredictable future, not trying to replicate the status quo.

When a Scaffold Becomes a Roadblock

A scaffold is a type of frame: a structure that influences how a student sees a particular learning situation. Some of our scaffolds help students see beyond the task or lesson to the larger value of the skills, knowledge, and dispositions they're developing. But other scaffolds significantly narrow students' views of learning. This is especially true in cases in which the scaffold does the work for students and/or is combined with bounded framing (e.g., "Just follow this template to complete the assignment. It practically writes the essay for you!").

Think about the following rationales for giving students writing templates or structures to follow. Which ones do you see as supporting students' long-term growth and independence? Which ones lead to transfer?

- To make writing easier.
- To give students practice with academic language.
- To make sure students have met all the assignment requirements.
- To model expert thinking.
- To make essays easier to grade.
- To establish clear expectations for academic writing.

We often think students need extra scaffolding when they struggle with writing. What students need is the procedural, conceptual, and conditional knowledge that empowers them to grapple with difficulty—and scaffolds can be an important way to help develop this knowledge. But only if they're framed for meaningful transfer. If the essay organizers and sentence starters are used primarily with the goal of helping students complete a task they seemingly can't complete on their own, chances are the learning students carry away with them is that writing is a matter of waiting for someone else to tell you what to do.

Handing students a template should not be our default response to struggle. Do students struggle when we ask them to write a summary paragraph or a rhetorical précis or an essay introduction? Sure. *We* struggle with these tasks. They're not easy. But we have other options for supporting developing writers besides putting the words on the page for them.

I become especially worried about what students are learning about the writing process when sentence frames are cobbled together into whole paragraph or essay templates.

We need to get better at asking what our students are learning *from* our scaffolds, not just what they're learning *through* them. Too often, the scaffold itself becomes the end students see. *Need to produce this type of text? There's a template for that.*

The procedural knowledge that many students develop from using the templates that teachers give them is that writing is a matter of filling in a preset form. Fill in these boxes, complete these sentence starters, choose a hook and a thesis from this menu of options, and voila: a finished essay. I've seen whole-essay templates that were little more than Mad Libs.

And I've asked students what they're learning about writing when they use these kinds of scaffolds. It's usually not what we'd hope. Sentence starters are typically intended to teach a combination of procedural and conceptual knowledge. They offer models of how to make certain moves in academic conversations, such as how to support a claim with evidence or address a counterargument. And they illustrate an important rhetorical concept: that academic discourse is characterized by particular language conventions.

But students don't usually tell me that they're learning about academic language or genre analysis or rhetorical moves when I ask them why they're using these structures to write. Instead, here's how those conversations go:

> **Me:** Why do you think you're using these templates?
>
> **Student:** [shrugs shoulders]
>
> **Me:** What are you learning about writing from these templates?
>
> **Student:** I don't know. I don't know how to answer that question. I don't really think about what I'm learning at the time.
>
> **Me:** What's the purpose of the templates?
>
> **Student:** To finish the essay.

We need to think carefully about the underlying beliefs about writing and learning our scaffolds engender.

Over-scaffolding is a cheat that doesn't help students win the game. It might accelerate the mimicry stage—for instance, by enabling students to more quickly imitate the conventions of academic discourse—but it doesn't help students develop the principles and processes that produce academic texts in authentic disciplinary contexts.

Framing Scaffolds for Transfer of Learning

We can frame scaffolds for transfer by clarifying the goals and principles behind our instructional strategies. What principles *can* students learn from templates and models? How about any of these "threshold concepts of writing" from *Naming What We Know* (Adler-Kassner and Wardle 2015, v–vi):

- Writing speaks to situations through recognizable forms.
- Genres are enacted by writers and readers.
- Writing is a way of enacting disciplinarity.

When templates are used with the purpose of helping students develop these kinds of understandings, they can contribute to deep and transferable learning. We need to make the deeper purpose of scaffolds clear.

When I use strategies like sentence frames with my own students, I explain why I'm doing this:

> This is just to get us started. When we're new to a task, we tend to need clear examples and procedures to follow. As we become more experienced, we're better able to make our own judgments and decisions.

I'll even share some of the findings from Benner's "From Novice to Expert" (1982), such as how novices rely on rules and step-by-step instructions while experts can adapt on the fly. It's important for students to imagine their growth, to see how their needs will change down the road. Situating our own instructional moves within this context of growth and change helps students understand that learning, like writing, looks different in different situations.

Look at each of the writing scaffolds in Figure 2.11. How do you know if and when your students could benefit from each type of scaffolding? To what extent does each scaffold help students develop a deep understanding of how to make rhetorical choices in different situations? What principles about written communication and language can be extracted from each scaffold? What kind of instructional framing would be needed to make this happen? What alternative forms of support could you provide to meet these same goals?

As you examine each scaffold, consider the extent to which it promotes mimicry or mastery and dependence or independence. See if you think any of these might result in "fakes" that are not "the product of a robust, flexible writing process" (Warner 2018, 5–6).

GST-TSG (Figure 2.11a): This "hourglass" scaffold offers students a formula for writing introductions and conclusions. Students first write a general statement, a specific statement, and a thesis statement for their introduction. They then reverse this order for their conclusion.

Paragraph template (Figure 2.11b): This scaffold provides ready-to-use sentence frames, transitions, and academic language and guides students through the construction of a paragraph.

Essay organizer (Figure 2.11c): This scaffold offers students step-by-step instructions for composing and organizing a multiparagraph essay.

> Students don't just learn knowledge and skills; they also develop principles and beliefs that guide their thinking in future contexts.

We need to ask ourselves if we're setting students up to outgrow our scaffolds or increasing their dependence on them. If you see the scaffolds in Figure 2.11 as potentially working against students' autonomy and transfer of learning, I have some modifications to suggest. Scaffolds should be stepping-stones, not barriers.

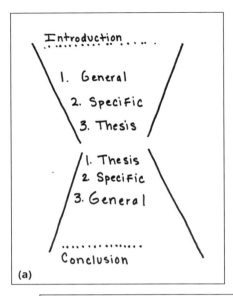

(a)

(b)

In my view, _____First, _____
_____. Another reason _____
_____.
Additionally, _____.
Although some people believe_____, the
evidence shows_____. That is why _____
_____.

(c)

1. General
2. Specific
3. Thesis

Reason 1

Reason 2

Reason 3

1. Thesis
2. Specific
3. General

FIGURE 2.11

To what extent are our scaffolds about success on school-based performance tasks rather than effective written communication? Can a scaffold accomplish multiple aims?

Do This, Not That: The Scaffolding Edition

The activities that follow are my version of "Do This, Not That"—or, to be less didactic, let's call this section "If you like this, you'll love that."

IF YOU LIKE SENTENCE FRAMES, YOU'LL LOVE SENTENCE UNPACKING AND BLACKOUT TEMPLATES!

Sentence Unpacking

This activity is adapted from the California State University's (CSU's) Expository Reading and Writing Curriculum (ERWC) and the California English Language Development Framework.

You'll need a selection of mentor sentences for this activity. The examples below were prepared by my colleague, Roberta Ching, using *We Should All Be Feminists* by Chimamanda Ngozi Adichie. The purpose of this activity is to help students analyze how different syntactic structures create meaning. When used with academic texts, sentence unpacking supports students in developing academic language.

> *Directions to Students:* Read each sentence and talk about what it means. Then unpack the sentence below in pairs or small groups. The sentences have already been broken into chunks for you. Take turns in your group talking about the meaning of each chunk. Share your understanding, but if no one knows the meaning of a word or phrase, look it up using Dictionary.com or Wikipedia if you agree it is essential for understanding the sentence. Then talk about the moves you see the writer making. Make sure you know what Adichie is arguing for. Then reread the whole sentence and collaboratively write a paraphrase.
>
> - "[Girls] grow up to be women / who cannot say what they truly think, / and they grow up— / and this is the worst thing we do to girls— / they grow up to be women / who have turned pretense into an art form."
>
> Paraphrase and describe this sentence. What is Adichie saying? What is she doing?
>
> - "Now imagine how much happier we would be, / how much freer / to be our true individual selves, / if we didn't have the weight / of gender expectations."
>
> Paraphrase and describe this sentence. What is Adichie saying? What is she doing?
>
> Now select a sentence that you found confusing and unpack it in your group. Read it aloud, break it into chunks, and then talk about what each chunk means. When you are finished, read the whole sentence aloud again. If you are still unsure of anything, ask your teacher.
>
> Remember: The purpose of this activity is to help you learn from the ideas and choices of other writers.

Blackout Templates

This next activity helps students learn academic language from the texts they read.

Excerpt #1

Shelly Eversley aptly summarizes part of the reason for my concern in her book ▓▓▓▓▓▓. Offering an anecdote about the time she ▓▓▓▓▓▓▓▓▓▓▓▓▓ ▓▓▓ barbershop in Baltimore, Eversley concludes that the ▓▓▓▓▓▓▓▓ "▓▓▓▓▓ ▓▓▓ cultural distinction" from the university campus, the ▓▓▓▓▓▓▓▓▓▓▓▓▓▓ ▓▓ intellectual ▓▓▓ currently work as professors. Because we participate in both sites, we suffer from the conflict that exists between them. So in order to get along on the (white) campus and in the barbershop, we must alter not the color of our skin but the ways we perform ▓▓▓▓▓▓▓▓▓▓. These racial performances are most often carried out through language, the ▓▓▓▓▓▓▓▓▓▓▓▓▓.

Eversley, for instance, was "▓▓▓▓▓ in her barber's chair" as "she listened to the men discussing their plans to [participate in and] make a political statement" during the Million Man March. In what she terms "▓▓▓▓▓▓▓▓▓▓ to student ▓▓▓▓▓," she expressed her belief that the march perpetuated the oppression of black ▓▓▓▓▓▓▓▓▓. "For a few seconds, the men seemed silent," she writes, "[but] then continued with their conversation." Because they didn't bother to persist (he whispered "Try it again, college girl"), she offered a picture of her thoughts." She explained that the "▓▓▓▓▓▓▓ and incomplete" of the ▓▓▓▓ "mirrored the logic of white supremacy."

Excerpt #2

Mills offers ▓▓▓ as an example in this regard in his ethnography of ▓ black barbershop on the South Side of Chicago.

Mills describes ▓▓▓ as "one of the regulars in the shop." But unlike other patrons, "his identity is shrouded in suspicion and innuendo," because "the barbers and many customers assume that Eric is gay." As a result, unlike other regulars who know, display, or join the discussion community, Mills writes that Eric "is silenced or disregarded in conversation. When [he] would initiate conversations, other would ignore him, ignore his questions, or entertain him for a short while only to move quickly to other topics." Instead of engaging Eric, they would "▓▓▓▓▓▓▓▓▓▓ by his ▓▓▓▓▓▓▓▓ voice."

Mills doesn't describe the ▓▓▓▓▓▓▓ of Eric's voice and ▓▓▓▓▓, but it's conclusive that for them his masculine performance is insufficiently heterosexual. What's interesting about the ▓▓▓▓▓▓▓▓▓▓▓▓▓▓ of Eric's sexuality is that it rides not on what he feels but on how he acts. On this Mills is clear: "Eric is not attracted to me," says to the other ▓▓▓▓▓, he says. "The performance of his sexual identity is the way they perceive in the shop." Eric's "offensive, inappropriate performance" disrupts "▓▓▓▓▓▓▓ the boundaries of blackness, between black masculinity and black speech," Mills writes, "and beyond the narrow definitions of masculinity."

My personal history is replete with anecdotes like ▓▓▓▓▓▓ and experiences like Eric's, and I'm trying to keep them from adding up, which is why I three privacy on the closed in the barbershop.

FIGURE 2.12

Blackout templates created from the Preface to *Your Average Nigga: Performing Race, Literacy, and Masculinity* by Vershawn Ashanti Young

Directions to Teachers: Start by choosing a mentor text that can serve as a model of how writers engage other writers in academic conversations. Look for texts that perform the moves your students are learning, such as lead-ins to direct quotations, paraphrase, summary, synthesis, etc. Make copies of the mentor text and distribute to students along with black pens or markers.

This activity is designed to help students with reading-based writing tasks, including research papers and synthesis essays (see Figure 2.12).

Directions to Students: This activity is designed to help you identify a writer's moves in a mentor text—in this case, the way that writer introduces and synthesizes the words of other writers. The text you will be using for the blackout portion of the activity is an excerpt from _____. By blacking out the writer's (or writers') content and leaving only their transitions, lead-ins, and signal words, you will create "found templates" for citing, summarizing, and synthesizing the views of other writers.

STEP ONE: Read the excerpt. Pay special attention to the functional language in the text (i.e., the signal words and transitions that connect the writer's or writers' ideas, rather than the ideas themselves). Then use a marker or dark pen to cross out the specific content of the passage, leaving only the functional language the writer uses to introduce, explain, and synthesize the sources. In other words, you will be blacking out the "bricks" in this passage and leaving only the "mortar." The remaining functional language (i.e., the "mortar") will become the basis for your reconstructed paragraph. You now have your blackout template.

STEP TWO: Use your blackout template to compose a paragraph in which you cite, summarize, and synthesize the views of other writers you plan to engage in your own writing. Feel free to rearrange and modify the moves you found in your mentor text.

Remember: The purpose of this activity is to show you models of some language and moves common to academic discourse. Keep in mind that language conventions change over time. You can use the templates to practice some of these moves using academic language, but remember that the best way to learn how people in a community or discipline communicate with each other is to study mentor texts. See if you can find some authentic examples of this kind of language in action.

IF YOU LIKE PARAGRAPH TEMPLATES, YOU'LL LOVE COLLABORATIVE TEXT RECONSTRUCTION!

Collaborative Text Reconstruction

This activity is adapted from the CSU's Expository Reading and Writing Curriculum and the California English Language Development Framework.

Collaborative Text Reconstruction is an additional strategy for helping developing writers learn how language works. The goal of this activity is to elicit a paragraph of student writing based on a mentor text. Using these paragraphs, teachers can informally diagnose students' strengths and weaknesses in the area of sentence construction. At the end of the activity, students will edit their paragraphs, applying what they have learned about grammar, usage, and mechanics. They will then compare their paragraphs with the original, paying particular attention to verbs, subjects, and sentence structure.

Directions to Teachers: Prepare for this next activity by choosing a mentor text in the genre your students will be producing. You'll be reading a paragraph from this text aloud.

Directions to Students: In this activity, you will be reconstructing a paragraph your teacher reads aloud to you based on notes you have taken. Try to take notes on both the content of the paragraph and the moves it makes (e.g., transitions, sentence types, verb choices).

1. Take out a blank sheet of paper.

2. Listen as your instructor reads a selected paragraph at a normal rate of speed. Then take notes while your instructor reads the paragraph again; the notes will be essential when composing your paragraph.

3. Reconstruct what you heard using your notes or the keywords. Compare what you have written with other students and make changes as necessary.

IF YOU LIKE ESSAY ORGANIZERS, YOU'LL LOVE DESCRIPTIVE OUTLINING!

Descriptive Outlining

Finally, if you like sharing essay organizers or sample outlines with your students, I think you'll love descriptive outlining. This strategy develops students' ability to understand not only what writers are saying but also how they are saying it—in other words, the moves they make to accomplish various rhetorical aims. Your students will need a mentor text for this activity. Models of student and professional writing both work great. See Chapter 7 for a full explanation of descriptive outlining, including sample purpose statements.

Here's the basic procedure (adapted from the CSU's Expository Reading and Writing Curriculum).

Directions to Students: In addition to summarizing text as you read, proficient readers also think about why the author included sections, or chunks, of text in the first place. In this activity, you will be thinking about the author's potential purpose for each section.

STEP ONE: Start by drawing a line across the page where you think the introduction ends. Then draw a line above where you think the conclusion begins. Now divide the remaining text into sections that make sense to you, keeping in mind that one functional "chunk" could include multiple paragraphs (e.g., an introduction that is three paragraphs in length).

STEP TWO: Summarize what the writer is saying in each section.

STEP THREE: Determine and write the purpose(s) for each section. What do you see the writer doing in each chunk? What is the writer trying to accomplish? What are the effects of the writer's choices?

Conditional Knowledge for the Teaching of Writing

Conditional knowledge is also important to ethical and effective instructional decision making. The choices we make as teachers depend on explicit or implicit conditions. How do we know if or when students need a sentence frame to support their writing? Have we practiced formative assessment? Examined our assumptions about students' needs or abilities? Aligned our goals with our methods? We need to take a critical look at the conditions under which we decide to give some students templates but others choices. Teaching writing for transfer means giving all students space to exercise their agency.

Knowing what *not* to do when—when to hold back, keep quiet, or forgo the sentence frame—can be just as important as knowing what to do.

Leveraging Prior Learning: The Importance of an Assets-Based Approach

Taking an assets-based approach is part of how we provide expansive framing. We're not only looking ahead to where students are going; we're also looking back to where they've been and to the resources and personal strengths they carry with them. If we want students to act as "agents of integration" (Nowacek 2011, 3), we need to help them value and leverage their prior learning. Unfortunately, students sometimes hear the opposite message in school: "Don't bring in your personal experience." "Don't write that way in this class." "Stay within the four corners of the text." Focusing on students' "misconceptions" can make them more afraid of being wrong. I'm afraid we're to blame for some of our students' reluctance to integrate their skills and knowledge and leverage their prior learning.

Because of its suggestion of student (and sometimes teacher) deficit or ineptitude, I don't love the idea of "negative transfer"—a name researchers have given to the "performance interference" (Yancey, Robertson, and Taczak 2014, 55)—that happens when "learning from one situation [is] inappropriately applied to a new situation" (Beaufort 1999, 181). The five-paragraph essay, a form widely derided by college writing instructors, has become the poster child for negative transfer.

I worry that framing the high-school-to-college transition in this way can actually impede transfer of learning and educational equity. If students perceive that their prior learning and experiences—including, perhaps, their home language and culture—are not valued and relevant in higher education and, indeed, that they must erase what they already know in order to achieve more sophisticated understandings, they may revert to waiting for an instructor to tell them the new rules of the game instead of looking for opportunities to make their own intellectual connections. We want students to recontextualize and repurpose their previous education, not unlearn it.

In *The Rhetoric of Reason*, James Crosswhite reminds us of the pedagogical commitments we make if we allow ourselves to take a deficits-based view of learning: "The difference between thinking of people as being deficient, and thinking of people as having abilities and potential that need cultivation, training, and developing is enormous, and it leads to radically different educational approaches and attitudes" (1996, 5).

Inclusive teaching and transfer of learning both involve viewing *all* prior knowledge, skills, and dispositions as *assets* with the potential to be meaningfully redeployed in new situations. This means that even knowledge of how to write a formulaic five-paragraph essay can be a helpful starting place if it gets changed up for a new purpose. We can tell students, "Good! You already know how to write using this structure. Now let's build on it and see where you can go."

> Students' transfer of learning may not look the way we want it to at first. And that's OK. If we approach rhetorical reading and writing as acts of creative problem solving, then we should expect students to have their share of productive "fails."

Designing Instructional Units

Transfer of learning should inform instructional decision making. How do we know when our students can do more on their own? When less scaffolding is needed? If we teach for transfer, we work to move students toward independence, and we give students opportunities to make transfer choices.

I've learned a great deal over the years about teaching writing for transfer through my work with the CSU's Expository Reading and Writing Curriculum. Rhetorical thinking and decision making are central to the curriculum's approach. The ERWC Assignment Template (see Figure 2.13), in particular, has changed my thinking about instructional design—especially in regard to students' development as independent writers. The template is built to help students transfer learning from reading to writing—to read like writers and write like readers.

If you're looking for a way to bring together all the rhetorical writing competencies this book addresses into one unit, the ERWC Assignment Template is a great planning tool. Developed through a collaboration between K12 educators and college faculty, the template moves students through an integrated, recursive process of reading and writing rhetorically. You can find more information about the ERWC at https://www2.calstate .edu/CAR/Pages/erwc.aspx.

In the Assignment Template Overview that follows (Figure 2.13), John Edlund, Professor of Rhetoric at California State Polytechnic University, Pomona, and one of the developers of the ERWC, offers teachers some guiding questions for curriculum development.

ERWC Assignment Template Outline with Key Questions for Module Development

(used with permission)

Reading Rhetorically	**Preparing to Read**	– **Getting Ready to Read** (What could students do to help access background knowledge relevant to the text?) – **Exploring Key Concepts** (What important concepts or questions in the text could students think about before reading it? What tasks or activities would help them do this?) – **Surveying the Text** (What do you want students to notice in or about the text before they read?) – **Making Predictions and Asking Questions** (What predictions or assumptions might readers make about the content or arguments of the text? How can you help students make useful predictions?) – **Understanding Key Vocabulary** (What words in the text are crucial to understanding, yet might be difficult for some students? How can you help students gain experience with these words?) – **Creating Personal Learning Goals** (How can you help students situate themselves within the learning goals of the module and set their own personal learning goals? You might ask questions such as "What do these learning goals mean to you?" and "What do you want to work on while you do this module?")
	Reading Purposefully	– **Reading for Understanding** (As students read "with the grain" to understand the text, are there key points or features you want them to notice? How can you help students grasp these key points?) – **Annotating and Questioning the Text** (What can you do to help students begin a dialog with the ideas, assumptions, and arguments of the text?) – **Negotiating Meaning** (How can you help students identify and overcome the features of the text that cause them difficulty, in both individual and group contexts?) – **Examining the Structure of the Text** (What should students notice about the structure of the text? How can you help them analyze it?) – **Considering the Rhetorical Situation** (How can you help students identify the basic elements of the rhetorical situation of the text and make connections between that situation and the rhetorical choices made by the author?) – **Analyzing Rhetorical Grammar** (Which words, grammatical patterns, sentence structures, or other linguistic features that are prominent in this text would be productive to analyze? How can you help students notice these features, model them, and use them in their own work?) – **Analyzing Stylistic Choices** (Considering the audience for this work, what are the likely effects of the author's specific choices of words, sentence structures, organizational strategies, or use of devices such as symbolism, metaphor, metonymy, synecdoche, irony, or other tropes and figures? How do narration and point of view affect the reader's engagement with the text? How can you help students notice these features?)
	Questioning the Text	– **Summarizing and Responding** (How can you help students express the ideas and arguments of the text in their own words and clearly articulate a response?) – **Thinking Critically** (How can you help students notice and question the arguments, evidence, and rhetorical decisions made by the author?) – **Synthesizing Multiple Perspectives** (How can you help students track the different positions taken by different authors? How can you help students analyze differences and similarities in the assumptions, values, and worldviews of the authors of the texts they are reading while also clarifying their own perspectives?) – **Reflecting on Your Reading Process** (How can you help students reflect on the problems they had reading this text, the discoveries they made about reading strategies, and their progress on their personal learning goals?)

FIGURE 2.13

Expository Reading and Writing Curriculum (ERWC) 3.0 Assignment Template Overview

Preparing to Respond	**Discovering What You Think**	– **Considering Your Task and Your Rhetorical Situation** (Considering the issues and questions of the texts and the learning goals of the module, what type of writing assignment will be most effective in helping students participate in the ongoing conversation? How can you design the assignment to create a believable rhetorical situation in which students can find a voice and a purpose? How can you help students analyze the task for clues about audience, purpose, and occasion for composing? How can you help students analyze the knowledge, values, and assumptions of their audience in the context of the task?) – **Gathering Relevant Ideas and Materials** (How can you help students revisit their notes, summaries, annotations, and other materials to find ideas, expert opinions, statistics, and other facts relevant to their rhetorical situation?) – **Developing a Position** (How can you help students consider possible positions on the issues raised by the text and decide what stance they will take and how they will support it?)
Writing Rhetorically	**Composing a Draft**	(Note: The composing process unfolds differently for different writers. The concerns in this section may be fulfilled in a nonlinear fashion. In whatever order the process unfolds, students should have a draft of their document by the end of this section.) – **Making Choices about Learning Goals** (How can you help students revisit the goals they set earlier in the module and set new learning goals for their development as writers?) – **Making Choices as You Write** (How can you help students make moment-by-moment choices about implementing genre conventions, selecting relevant and compelling evidence, and discovering the most effective organizing strategy for their text?) – **Negotiating Voices** (How can you help students learn to quote, paraphrase, and summarize their sources appropriately and document them accurately? How can you help students represent the dialog between their own views and their various sources?)
	Revising Rhetorically	– **Analyzing Your Draft Rhetorically** (How can you help students identify and evaluate the rhetorical choices made in their draft in light of their rhetorical situation?) – **Gathering and Responding to Feedback** (What kinds of feedback do students need from their instructor and their peers in order to improve their texts? How can students learn to turn feedback into revision?)
	Editing	– **Editing Your Draft** (How can you help students find and correct grammatical and mechanical errors? How could students connect the rhetorical grammar analysis they did earlier in the module with sentences in their own draft?) – **Preparing Your Draft for Publication** (How can you help students effectively format their work in their chosen medium to share with their intended audience?) – **Reflecting on Your Writing Process** (How can you help students think about what they have learned from writing this assignment and how they can improve future writing that they do?) – **Reflecting on Learning Goals** (How can you help students reflect on their progress on the learning goals of the module and their own personal learning goals?)

FIGURE 2.13 (CONTINUED)
Expository Reading and Writing Curriculum (ERWC) 3.0 Assignment Template Overview

Flexibility is a key principle behind the template's design. Edlund (2018) explains, "The template is a tool kit. But a tool kit lets you take whatever tool you need when you need it. It doesn't say, 'now it's time for a screwdriver.'"

I've found the Assignment Template to be useful also for creating individual lessons on particular writing skills, such as gathering evidence or integrating sources. You'll find more great teaching ideas and resources at Edlund's blog, *Teaching Text Rhetorically* (https://textrhet.com).

Conclusion: Stepping Back, Letting Go

Transfer theory explains why so many of us chafe at mandates and formulas we intuitively know are not good for our students. It also offers insights into how we can teach in ways that support students' long-term flourishing, ways that help them succeed not just on a test but in life.

Teaching writing for transfer is ultimately about letting go—about stepping back as teachers, so students can step up as expert learners.

CHAPTER THREE

Preparing to Enter the Conversation

. . . we find ourselves in a scenario in which civic life is becoming more divisive and rancorous as the United States faces serious 21st-century challenges that require cooperation and compassion.

—NICOLE MIRRA

Students learn to write by talking to one another.

—THOMAS M. MCCANN

Entering an academic conversation in an informed and productive manner takes a fair amount of prep work. It's one thing to put in your two cents, quite another to contribute to a discussion in a way that deepens and extends a community's thinking and moves it toward effective action. Writing is a form of rhetorical action. To act effectively, we have to know what needs to be done: what problems to solve, what questions to answer, and what others have already done to address the issue. We have to figure out how to build on existing efforts while adding something new. And we need to understand the cares and concerns of the people involved. This is the mindset shift I'm pursuing with my students: that we practice academic argumentation not so we can win, but so we can help.

This chapter thus focuses on the inquiry, discussion, and dialogue skills that are essential to effective communication and problem solving. In Appendix G, you'll find a diagnostic writing prompt (and some prompt-writing guidelines) that you can use to identify additional ways to prepare your students to make productive contributions to written conversations.

Are We Preparing Students for the Future We Want to See?

With some of the current approaches to argument writing being driven by the Common Core State Standards, I think we're in danger of leading students to see argument not as a conversation but as the kind of dog-eat-dog competition Deborah Tannen describes as a social problem in *The Argument Culture*. According to Tannen, this destructive approach to argumentation results in a "pervasive warlike atmosphere that makes us approach public dialogue, and just about anything we need to accomplish, as if it were a fight" (1999, 3). We see this in "Oh yeah?!" approaches to argumentation that teach students how to attack their opponents' claims. One argument worksheet I saw on Pinterest was even decorated with boxing gloves. Instead of postponing judgment and listening with the purpose of understanding, disputants aggressively declare their resistance to persuasion:

"You can't make me believe . . .!"

"There's no way you can tell me . . .!"

"You can't convince me . . .!"

"I couldn't disagree more!"

There are historical reasons our culture sees argument as a form of agonism, a centuries-old phenomenon in Western culture that Walter Ong writes about in *Fighting for Life: Contest, Sexuality, and Consciousness*. The *Oxford English Dictionary* defines *agonism* as "a strenuous struggle, a combat, a competition." In the traditional approach, male students were trained to take one of two competing points of view (Ong 1981, 118). They learned tactics for offense and defense. The goal was defeating an opponent, not solving complex problems together.

This approach reinforced the social hierarchy and male dominance by rewarding aggression. Communication studies scholars Josina Makau and Debian Marty describe the traditional adversarial process as taking place "between privileged men of similar background and stations in life" (2013, 12)—a model that has been dismayingly persistent. Research suggests that male students and socioeconomically privileged students continue to dominate classroom discussions (Crocco et al. 2018, 68–69).

The 1968 Vidal-Buckley debates are a textbook example. The televised debates between liberal thinker Gore Vidal and conservative columnist William F. Buckley famously devolved into name calling and threats of physical violence. *Best of Enemies*, the 2015 documentary on the series of debates, describes the encounters in language redolent with agonism.

In the documentary, the debaters are depicted as combatants "await[ing] the sound of the bell." Buckley is characterized as "readying himself for his attack on his intellectual prey of the moment" (2015). Vidal boasts of his own debating prowess: "I do this so well and so terminally, that I have left the bleeding corpse of William F. Buckley on the floor in Chicago." According to the narrator, the breaks between the series of debates gave Buckley and Vidal "time to restock their arsenal" (2015). This was debate as blood sport, not argument as inquiry.

Best of Enemies demonstrates that highly educated individuals—indeed the premiere public intellectuals of their day, men supremely proficient in the critical reasoning skills valued by the Common Core State Standards—can still fail to understand each other.

We need to be careful not to oversell the problem-solving capacities of the logical thinking skills we teach. Without a genuine desire to engage and understand diverse perspectives or the ability to listen nondefensively, advanced argument and reasoning skills are likely to cause as many problems as they solve. One study of classroom debates, for example, found that "students mirror the incivility plaguing our national politics: talking past one another, using evidence selectively, and valuing being 'right' over engaging across differences to build common ground" (Crocco et al. 2018, 69). Adversarial interactions erode trust and motivation. They also undermine the inquiry process. Faced with combative opponents, participants hunker down to defend their own positions instead of wanting to know more about other viewpoints.

> Teaching writing as ethical and effective communication and problem solving starts with framing prewriting (or *invention*) as collaborative inquiry.

How we teach argumentation not only impacts the writing skills students develop but also affects the kinds of relationships we build in our classrooms, which in turn, affects our capacity for collaborative problem solving. We need to remember that we're preparing students to enter a conversation, not a boxing ring.

Attaining a Deeper Understanding: The Importance of Inquiry

Through inquiry, we learn what others have already done to address a problem and how we can build on their efforts. I like to use a concept map (Figure 3.1) to help students explore the idea of inquiry (see Janet Allen's *Words, Words, Words* [1999] for the origin of this activity). Mapping is a good strategy for moving students beyond a surface understanding of a concept. In this activity, students work collaboratively to identify the essential characteristics of *inquiry* and to generate short lists of examples and nonexamples. For the nonexamples, they brainstorm things that are *not* inquiry based. Students also compose an example sentence about inquiry and write a definition and synonyms, using knowledge gained through reading, research, and discussion to complete their map.

130

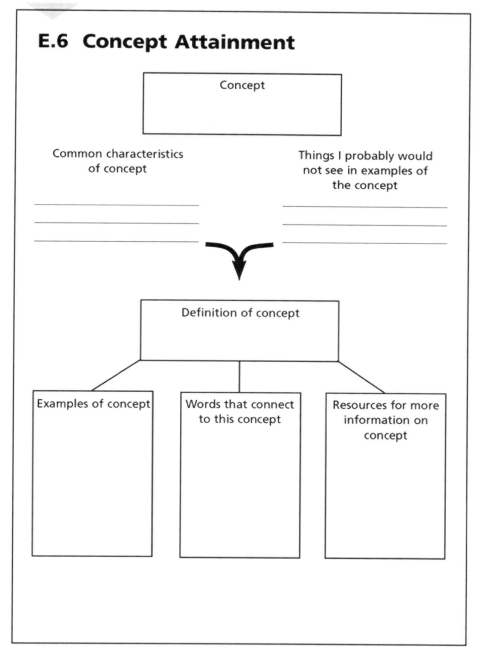

FIGURE 3.1

Concept attainment graphic organizer from *Words, Words, Words*, by Janet Allen (1999). Reproduced with permission

I'm always pleased by what my students come up with. Viviana's and Anahi's maps, for instance, emphasized the importance of intellectual curiosity and investigative skills. They listed "research," "answering a question," "follows a method," "step-by-step," and "searching" as essential characteristics of inquiry. Their examples included "surveys" and "reading." Yazmin identified "writing, talking, annotating, summarizing, and making connections" as examples of inquiry. Her synonyms included "finding out" and "looking for information," and she defined inquiry as "research in which you look for answers from different sources and you put it together."

The example sentences students choose are equally impressive. Joel wrote the following apt sentence in his concept map: "The best inquiry comes from curiosity and investigations on issues that we care about."

But perhaps my favorites are the nonexamples. Students have identified "plagiarism," "following rules," "taking a test" (both the DMV and SAT have been mentioned), "yes or no questions," and "random guessing" as being the opposite of inquiry. One student gave "no curiosity" and "no exploration" as his nonexamples. Starting our work with this shared understanding makes a tremendous difference in our approach. Instead of deciding what they want to say and dropping their content into a ready-made structure, students treat writing itself as an act of discovery.

Pathos as Inquiry

My commitment to argument as inquiry and problem solving is yet another reason I'm concerned by approaches to argumentation that treat emotional appeals as fallacious or manipulative. People's feelings are important data points. They're part of the evidence we consider when we draw conclusions and choose communication strategies. Much damage is done when people aren't interested in how others feel.

John Edlund, a professor of rhetoric at California State Polytechnic University, Pomona, notes how pathos functions as both a persuasive strategy and a method of inquiry. Asking questions about our audience's needs, emotions, and experiences helps us communicate more effectively. This inquiry work can also change our own view of an issue. Edlund writes,

> If we know why the people we are trying to persuade are angry, we may become more sympathetic and may see our own position in a different way and make different arguments. As we become more open to the arguments the other makes, dialogue becomes more possible and we may become more persuasive because of it. (*Teaching Text Rhetorically*, January 12, 2018)

Pathos helps us understand where other people are coming from—a precondition for productive dialogue. As James Crosswhite notes in *Deep Rhetoric*, "There is no understanding without *pathos*" (2013, 183).

Considering the Rhetorical Situation

Asking questions about the rhetorical situation is a central part of this inquiry work. A rhetorical situation is a situation that can be changed by rhetorical action. Before students take action, they need to understand what they're getting themselves into.

After introducing your students to key components of a rhetorical situation—including audience, purpose, genre, and occasion (see Chapter 1)—you can expand their understanding through the following activities.

TAKING RHETORICAL ACTION

Directions to Students: How do you know what to do in each of the following situations? Which of these situations are rhetorical situations (i.e., a situation that can be changed by effective communication)? With someone near you, discuss the extent to which rhetorical action is needed in each scenario.

1. Driving alone on an icy road
2. Asking your boss for a raise
3. Getting lost with your family in a major airport
4. Writing an email to your teacher asking to be excused from a test
5. Trying to repair a leaky faucet by yourself
6. Persuading a coach to let you play a new position
7. Giving a toast at a wedding or birthday party
8. Filling out a form for a new library card
9. Filling out a job application
10. Making an online purchase

Here's what a few high school students I worked with said:

- "Fixing a leaky faucet by yourself is *not* a rhetorical situation because if you are trying to accomplish something on your own, effective communication is not necessary (who would you even communicate with?)"

- "Asking your boss for a raise is a rhetorical situation because what you say can have a huge impact on if you get the raise."

- "I would say that in most situations, writing an email to a teacher to be excused from a test is a rhetorical situation. You need to have the email be equal parts formal and concise, respectful and pleading. If you can make your teacher have sympathy for your cause, they will be more obliged to do what you ask. Therefore, persuasive communication is beneficial in this situation."

Your students will probably want to respond to some of these scenarios by saying, "It depends." For instance, if they think it'd take strategic communication (perhaps with their own family members) to solve the problem of being lost at an airport, they might identify number 3 as a rhetorical situation—that is, a situation that can be impacted by rhetoric. This is good. The point is for students to start thinking about the way our communication choices—both verbal and nonverbal—can affect the outcomes of particular situations.

It's also helpful to know that we don't have to be on high alert all the time. There are lots of situations when our rhetorical brains are off duty. But in those scenarios when rhetorical action *is* needed, we want students to be able to activate their rhetorical thinking skills. If they're not considering their ethos, audience, genre, purpose, and occasion—but they should be—they'll likely be unhappy with the results they get.

Asking students to consider *when* they need to do this kind of intellectual work develops conditional knowledge. The National Research Council notes that "knowledge must be 'conditionalized' in order to be retrieved when it is needed; otherwise, it remains inert" (2000, 49).

> Knowing when to think and act rhetorically is a key part of postsecondary success.

RHETORICAL PROBLEM SOLVING

The following exercises invite students to think through scenarios that present rhetorical problems. Ask your students how they would respond in each situation. They can share their ideas through a quick-write or pairs conversation. Encourage students to consider the exigencies and constraints of each rhetorical situation.

Scenario 1

Directions to Students: Imagine you are a member of your school's leadership class, and you've been asked to invite a well-known writer or artist to serve as your commencement speaker at your graduation ceremony. This could be a poet, young adult novelist, rapper, or anyone else you think might be a suitable and inspiring speaker for this occasion. First, identify a person you'd like to invite. Assume that this person receives loads of invitations for commencement addresses. What do you need to know about this famous—and busy—person in order to persuade them to be your speaker? What does this person need to know about you and your school? What's the best way to invite this person?

Scenario 2

Directions to Students: Imagine you are applying to a scholarship that requires you to write a speech in response to this prompt:

"You have been invited to address a Joint Meeting of the United States Congress at the Capitol Building in Washington D.C. All 100 U.S. Senators and 435 U.S. Representatives will be in attendance. Write your speech. (250–500 words)"

Notice that the prompt does not identify a specific topic for you, so you are free to choose your own subject. What do you need to do first? How will you decide what to write about? How will you figure out the most effective style and structure for your speech?

Scenario 3

Directions to Students: Imagine you have inadvertently offended a coworker. You've been publicly complaining about a new product without realizing that your colleague was the one who developed it. Your colleague is hurt and embarrassed by your negative comments. To do your own job effectively (and because you are a nice person), you need to preserve a good professional relationship with this person. What's the best way to apologize to your colleague for your remarks while still being honest about your concerns? Remember: Your goal is to improve both your relationship and the product.

Bonus Scenario

Directions to Students: Imagine your job is to select music for different businesses to play while their customers are on hold. This will be the music callers listen to while waiting on the phone. What kind of music would you choose in response to the following situations? What feeling or implicit message should the music communicate in each case? Consider the purpose of the music (e.g., to energize, reassure, discourage, build anticipation, convey a professional image, etc.).

- A health insurance company that's trying to attract new members

- An upscale restaurant that offers modern and edgy cuisine

- The ticket office for a Halloween haunt at an amusement park

- A school district that wants to portray a more academic image

- A tech support service that deals with frustrated customers

- A pharmacy that doesn't have time or staff to help people on the phone (and wants callers to hang up)

Consider what else you might need to know about the company or its customers before recommending hold music.

Keep in mind that there can be many different ways to respond to the rhetorical problem effectively. Taking an inquiry-based approach means we're not teaching to one right answer. See Appendix B and Appendix C ("Choosing a Logo for an Animal Shelter" and "Collaborative Problem Solving") for additional activities on rhetorical problem solving.

As the preceding exercises show, a transferable process for rhetorical problem solving involves asking key questions:

- What's the problem? (exigence)

- What do you want to do about it? (purpose)

- Who has the power to make this change? (audience)

- What's the best way to reach this audience? (genre)

- Why is now the right time to act? (*kairos*)

Chapter 7 explores these questions in greater detail.

Additional Opportunities for Rhetorical Problem Solving

- grant writing
- scholarship applications
- requests for letters of recommendation
- requests to work with an organization for a community service project
- requests for interviews

Procedural Knowledge for Rhetorical Problem Solving

In academic contexts, we prepare to take effective rhetorical action by asking those who, what, when, where, and why questions about the situation we're about to enter:

- What makes this discussion timely and important right now?
- What's at issue? What's the unmet need that calls for a response?
- What problem can be addressed by rhetorical action?
- Who are the stakeholders in this conversation? What are their needs, interests, priorities, beliefs, and values? Why do they care?
- What's the context? Where and when is this conversation happening?

The answers to these questions offer students a snapshot of the conversation they're getting ready to join. I'll offer some strategies later in this chapter for helping students dig into the specifics of these questions, but I think it's useful to start with the big picture. As students develop a habit of thinking rhetorically, they'll be able to focus on the most relevant questions for particular situations—and eventually do so without teacher support. See Figure 3.2 for a planning tool for taking rhetorical action you can share with your students. Figure 3.3 shows a student sample.

Teachers have some inquiry work of our own to do. Thinking about the following kinds of planning questions can help us design effective learning experiences:

- How will we motivate students to enter the conversation?
- How will we prepare them to be informed and responsive contributors?
- How will we help students identify an authentic purpose for writing?

The answers to these questions form the basis of responsive teaching.

1. What's the need or problem? (exigence)	**2.** What do you want to know about it? (question)
3. What do you want to do about it? (purpose)	**4.** Why is now the right time to act? (*kairos*)

FIGURE 3.2
Planning tool for taking rhetorical action

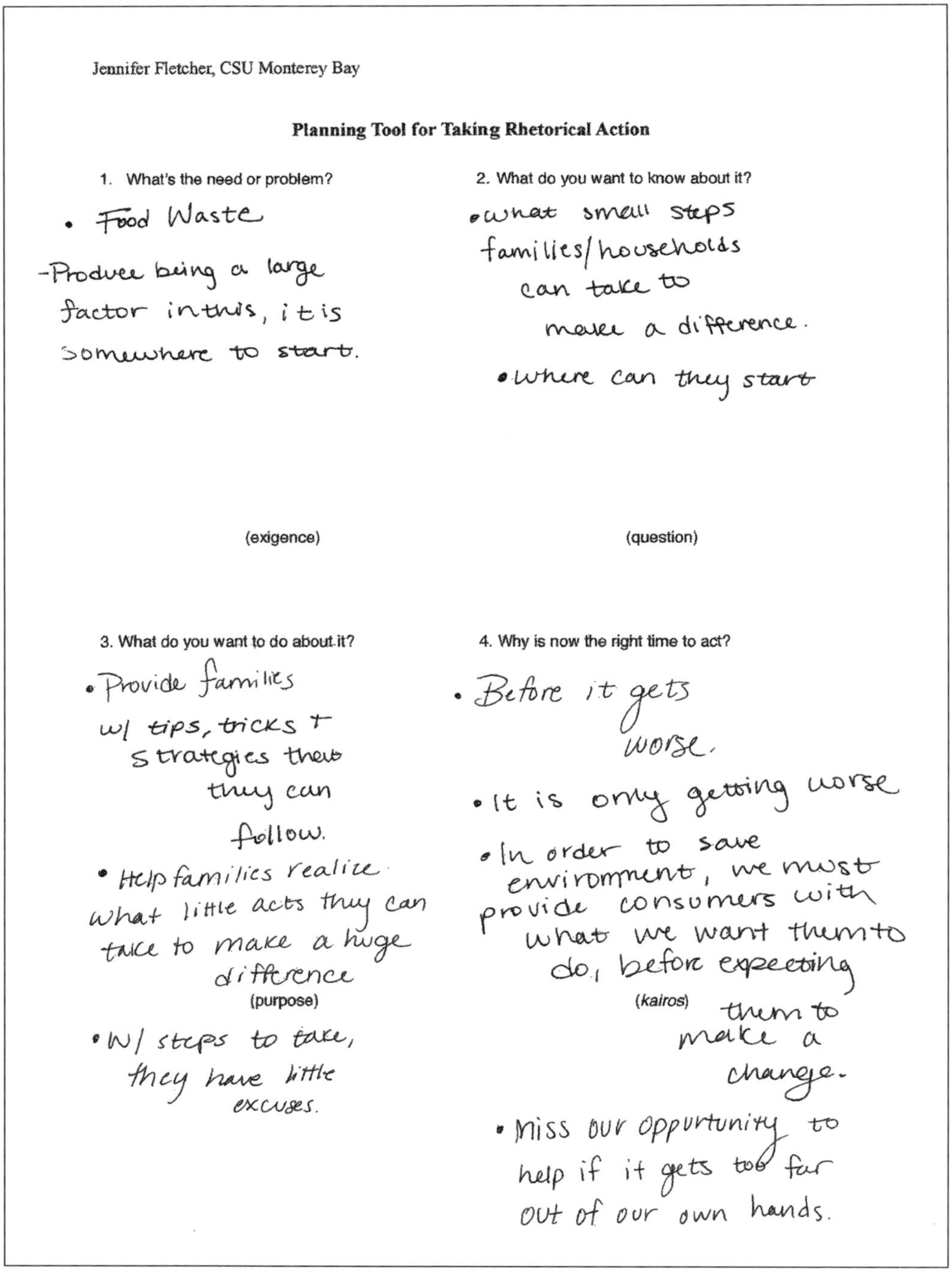

Jennifer Fletcher, CSU Monterey Bay

Planning Tool for Taking Rhetorical Action

1. What's the need or problem?

- ~~Food~~ Waste

- Produce being a large factor in this, it is somewhere to start.

(exigence)

2. What do you want to know about it?

- what small steps families/households can take to make a difference.

- where can they start

(question)

3. What do you want to do about it?

- Provide families w/ tips, tricks + strategies then they can follow.

- Help families realize what little acts they can take to make a huge difference

(purpose)

- W/ steps to take, they have little excuses.

4. Why is now the right time to act?

- Before it gets worse.

- It is only getting worse

- In order to save environment, we must provide consumers with what we want them to do, before expecting them to make a change.

(kairos)

- Miss our opportunity to help if it gets too far out of our own hands.

FIGURE 3.3

Student example of planning tool for taking rhetorical action

My colleague, Nelson Graff, uses the following questions to help his students think about rhetorical situations:

What is the discourse about?

Why is the discourse needed?

What is the discourse trying to accomplish?

Engaging in Productive Dialogue

Dialogue is a form of inquiry; it's a way of learning more about ourselves and our world. The mindset we bring to a conversation is at least as important as the literacy skills we bring. If we're not willing to work with others to promote understanding and resolve issues, we can't make a positive contribution.

Daniel Yankelovich's highly influential book, *The Magic of Dialogue: Transforming Conflict into Cooperation* (1999) offers several ways to develop a mindset for dialogue. Yankelovich calls dialogue "a process of successful relationship building" and "a practical everyday tool" (1999, 15). At its core, dialogue is a method for promoting mutual understanding. Yankelovich identifies three distinctive features of dialogue:

1. Equality and the absence of coercive influences

2. Listening with empathy

3. Bringing assumptions into the open

Yankelovich says people typically have two reasons to engage in dialogue: "to strengthen social relationships and to solve problems" (1999, 12). These purposes are shared by politicians, businesspeople, community leaders, and many others whose work depends on successful collaboration. Dialogue has almost limitless transfer value.

Among the many forces Yankelovich identifies as driving an increasing need for dialogue in the business world is one I find especially compelling: "The need to stimulate the maximum amount of creativity, innovation, and initiative in coworkers, rather than simply expecting them to show up and obey orders" (1999, 13). Isn't this why we teach? To stimulate creative and critical thinking, not to train our students to take orders?

Using the work of philosopher Martin Buber, Yankelovich identifies several behaviors that are *not* characteristic of effective dialogue:

- Tuning out views we disagree with

- Preparing a rebuttal instead of listening to what someone is saying

- Seeking only to reinforce our own prejudices (1999)

These communication practices discourage innovation and collaboration. We won't be serving the best interests of our students or our society if what we teach kids only increases "polarization, acrimony, demonization, and other forms of fracture" (Makau and Marty 2013, 1). What's more, this kind of combative debate is significantly different from the types of written conversations students typically encounter on the job or in higher education. Our goal shouldn't be to teach students how to fight with evidence; our goal should be to help students engage in reasoned intellectual inquiry.

James and Merickel make this point nicely in their work on argument and literature:

> In an academic setting [. . .] argument means more than confrontation. Academic argument implies a reasoned approach to issues. In an academic community, people also hold opposing viewpoints, but they debate in order to modify and strengthen their positions. Through the deliberative and respectful exchange of viewpoints, each side "wins" by attaining a deeper understanding of the issue. (2005, 1)

Teaching for transfer means we don't skip over the messages we send or principles we foster by our approach. It means we critically engage the long-term understandings and values we cultivate when we do things like teach arguments through binary thinking. Telling students that an issue has two sides (and only two sides) and assigning students the affirmative or negative stance sets students up to see the world through a win/lose framework.

This isn't the way of being in the world I want for my students. And it certainly isn't how I want to approach workplace problems with my colleagues or disagreements with my family. Instead, the principle I want to cultivate is that we need to understand before we argue.

> See the National Coalition for Dialogue and Deliberation videos at http://ncdd.org/rc/item/4015

Promoting Dialogue Across Differences

In *The Rhetoric of Reason*, James Crosswhite says that argument is "a communicative process" and a form of "call and response" (1996, 51). The back-and-forth exchange of questions and answers between people who care about the same issues is the conversation. Framing academic discourse as a conversation acknowledges the collaborative and dialogic nature of academic work.

This doesn't mean that we avoid difficult conversations. Quite the contrary. There's a difference between combative communication and productive advocacy. We can agitate for social change in a manner that promotes engagement rather than withdrawal or dismissal.

In its Resolution on Contemporary Discourse and the English Language Arts Classroom, the National Council of Teachers of English (NCTE) affirms the importance of engaging diverse voices and views: "Respectful disagreements develop not only empathy but also engaged, responsible citizens" (2017). The more angles of approach to solving a problem, the better. In *Academic Conversations*, Jeff Zwiers and Marie Crawford give the example of two students who have different ideas about the same issue. "As they converse," Zwiers and Crawford write, "they form a mutual understanding by conceding some points and adding others from the partner" (2011, 81). Through dialogue, the students "build stronger ideas that are less black and white" (81).

> Visit http://dialogueand deliberation.com for resources on teaching dialogue.

Writing that starts with inquiry and dialogue is usually the kind of writing we want to keep reading. Such writing gives us a sense of being in a live conversation with real human beings who can teach us something new about ourselves or our world.

> Teaching for transfer means we don't skip over the messages we send or principles we foster by our approach.

SOCRATIC SEMINAR: INNER/OUTER CIRCLES

Discussion and peer interaction are essential preparation for writing. When we use a strategy like the Socratic seminar to collaboratively explore an issue, we help students develop their skill in dialogue while deepening their thinking. The purpose of a Socratic seminar—an open-ended discussion of a text or topic led by students' questions—is to build up mutual understanding through extended inquiry.

I arrange students in two concentric circles and place a couple of empty chairs as "hot seats" in the inner circle to allow students in the outer circle to join the discussion. The inner circle has a free-flowing discussion based on a central question and grounded in a shared set of readings. Subsequent questions are generated by the students. Students in the outer circle listen and take notes, jumping into the hot seat (and then promptly leaving) if they want to pose a question or make a comment. If I want to speak, I sit in the hot seat, too. This structure allows students to experience being both a listener and a participant. We conclude the seminar by freewriting on this reflective prompt: How did your thinking change based on this discussion?

Read the abbreviated transcript that follows from one of our Socratic seminars and see what you notice about the dispositions and communication practices students brought to this discussion. Students prepared for this discussion on waste management and consumerism by reading the op-ed article "Waste More, Want More" by Andrew Lam (2012), the author of an award-winning collection of essays on the Vietnamese diaspora and a frequent contributor to National Public Radio. They also completed a planning tool for Socratic seminars (see Figure 3.5 later in the chapter).

> **Miguel:** I have a question to start. Why do you think that despite being only 5 percent of the world's population the United States uses 30 percent of the world's resources and generates 70 percent of the world's trash?

Ben: I think we buy a lot of things we don't really need. Then we don't want them anymore, and that creates excess waste. It could be cars, could be toys when you're a kid.

Anna: When people first started talking about this problem, there was a lot of excitement about reduce, reuse, recycle. People were going to make things for themselves. But now it seems like people lost interest.

Sara: It goes back to when we were first industrializing, and everybody was so excited because we were finally making things for ourselves. And that was great, but we've kind of kept that mentality. We're a very materialistic society. Whatever we don't use just goes to waste. We should be spreading more of the resources around.

Miguel: So are you saying that we're taking more than our share?

Sara: Yeah, I think we should be spreading things around more, but also we should realize that having stuff isn't the most important thing in life. It's love and spending time with family and friends and just enjoying life that's important.

Alyzha: Why do you think we keep falling into this trap? If we're aware of what we're doing, why do we keep ignoring the problem?

Miguel: I don't think we really are aware of the problem. I didn't know until today that the United States produces most of the world's garbage, and that kind of upsets me. It makes me wonder why this isn't very well known. I think people aren't aware of how this will affect wildlife.

Ben: That Pacific Garbage Patch has gotten way bigger now. I think now it's like the size of France.

Sara: I think people do know about the problems. We get all these reminders and videos on our phones telling us not to waste, but the phones themselves are things we have to have. The news comes in on your phone or your TV or your tablet or whatever. That's like a paradox.

Ben: You're saying you see all this information on your phone, right? Could that maybe be a solution we can talk about? Like education? I didn't know there was something that large in the ocean. Do you think there's a reason why, a purpose, that this information isn't reaching people or having an impact?

Christina: People with power and money.

Ben: Could you say more?

Christina: Well, the people who make phones and tablets want to sell their products. So we get the information, but we also get ads that make us just want to keep buying more new stuff.

Me (from the hot seat): The little that I've read about this is that people are not apathetic; they really do care, and they're also informed. As you've said, we have all these ways to access information. So they know and they care, but they're still not changing their behavior. What then is the core problem we should address? What's the mechanism that's preventing change?

Ben: People don't advocate or want to do anything about it because they don't see that it's that big of an issue.

Miguel: I agree. I think when you're only one person it's very hard to think you're making a difference. I think when you see big groups measuring food waste in the cafeteria, you feel like change is possible. Honestly, you can't really do much when you're alone.

Melissa (from the hot seat): I think there's also the reality of people's lives. People don't want to change because it's not convenient. Like I'll still buy bottled water at a game if I forget to bring my own water bottle.

Christina: To add to that, I think we need to make it easier for people to reduce their trash and food waste. It can be hard for working parents to pack zero-waste lunches for their kids. It's like the idea of seeing more people making a change. If big groups are doing it, and it's convenient, you have more support.

What did you notice? Did you see evidence of dialogic communication skills? Did students work to negotiate meaning? Did they identify differences in viewpoints? To what extent did they develop a more complex understanding of a shared problem?

This particular Socratic seminar moved from an exploration of the causes of consumerism and waste production (e.g., industrialization) to a consideration of factors influencing social change (e.g., convenience, group effort). Some ideas that were introduced, such as the role of education, needed more clarification and elaboration. You can probably think of additional discussion moves that would have taken this conversation even further.

When I first learned about the Socratic seminar at a literacy conference many years ago, the presenter introduced this strategy by examining the distinctions between dialogue and debate. I use this same approach with my own students today. Drawing on the work of social scientist Daniel Yankelovich, I share key characteristics of dialogue and invite students to make their own comparisons between dialogue and debate. One of my classes generated the T-chart shown in Figure 3.4.

DEBATE	DIALOGUE
Closed-ended	Open-ended
Seeks one right answer	Tolerates ambiguity
Rejects other viewpoints	Makes new connections
Divided into pro/con	Explores multiple perspectives
Escalates the conflict	Seeks common ground
Competes for victory	Collaborates in constructing meaning
Values individualism	Values interdependence

FIGURE 3.4
Differences between debate and dialogue

These comparisons also help establish the protocol for our discussion. If we know our goal is to surface all the unique perspectives and experiences in the room, then we're more willing to let others have their say. A shared appreciation for the value of inquiry informs our norms. These include the following:

- Listen with the purpose of understanding.
- Allow others to completely finish talking before you respond.
- Use the word "and" instead of "but."
- Wait to see if others want to respond before jumping in.
- Remember that everyone wants to be heard.
- Consider how others are affected by the problem and the solution.

When I propose these norms to my students and call for their adoption (they're not norms if I impose them), I also invite students to amend my list. I liked Jacqui's amendment so much that I've included it in my proposed list of norms ever since: "Promote equity of voice and participation."

It takes a bit of modeling and coaching to put these norms into practice, so I act as a note taker during our initial Socratic seminars, and we assess our performance after each discussion. Sometimes the norms need to be tweaked to encourage more participation. Other times I have to remind students to listen supportively. Lapsing into debate also calls for redirection since the purpose of the seminar is to engage in inquiry rather than critique. As Yankelovich says, "those who practice dialogue have come to see that the worst possible way to advance understanding is to win debating points at the expense of others" (1999, 38). We don't want to be judged or told we're wrong when we're just trying to learn.

If students need extra support and guidance, I've found it helpful to use additional norming strategies. Zwiers and Crawford (2011) suggest building a norms checklist with students on their communication values and practices. This activity works well after a

Socratic seminar as a self-evaluation and reflection tool. Here are some checklist items Zwiers and Crawford offer as examples:

- I am critical of ideas, not people.
- I strive to confirm that I value others, even if I challenge their ideas.
- I know that I am valuable even if others criticize my ideas.
- I converse, disagree, and challenge in order to learn, not to win.
- I listen respectfully to all sides, even if I disagree.
- I work to understand all sides and perspectives of an issue.
- I change my mind when evidence and reason convince me. (2011, 53)

The authors also recommend role-playing these behaviors and training students to encourage and compliment each other, thereby building mutual trust and respect (2011, 83).

Activities like the Socratic seminar are rich in transfer potential. We can build on what students learn from productive class discussions by framing writing as a dialogue with other writers. Doing so helps students generate new insights and solutions instead of getting entrenched in polarizing debates.[1] Researchers have also documented the numerous ways discussion benefits writing. In *Transforming Talk into Text: Argument Writing, Inquiry, and Discussion, Grades 6–12*, Thomas M. McCann notes that "a substantial body of research in the teaching of writing reveals that frequent purposeful interactions among peers, as part of the writing process, positively affects the quality of the writing that students produce" (2014, xiii).

Try using the planning tool for Socratic seminars (Figure 3.5 and Figure 3.6) and the following resource, "Checklist for Listening to a Socratic Seminar," to further develop your students' skills in dialogic communication.

Directions to Students: Use the planning tool to prepare for your Socratic seminar. Write notes in each box in response to the questions.

- - - - - - - - - - - - - - - - - -

1. *In light of examples such as the brilliant Parkland students—who in 2018 so compellingly leveraged their debate skills to advocate for changes in gun control legislation after a school shooting killed 17 people—I want to acknowledge the importance and impact of oppositional forms of argument. Debate has a place in academia, civic life, and advocacy work. Respectful and constructive forms of rebuttal are essential to the deliberative process. What dialogue does for comprehension, debate does for critique.*

What's the need or problem?	What do you want to know about it?
(exigence)	(questions)
What have others already done to address this need or problem?	What do the people involved care about?
(reading selections)	(pathos)

FIGURE 3.5

Planning tool for a Socratic seminar

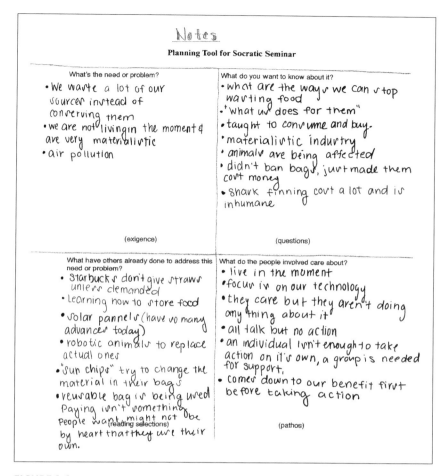

FIGURE 3.6
Student sample of a planning tool for a Socratic seminar

CHECKLIST FOR LISTENING TO A SOCRATIC SEMINAR

This checklist works for the inner/outer circles model of Socratic seminars. Students in the outer circle use the checklist to record the communication practices and habits of mind they observe among the discussion participants in the inner circle.

Directions to Students in the Outer Circle: As you listen to the Socratic seminar, keep track of what students do during the discussion. Place a check mark by the communication practices and habits of mind you observe. Consider the extent to which each one can help you make informed and responsive contributions to academic conversations.

___ Assume the best intentions

___ Postpone judgment

___ Ask questions that move the conversation forward

___ Probe different points of view

___ Build on others' ideas

___ Identify needs and opportunities

___ Make connections to the readings

___ Explain the urgency of an issue

___ Explore the context

___ Consider implications and impact

___ Paraphrase or summarize others' viewpoints

___ Listen empathically

___ Consider the evidence

___ Respond to the cares and concerns of others

___ Demonstrate curiosity

___ Clarify definitions

___ Find common ground

___ Offer a personal response

___ Bring assumptions into the open

___ Be open to new ideas

___ Promote equality and inclusion

___ Allow time for others to respond

Reflective Quick-Write: Which of these practices do you also use when you write? Focus on three or four you think are especially important. What effect do these have on how and what you write? In what other contexts or settings could they be helpful?

> With any kind of learning experience, including classroom debates, the essential questions to ask are these: What are the most transferable skills this activity develops? How do I frame this activity to foreground these skills?

Practicing Inquiry: The Believing (and Doubting) Game

The believing game is a dialogue between reader and writer. As readers, we say, "Talk to me, writer. Help me understand your point of view." In *Embracing Contraries*, Peter Elbow describes the believing game as a willing suspension of disbelief. He talks about "methodological belief" (1986, 255) meaning this is a method—a strategy—for accessing text. When we play the believing game as readers in preparation for responding as writers, we work to understand a text on its own terms and save the criticism for later.

Following are my rules for how to play, adapted from Elbow.

HOW TO PLAY THE BELIEVING GAME

- Postpone judgment.

- Listen with the purpose of understanding.

- Try to see the writer's point of view.

- Read with the grain.

- Understand the text on its own terms.

I'm often asked what it means to try to understand a text on its own terms. I think of it this way: We let the writer set the terms for discussion. That means we accept the writer's definitions for key words or ideas, as well as the writer's priorities and world view. Through close and careful reading, we try to understand the text as it is, not as we'd like it to be. But only temporarily. Only, that is, until we've given the writer's thinking a fair hearing, and we believe we can responsibly summarize the writer's main points.

Playing the believing game takes the issue of emotional manipulation off the table, at least for the time being. We're not on our guard against a writer's attempt to manipulate us when we're trying to understand a text on its own terms. Instead, we assume that the writer's feelings and our feelings are important data points. We attempt, in Elbow's words, to *"enter into"* what we read and *"experience* or *feel the force* of new ideas and texts" (285) (original emphasis).

> Playing the believing game is like telling a writer, "I'll take your word for it."

The doubting game is another form of inquiry. When we read against the grain, we invite other views and voices into the discussion, including our own inner skeptic. Now we ask, "What do others say? Are there different ways of seeing this?" Elbow associates doubting with "refusing, saying NO, pushing away" and with "interrupting and making noise" (266). Now's the time for students to put their debating skills to good use. The doubting game affords students practice rebutting the words of other writers, but this is rebuttal as a means to an end, not an end in itself. The ultimate goal is critical inquiry that leads to new understandings.

Here are the rules for the game:

HOW TO PLAY THE DOUBTING GAME

- Resist the authority of the text.

- Question the writer's assumptions.

- Read against the grain.

- Critique the writer's evidence and reasoning.

- Consider other perspectives.

Both approaches deepen our understanding of a text and its context. The different ways of reading help writers prepare to enter a conversation through open-minded inquiry.

This ability is critical to effective democratic participation, as we know all too well. Makau and Marty (2013) describe a common problem in civic discourse: "Already committed to their convictions, partisan politicians sometimes refuse to listen attentively, ask critical questions, or carefully evaluate any dissent" (196). Practicing the doubting and believing game can move participants past this kind of impasse.

> How we teach students to engage the views of others in face-to-face conversations has important implications for how they learn to engage the views of others in written conversations.

Ways to Play the Doubting and Believing Game

1. Annotation: Invite students to annotate texts as they read with and against the grain.

2. Discussion Norms: Ask students to listen with the purpose of understanding and consider multiple perspectives.

3. Quick-Writes: Encourage students to summarize a writer's position on its own terms and/or to critique that position.

4. Pairs Conversations: Ask students to turn and talk to a partner about their understanding of a writer's claims; then invite pairs to question and critique those claims.

Exigence: Finding a Reason to Write

Exigence is the word contemporary rhetoricians use to describe the need or problem that motivates us to write (Bitzer 1999 [1968], 219). A rhetorical exigence is a "defect" or "obstacle" that can be changed by rhetorical action (Bitzer 1999 [1968], 221). Once students understand the problem, they can decide what they want to do about it. Identifying an authentic purpose for writing is an important step in preparing to enter a conversation.

Starting with the concept of exigence can flip students' approach to writing. Instead of just producing reasons and evidence to support a position—work that can be done whether it is meaningful and needed or not—students engage in a process of inquiry and deliberation framed around an essential question: *What is the problem that needs a solution?*

The exigence drives the writer's purpose. Sometimes students are confused by the distinction between purpose and argument. Isn't the writer's purpose to make the argument? Not exactly. Writers write for a variety of purposes: to affirm our shared values, to challenge our thinking, to promote justice, to entertain, to comfort, to condemn. Sometimes writers can have the same message but different purposes. In other words, they can say the same thing but try to accomplish something different. If they are writing to an audience that already agrees with their central claim, they will likely have a different purpose than if they were writing to an audience that disagrees with them. In the first case, they are not writing to change what their readers think or know about the world but rather to change what they do in response. Writing to move someone to action is a different purpose from writing to change someone's view of reality.

I'll give you an example. The former *New York Times* columnist Bob Herbert wrote several op-ed pieces on the use of racial profiling by law enforcement. The problem of racial profiling was the main exigence for Herbert's rhetorical action. Herbert's repeated claim was that this practice was an outrageous and unconscionable violation of civil rights—a claim that most of his progressive *NYT* readers probably already agreed with. If Herbert wasn't writing to inform (assuming that what he was saying wasn't news to his audience), what then might he be doing? There are several possible purposes for his articles:

- Intensify pressure on political leaders
- Move readers to action
- Act as a witness to oppression
- Express empathy for victims

> *What is the problem that needs a solution?* Starting with this question helps students take effective rhetorical action.

All of these are rhetorical attempts to change something that is "other than it should be" (Bitzer 1999 [1968], 221)—whether that something is oppression, indifference, or inaction.

Stasis Theory: Choosing a Conversation to Join

In the chapter opening, I said that effective rhetorical action involves knowing what questions need to be answered. We listen for the real questions at issue in a community, so that we can make a productive contribution. If we skip this prep work, we can wind up arguing at cross purposes or forcing our own agenda.

So, to sharpen the focus of students' inquiry process, I introduce them to stasis theory, a classical strategy for identifying the question(s) at issue in an ongoing conversation. Makau and Marty explain that an "*issue* arises whenever there is a clash between two or more claims" (2013, 118). A question at issue is a central point of contention. The stasis, or sticking point, is a conflict that can be resolved through informed and thoughtful decision making. Find the stasis, and you've found a conversation to join.

Identifying the question at issue requires summary and synthesis skills. Writers must carefully listen to a conversation to determine what others are saying and how those viewpoints are related. A question is *at issue* when it is the *shared* concern of a group. While individuals may (and probably do) have different answers to that question, the question itself represents the common touchpoint that allows them to engage each other in discussion. Stasis theory gives writers a way to meet in the middle.

Discovering this shared concern is critical. If a community can't agree on the point of stasis, it can't move forward with deliberations. You've got to have a match—at least in terms of the questions being asked—so you can get to work on the solutions.

Drawing on the work of people like Andrea Lunsford, John T. Gage, George Hillocks, and John Edlund, I share the following four stasis theory questions with my students as a general introduction to this strategy:

Question of Fact: What happened? Is it real?

Question of Definition: What is it? What do we call it? How do we classify it?

Question of Quality: Is it good or bad? Right or wrong?

Question of Policy: What should we do about it?

The first step in the stasis process is figuring out where the disagreement is. If people agree on the facts and the definitions but disagree about how to judge something, then the conversation starts with a question of quality. As Linda Flower notes, "difference, rival hypotheses, and conflicting realities" are resources for inquiry (2008, 40). If you've had your students track related arguments across a set of readings, try revisiting those texts to see if they address a shared question at issue. If they do, those texts are in stasis with each other.

> We can't engage in dialogue if we don't find common ground.

Imagine the different conversations that can emerge when this strategy is applied to a text such as the Declaration of Independence:

STASIS THEORY QUESTIONS FOR THE DECLARATION OF INDEPENDENCE

Fact

- How has the Declaration of Independence shaped American culture and identity?
- What social and political constraints did the Founders face in drafting the Declaration of Independence?
- Are these ideals still influential in American society today?

Definition

- What is the nature of American independence?
- What are the key features of this concept?
- How do we define what it means to be an American?

Quality

- What is the value of the Declaration of Independence? In what ways, if any, is it still important?
- To what extent has a failure to uphold the ideals of the Declaration of Independence harmed our country?

Policy

- To what extent should American leaders embody and uphold the ideals of the Declaration of Independence?
- To what extent should the Declaration of Independence still serve as our nation's creed?

The beauty of these questions is the integrative thinking they spark. The answer to one type of question often compels us to pursue or revisit other types of questions. A destructive failure to uphold the ideals of the Declaration of Independence, for instance, might force us to redefine what it means to be American. Stasis theory helps us both discover and generate meaningful discussion.

Cristina, one of my first-year students, applied stasis theory to her research on stereotype threat. She started by asking, "What is a stereotype?" and "What is stereotype threat?" and then moved into an examination of the impact of stereotype threat on learning and performance. From there, she turned her attention to an evaluation of this impact, asking, "What are the costs of stereotype threat?" That question took her to a consideration of policy: "What should teachers and students do to reduce stereotype threat?" The threaded questions offered an unfolding series of insights.

> In *Community Literacy and the Rhetoric of Public Engagement*, Linda Flower writes, "Discovery starts with the articulation of difference" (2008, 40).

I often find with my own classes that the stasis questions guide students toward more sophisticated understandings and more authentic purposes. Cristina's research, for instance, moved her from identification to evaluation to advocacy—in other words, from surface to depth to action. That's the magic of stasis theory; the progression of questions can change our thinking.

Teaching *Kairos* as an Invention Strategy

A consideration of *kairos*—or the opportune moment—is another means of invention.

Like stasis theory, the concept of *kairos* helps writers generate questions and ideas worth exploring. *Kairos* is the "Why now?" of a conversation. Crowley and Hawhee explain that *kairos* "points to the situatedness of arguments in time and place and the way an argument's sustainability depends on the particulars of a given rhetorical situation" (2009, 48).

For Crowley and Hawhee, a *kairos*-based rhetoric is an inquiry-based rhetoric. They explain, "[K]airos requires that rhetors view writing and speaking as opportunities for exploring issues and making knowledge. A rhetoric that privileges *kairos* as a principle of invention cannot present a list of rules for finding arguments ..." (2009, 48). By considering the *kairos* of an issue, students sharpen their investigative skills as they work to discover the contexts, viewpoints, and events that make the issue relevant and important right now. This exploratory work is at the heart of the invention process.

> *Kairos* can be defined as knowledge of "what to say when" or "the right words at the right time." *Kairos* also involves understanding what is fitting and proper for a particular occasion. Many scholars see this kind of conditional knowledge as essential for transfer of learning.

Awareness of *kairos* also helps us to be aware of turns in the conversation. We're on the watch for new arguments and new voices because we understand that the conversation is always changing. And if the *kairotic* moment doesn't yet seem right for the issue we want to address, we look for a way to create an opening. Part of our skill set as rhetors is knowing how to shift our audience's focus when needed.

EXPLORING THE *KAIROS* OF A RHETORICAL SITUATION

Crowley and Hawhee (2009) provide several questions that can help students explore the currency and immediacy of an issue. Notice how these questions encourage nuanced analysis:

1. Have recent events made the issue urgent right now, or do I need to show its urgency or make it relevant to the present? Do I need to research the history of this issue?

2. What arguments seem to be supported by what groups at this time? That is, which communities are making which arguments? How are their interests served by these arguments?

3. Where are these arguments being made? What media and venues are people using to make these arguments? Does one group or another seem to be in a better position—a better place—from which to argue? In other words, what are the power dynamics at work in an issue?

4. What lines of argument would be appropriate or inappropriate considering the current needs and values of the audience?

5. What other issues are related to the discussion of this issue right now, in this place and in this community? Why? (Adapted from Crowley and Hawhee, *Ancient Rhetorics for Contemporary Students*, 2009, 52.)

These critical thinking questions deepen students' understanding not only of the rhetorical situation, but also of their own response, often pointing the way to qualifications or concessions they may need to make. Considering the time, place, and social dynamics of arguments prepares students to make informed contributions.

> The classical idea of *kairos* is closely related to the concept of exigence in contemporary rhetoric. The nature of the problem (the exigence) impacts the means and opportunities rhetors have for addressing it.

Conclusion: The Ultimate Goal

Preparing to enter real-world conversations in a responsive and responsible manner starts with how we engage the words and ideas of others in the writing we do for school. If we learn academic argumentation as just a game of parry and thrust—a counterpoint for every point and a rebuttal for every claim—we're not adequately prepared to promote healthy public discourse. Shouting matches of the kind public relations president James Hoggan describes in the book *I'm Right, and You're an Idiot* (2016) fail to produce the thoughtful, analytical decision making needed to address complex problems.

It is dialogic, not divisive, communication that will best prepare our students to adapt and thrive in an interconnected global society. The stakes have never been higher.

Entering the conversation is important. Doing so in a civil, informed, and productive manner is critical.

CHAPTER FOUR

Negotiating Different Voices and Perspectives

The classroom should be a space where all voices are recognized, where difficult conversations can be explored, and where communication in all its forms—written, digital, oral, visual—is used as a tool to help people enact their ideas and interact with each other.

—NATIONAL COUNCIL OF TEACHERS OF ENGLISH (NCTE) RESOLUTION ON CONTEMPORARY DISCOURSE AND THE ELA CLASSROOM

Academic writing is at its root a conversation among scholars about a topic or question.

—*MLA HANDBOOK*, 8TH EDITION

Responsibly negotiating different voices and perspectives in an academic conversation is not a trivial matter. Listening across our differences is one of the hardest things we do in any communication context. I think it's also the most important literacy skill students can take with them into their future lives and relationships. At the risk of downplaying the value of the other chapters in this book, I would argue that no other skill is as essential to twenty-first-century problem solving as the ability to interpret and integrate multiple sources of information, including the experiences of people who are different from ourselves.

My experience also tells me that this is one of the most difficult skills to teach. I probably get more of those "How do I this?" questions in relation to source-based writing than just about any area of composition I teach. Many students continue to struggle with how to paraphrase, summarize, synthesize, and cite sources well into their college careers. Mastery can be elusive.

This chapter is thus about moving the needle on one of the toughest challenges we face as writing teachers: helping students develop a *deep and principled* understanding of how to responsibly engage and respond to sources in written academic conversations. In a rhetorical approach to texts, the reading-writing connection describes more than just the sequence of instructional activities. Because students are practicing writing as communication, they're doing more than just *using* the words of other writers in their essays. They're doing this, of course, but they're citing sources as part of an earnest attempt to really understand what other people are saying and to respectfully and knowledgeably respond to those viewpoints.

Rhetorical Empathy and the Democratic Exchange of Ideas

Linda Flower explains that "talking across difference will demand rhetorical empathy, an attempt not only to listen and understand others but to present our views in words that speak to them" (2008, 36). This is one of the areas where the Common Core State Standards is well aligned with what college faculty expect of entering students and what employers value in recent graduates. Notice, for instance, what the substrands of the Common Core Standard for Speaking and Listening say about comprehension and collaboration (CCSS.ELA-Literacy.SL.11-12.1):

- Come to discussions prepared, having read and researched material under study; explicitly draw on that preparation by referring to evidence from texts and other research on the topic or issue to stimulate a thoughtful, well-reasoned exchange of ideas. (CCSS.ELA-Literacy.SL.11-12.1.A)

- Work with peers to promote civil, democratic discussions and decision-making . . . (CCSS.ELA-Literacy.SL.11-12.1.B)

- Propel conversations by posing and responding to questions that probe reasoning and evidence; ensure a hearing for a full range of positions on a topic or issue; clarify, verify, or challenge ideas and conclusions; and promote divergent and creative perspectives. (CCSS.ELA-Literacy.SL.11-12.1.C)

- Respond thoughtfully to diverse perspectives; synthesize comments, claims, and evidence made on all sides of an issue . . . (CCSS.ELA-Literacy.SL.11-12.1.D)

These standards articulate the competencies most college faculty and employers would agree are essential for effective communication and collaborative problem solving.[1] Students derive maximum benefit from instruction in these speaking and listening competencies when they can transfer their learning to written communication.

- - - - - - - - - - - - - - - - - -

1. See, for instance, the American Association of Colleges & Universities' survey of employers (https://www.aacu.org /leap/public-opinion-research/2015-survey-falling-short) and their Liberal Education and America's Promise (LEAP) initiative.

Like the Common Core State Standards, the National Writing Project (NWP) also promotes the respectful engagement of diverse perspectives as a foundational practice for democratic participation. In an article describing the NWP's College, Career, and Community Writers Program (C3WP), Linda Friedrich, Rachel Bear, and Tom Fox explain that "the NWP's approach to argument writing starts with having students understand multiple points of view that go beyond pros and cons and are based on multiple pieces of evidence, which ultimately enables students to take responsible civic action" (2018, 19).

> A rhetorical approach to argument writing helps students learn how to take different perspectives, not just take a side.

Beyond doing our best to establish inclusive learning community norms (see Chapter 3), we can also keep in mind that this is developmental work that takes time and mentoring.

Learning at the Threshold

There are special steps teachers can take to support students as they progress from novices to experts, including being aware of different mile markers along the journey.

One eighth-grade girl I talked with said that source-based writing is hard because "most of the time [the source] doesn't fit. You just have to do it because that's the assignment." She added, "Sometimes you just have to stick the quotation in." A ninth-grade boy I spoke with told me what was challenging about using sources was "finding information," "writing from stuff you didn't write," and "mixing your information with their information." These comments give us a good idea of our starting place.

Remember, too, that novices often use mimicry as a coping strategy and will substitute easier tasks for more complex ones. Other common beginner moves in source-based writing include the following:

- Quoting or paraphrasing a source without comprehending it
- Imitating the form of parenthetical citations without understanding the principles or purposes of documentation conventions
- Using academic transitions or lead-ins without understanding their meaning
- Plagiarism

Essays that are quote-heavy but not content-heavy are also signs that students haven't yet developed a deep understanding of how to engage diverse perspectives. So are essays that just list sources. Beginners often just paraphrase a single claim when they're not sure how to unpack the full implications of a writer's viewpoint.

When we see these kinds of responses to academic conversations, we know our students could benefit from additional instruction in understanding and negotiating textual voices. This involves going beyond scaffolding that just teaches students to imitate the surface features of source-based writing, such as telling students that they have to have two quotations in each paragraph or giving students a rubric that quantifies how many sources they have to include.

Expert writers have mastered more than just the mechanics of source-based writing; they also have a deep understanding of the concepts and principles that guide these practices in authentic discourse communities. Concept building is thus one of the ways we help students develop expertise.

Seeing Sources as People

One of the concepts that can have the greatest impact on students' approach to source-based writing is the idea that sources are people. People who have rich reading lives often speak of books as old friends. This is how I want students to feel about the sources they cite in their academic writing. I want them to have a warm affection for—or at least a personal interest in—the writers whose words they consider important enough to include in their own compositions.

However, getting students to see sources as people, let alone friends or acquaintances, takes some doing. Novices tend to see sources as something to use, not someone to listen to. But if we want students to transfer what they learn from source-based writing to real-world problem solving, then we have to show students the larger value of this work. We need to help them see that they are developing valuable communication skills that will help them resolve conflicts and practice collaborative decision making.

Engaging in productive dialogue is as important in written communication as it is in face-to-face conversations. In *Holding on to Good Ideas in a Time of Bad Ones*, Thomas Newkirk makes an astute observation that illuminates a core practice of our discipline:

> There is a wonderful tradition in academic quotation that puzzles most beginning students: we use the present tense even if the author is long dead . . . As long as we quote them, they remain alive and present . . . (2009, 12)

If we didn't see sources as people—and see ourselves as engaging these people in dialogue—this convention would make no sense. The act of quotation brings writers and conversations to life.

If you, like me, have ever been dismayed when you ask students for the source of some information they've cited only to have them respond, "Google," then we share this common challenge: helping students see the humans behind the search results. That involves taking a closer look at what those humans are saying, how they do their work, and where their way of thinking comes from.

When students start to see sources as voices in a conversation—and not just tools or resources for completing academic assignments—they understand that more is at stake than just a grade. When we sincerely engage the views and experiences of other people, we have to accept a higher level of responsibility for our actions because what we say and do in response to the words of others has real consequences.

Seeing Sources as Mentors

Another transformative concept that can help students develop greater expertise is the idea that writers and scholars don't work in isolation.[2] They rely heavily on others to help them do their work. Writers' acknowledgments of their intellectual debts make manifest the back-and-forth exchange of participants in academic conversations. I'm always happy when I find examples of these tributes I can share with my students. In *The Rhetoric of Irony*, for instance, Wayne C. Booth explicitly calls out his debt to D. C. Muecke's *The Compass of Irony*:

> I wish that I could have read Mr. Muecke's book before I wrote the first draft of mine; his help is evident everywhere in this final version, and I have again and again been tempted to say to my reader: go read Muecke and then we can carry on from there. (1974, xiii)

This is precisely what we do when we enter an academic conversation; we go and read a bunch of other thoughtful writers and then we carry on the discussion from there. One of my favorite places to trawl for reading recommendations is in the acknowledgments section of scholarly books. I figure the people a writer thanks have clearly been a big influence on their thinking and could probably help me sort out my ideas, too.

Getting to Know Your Sources

Writers who really know their sources are better prepared to help their readers understand the significance of those sources. These are the questions I want students to be able to answer about their sources:

- Why are you citing this source?
- Who wrote this source? What does the reader need to know about the writer(s)?

----

2. The report by the Intersegmental Committee of Academic Senates (ICAS) makes this point nicely: "[College faculty and students] think with, around, and against other thinkers in a culture of academic literacy" (2002, 12).

- What's the nature of this source?
- What does it contribute to the conversation?

Knowing the answers to these questions will help students position their sources more effectively in their writing.

In a class I teach for future teachers, one of my students cited Kaplan University in her research paper on grammar pedagogies. This was an interesting choice, full of potential. But the student hadn't yet situated Kaplan in relation to the other sources in her paper, all of whom were educational researchers. Kaplan University is a for-profit university focusing on professional training and distance learning. Its parent organization, Kaplan Inc., is a for-profit corporation typically known for test prep. What role might Kaplan play in the conversation on how to develop K12 students' academic language skills? How is this source different from scholar-teachers such as April Baker-Bell, Vershawn Ashanti Young, Harry Noden, Lily Wong Fillmore, and Constance Weaver, some of the other voices in the ongoing conversation on grammar instruction?

My student and I talked about how it could actually be quite interesting to have a for-profit educational corporation present in the discussion, but that, as the conversation host, she'd need to situate her sources appropriately and make sure her audience knows who they are.

CITATION YEARBOOK

When the straightforward approach doesn't work, I try a backdoor to concept building. One such activity is the "Citation Yearbook." In this activity, students create a list of yearbook superlatives for the sources in their list of works cited. They include pictures, too. This is the kind of creative activity I use in the hope that my students will say, "OK, I see it now." To make learning memorable and transformative, we have to make it visible.[3]

The purpose of the "Citation Yearbook" is to help students see their sources as real human beings (at least, those that aren't corporations). A whole host of writing ills are cured once this happens—chief among these is plagiarism. Notice, for instance, how the "yearbook photos" in Figure 4.1 bring the sources my student cited in her grammar paper to life:

----

3. *See, for instance, the work of Douglas Fisher, Nancy Frey, and John Hattie in* Visible Learning for Literacy: Implementing Practices That Work Best to Accelerate Student Learning *(2016).*

FIGURE 4.1

Photos for a "Citation Yearbook" (pictured from left to right: Deborah Dean, April Baker-Bell, and Vershawn Ashanti Young)

When students understand that writing is communication, they take greater care to get to know their sources and to help their readers get to know these sources, too.

Directions to Students: Create a list of yearbook superlatives for the sources listed in your Works Cited. The purpose of this activity is to more fully imagine the personalities and distinguishing traits of the people you're engaging in a written conversation. If possible, include "yearbook photos" of your sources.

Yearbook Superlative Categories

> Most Likely to Be an Undercover Agent
>
> Most Likely to Achieve World Peace
>
> Most Likely to Be President
>
> Most Likely to Be on a Reality Show
>
> Most Likely to Win a Nobel Prize
>
> Most Likely to Win a Pulitzer
>
> Most Likely to Survive the Hunger Games
>
> Most likely to Be a Supervillain
>
> Most Likely to Be Sorted into Gryffindor
>
> Most Likely to Be Sorted into Slytherin
>
> Most Likely to be Sorted into Ravenclaw
>
> Most Outspoken
>
> Most Unique

Best Style

Best Humor

Best Storyteller

Best Attitude

Best Selfie-Taker

Best Person to Be Stranded with on a Desert Island

Biggest Drama King/Queen

If the above categories don't seem to fit your sources, you can generate your own list of superlatives for the writers in your Citation Yearbook. What categories best capture the unique personalities and achievements of the sources you've invited to be part of the conversation you're hosting?

I loved the list of superlatives Esther created for the sources in her paper on food waste:

Most Likely to Achieve World Peace: White, Ajita. "Health Benefits of Eating Local Produce." *Down to Earth Organic and Natural*, 9 Mar. 2018.

Best Attitude: Union of Concerned Scientists. "Cars, Trucks, and Air Pollution." 5 Dec. 2014.

Healthiest: Carlson, Kristine. "The Benefits of Eating Locally Grown Foods." *UW News*. 29 Apr. 2015.

Most Likely to Live Longer: Blythman, Joanna. "Inside the Food Industry: The Surprising Truth about What You Eat." *The Guardian*, Guardian News and Media. 21 Feb. 2015.

Another standout list of citation superlatives was this one for a researched-argument essay on immigration:

Most Likely to Win a Nobel Prize: Vargas, Jose Antonio. "Vargas: Undocumented and Hiding in Plain Sight." CNN, Cable News Network, 30 June 2014.

Most Outspoken: Morrison, Pat. "Why Do People Cross the Border Illegally? It's Not What You Think." *Los Angeles Times*, 25 Nov. 2014.

Most Unique: Krogstad, Jens Manuel, et al. "5 Facts about Illegal Immigration in the U.S." *Pew Research Center*, Pew Research Center, 27 Apr. 2017.

I do these kinds of playful activities with my students because I'm trying to change their conceptual framework. Concept building is one of the hardest things we do as teachers. The idea that "writing is a social and rhetorical activity" is one of the threshold concepts that transfer researchers Linda Adler-Kassner and Elizabeth Wardle (2015, 17) discuss in the book *Naming What We Know: Threshold Concepts of Writing Studies*. In my experience, I've found this particular concept—that is, the notion that writing involves other people besides the teacher—to be especially challenging for students to grasp. When students are just focused on completing an assignment and earning a grade, they don't worry much about whether or not they've represented the views of others fairly. It often takes a big shift in thinking to alert students to the responsibilities they have to their sources and readers.

Hosting the Conversation

Hosting an academic conversation through writing is an act of synthesis that requires great skill and responsiveness. When students are new to source-based writing, they might refer to the subject matter of the sources they've read without directly engaging the views of other writers. This is a little like an eavesdropper at a party picking up on the topic of a conversation but then going home to mull over the topic alone. Engagement requires a response.

A responsible conversation host does not just list sources but engages the thinking of sources and puts them into dialogue with each other. Try using the graphic organizer shown in Figures 4.2 and 4.3 to prepare students to engage sources in their writing.

> The they say/I say model of academic argumentation (Graff and Birkenstein 2014) requires that we understand and explain other writers' arguments before we discuss the extent to which we agree or disagree with them. Writers who skip that first step—explaining others' arguments—end up using sources rather than responding to them.

CONVERSATION PLANNING NOTES

Directions to Students: Take a few minutes to think about how you want to engage your sources in your writing. Choose two sources to focus on for this activity. Be sure you have read these sources carefully. Identify the main ideas expressed by each source and record these "talking points" on the lines provided. Then generate a short list of questions you'd like to ask both sources, taking into account their similarities and differences. What can you do as a conversation host to promote the productive exchange of ideas?

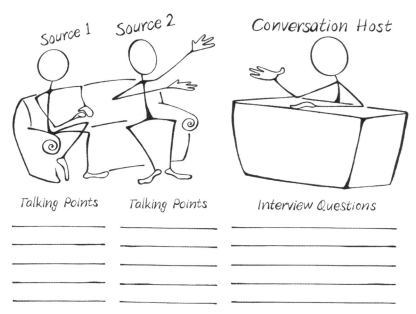

FIGURE 4.2
Conversation planning notes

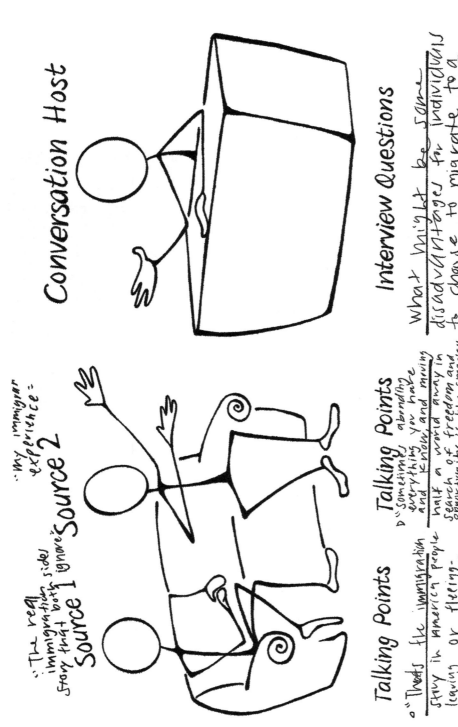

FIGURE 4.3

Student example of conversation planning notes

Figuring Out Who Is Saying What

Responsibly negotiating different voices and perspectives starts with figuring out who is saying what. Can we take a moment and acknowledge how hard this work is? For us and our students? Getting the "they say" (Graff and Birkenstein 2014, xxi) of an academic conversation right depends on close and careful reading. Often, we just have to slow down and give ourselves over to fully understanding a text. We can't rush this step and hope to fairly represent the views of others.

The wise Charles Bazerman (a professor of education at the University of California, Santa Barbara) offers this insight to students in *The Informed Writer: Using Sources in the Disciplines*: "People who listen closely and understand what other people say make more relevant responses" (1995, 45). It's easy to imagine why the contributions of someone who *doesn't* listen to what others have to say wouldn't be super helpful.

Academic texts present extra challenges. Because these sources are themselves a synthesis of and response to the work of others, they significantly increase the amount of textual negotiation and navigation students must do. Readers have to keep track not only of what the writer is saying but also what the writers' sources are saying and the extent to which the writer agrees or disagrees with these other voices in the conversations. That's a lot, especially for developing readers. No wonder, then, that students often become confused when they encounter multiple sources within a single text and mistake the view of a source the writer cites for the writer's own position.

In the grammar class I mentioned previously, for instance, my students have to work hard to distinguish summary writing from evaluative writing or policy recommendations. Many of the sources we read include a discussion of past approaches to teaching grammar, making it a challenge to discern when writers are explaining the views or practices of others and when they are stating their own position. One of my students said that he didn't agree with Constance Weaver's book, *Teaching Grammar in Context* (1996), because she focuses on memorization and recitation. While Weaver does describe the role of memorization and recitation in traditional grammar instruction, she does not advocate for this approach herself—a distinction not easily made without a full reading.

> Developing readers need support for grappling with complex texts.

We can help students practice figuring out who is saying what by studying mentor texts that negotiate different voices. A good one to use is Benjamin Nugent's (2012) *New York Times* article, "Who's a Nerd, Anyway?"—a reading I include in my argument unit on nerd identity and culture. As students read the opening paragraphs of the article, I ask them to consider the following questions:

- When is Nugent speaking for himself?
- When is he quoting, paraphrasing, or summarizing his source's views?
- How does he signal these shifts in viewpoint?

Here's the excerpt. I've marked noteworthy citation moves in bold and underlined those claims that Nugent seems to be making for himself. You could invite students to analyze this kind of multivoice text by highlighting different viewpoints in different colors.

Mary Bucholtz, a linguist at the University of California, Santa Barbara, has been working on the question for the last 12 years. **She has gone to high schools and colleges,** mainly in California, and asked students from different crowds to think about the idea of nerdiness and who among their peers should be considered a nerd; students have also "reported" themselves. Nerdiness, **she has concluded,** is largely a matter of racially tinged behavior. People who are considered nerds tend to act in ways that are, **as she puts it,** "hyperwhite."

<u>While the word "nerd" has been used since the 1950s, its origin remains elusive. Nerds, however, are easy to find everywhere. Being a nerd has become a widely accepted and even proud identity, and nerds have carved out a comfortable niche in popular culture; "nerdcore" rappers, who wear pocket protectors and write paeans to computer routing devices, are in vogue, and TV networks continue to run shows with titles like "Beauty and the Geek."</u> **As a linguist,** Bucholtz understands nerdiness first and foremost as a way of using language. **In a 2001 paper,** "The Whiteness of Nerds: Superstandard English and Racial Markedness," and other works, including a book in progress, **Bucholtz notes** that the "hegemonic" "cool white" kids use a limited amount of African-American vernacular English; they may say "blood" in lieu of "friend," or drop the "g" in "playing." But the nerds **she has interviewed,** mostly white kids, punctiliously adhere to Standard English. They often favor Greco-Latinate words over Germanic ones ("it's my observation" instead of "I think"), a preference that lends an air of scientific detachment. <u>They're aware they speak distinctively, and they use language as a badge of membership in their cliques.</u> **One nerd girl Bucholtz observed** performed a typically nerdy feat when asked to discuss "blood" as a slang term; she replied: "B-L-O-O-D. The word is blood," evoking the format of a spelling bee. She went on, "That's the stuff which is inside of your veins," humorously using a literal definition. <u>Nerds are not simply victims of the prevailing social codes about what's appropriate and what's cool; they actively shape their own identities and put those codes in question.</u>

We discuss the preceding questions, then work together to distinguish Nugent's views from Bucholtz's. When we use the highlighting strategy, we find that most of this passage represents Bucholtz's thinking but that Nugent does insert his own claims here and there. Doing this analysis together gives me important insights into when my students have to work hard to figure out who is saying what.

Building students' reading comprehension skills is important preparation for source-based writing.

> Just "using" or citing sources is not the same as sincerely working to understand and engage sources.

Quotation, Paraphrase, and Summary

Viewed through this conceptual framework (i.e., the idea that sources are people who deserve to be understood), the three ways of using the words of other writers that form the basis of source-based writing—direct quotation, paraphrase, and summary—can be thought of as three interpretive strategies. In other words, they are tools for figuring out who is saying what.

Each citation method has a different rhetorical function (Figure 4.4).

1. Quotation showcases a source's language choices when those choices matter.

2. Paraphrase seamlessly integrates a source's content with a writer's argument.

3. Summary offers a "big picture" of a source's main ideas or importance.

DIRECT QUOTATION	PARAPHRASE	SUMMARY
Adam Serwer argues, "The perennial image of the nerdy white suburban kid locked away in the basement with his boxes of comic books is no longer operative, because as America browns, the comic book audience is browning with it" (1).	In "What Color Is Your Superhero?" Adam Serwer argues that the stereotypical image of a comic book fanatic as a nerdy white kid no longer holds true for the diverse new generation of fans (1).	In "What Color Is Your Superhero?" Adam Serwer describes the increasing ethnic diversity of the comic book audience—a "browning" not yet fully represented by the limited number of heroes of color, such as Mr. Terrific, Static Shock, and Black Panther.

FIGURE 4.4
Quote, paraphrase, or summarize?

When students make their own decisions about whether to quote, paraphrase, or summarize, we want them to consider the following questions: What are you trying to do? Why are you trying to do this? What's the best choice in this situation? Different choices accomplish different ends. Social scientists, for instance, tend to use more paraphrase than direction quotation because their focus is on the content of their sources rather than the writers' language choices.

How we treat sources varies according to discipline. Different academic disciplines (e.g., biology, psychology, literary studies) follow different practices for engaging the work of other scholars—practices that reflect the special ways of thinking and working unique to those fields.

In addition to performing different disciplinary and rhetorical work, the choices also range in degree of difficulty, but all are ways of reading for understanding. And all can be used to synthesize the ideas of other writers. Showing students their options for engaging the words of other writers fosters rhetorical thinking.

QUOTATION

Let's start with the easiest. As Newkirk notes, direct quotation breathes life into a written conversation (2009, 12). The quotation marks show that someone else is talking at that moment. The host (the writer) has temporarily passed the microphone to a guest speaker, but both are present to the audience.

Beginners do a lot of fake it 'til you make it, which is OK, providing they don't confuse faking it with making it. Fake quotations are a common starting point. When students are new to this work, they sometimes do things like visit an online bank of quotations on a topic rather than carefully reading their sources. Finding a quote on loyalty from BrainyQuote or Pinterest doesn't do much to further the discussion of how loyalty functions in *Julius Caesar*. Younger students might also not understand what it means to quote a writer. An instruction to include direct quotations in their essay might send them searching for quotation marks in their sources (which is perhaps a good reason for teaching them their options for citing sources and letting them decide whether they quote, paraphrase, or summarize). Moving students toward genuine inquiry gets them over the beginner's crutch of mimicking the form of academic writing without engaging the substance of academic thinking.

It takes time and support to become an expert learner, but it helps to have a clear sense of the ultimate goal. The big understanding I'm trying to help students develop is that our job as academic writers is to contribute. We're there to help further everyone's understanding, including our own.

You'll find strategies for helping students introduce and contextualize quotations later in this chapter.

PARAPHRASE

Paraphrase is a bit more like a mention in a monologue. The host says, "So I was talking to so-and-so the other day . . ." and then relates what the person says. But only the host gets to stand in the spotlight.

In academic contexts, paraphrase is an important way to check for understanding; it is an "imitation or transformation" (Rabinowitz 1987, 17) of another writer's meaning. Paraphrases can differ significantly from the original text but still adequately demonstrate understanding. In the landmark work *Before Reading: Narrative Conventions and the*

Politics of Interpretation, Rabinowitz gives the example of a parent who says, "It's time for bed," and a child responding, "Is it really eight o'clock?" (1987, 16).[4] While the child's paraphrase is not synonymous with the parent's statement, it nevertheless demonstrates that the child understands what he or she has been told.

In fact, avoiding synonyms in paraphrases can be an excellent way to imitate or transform a source's statement. Less experienced students often translate "write this in your own words" as "use a thesaurus to find a synonym for each word in the original"—a transformation that does *not* adequately capture the meaning of this common teacher direction. Paraphrase as parade of synonyms can result in an imitation that does little to further the student's understanding of the original quotation.

What counts as an adequate paraphrase? An adequate paraphrase fairly and responsibly represents a person's meaning. There's a moment in the 2017 *Lego Batman Movie* that struck a chord with me. See if the following dialogue rings any English teacher bells for you, too (Figure 4.5):

Batman: We are gonna steal the Phantom Zone projector from Superman.

Robin: [frowns] Steal?

Batman: Yeah. We have to right a wrong. And sometimes, in order to right a wrong, you have to do a wrong-right. Gandhi said that.

Robin: Are we sure Gandhi said that?

Batman: I'm paraphrasing.

FIGURE 4.5
"I'm paraphrasing."

---

4. *If you want to help your students determine the influence and impact of a source they are citing, you can have them use Google Scholar to identify how many times that source has been cited by other writers. Rabinowitz's* Before Reading, *for instance, had been cited 1,218 times as of January 12, 2021, when I last edited this chapter. That's a significant contribution to the field.*

Sometimes this is about as close as students get to an accurate paraphrase. As one of my colleagues has said, you can make a square peg fit into a round hole, but you have to do violence to the peg. We don't want our students doing violence to the sources they cite in order to get them to fit their own arguments.

Thinking rhetorically about citation strategies changes how we view and evaluate paraphrase. Rabinowitz notes, "Different kinds of imitations are adequate under different circumstances, since the imitator's decisions about which features are essential

> Ask students if their paraphrase is reasonable in the context of the whole text.

and which are secondary will depend in part on his or her purposes" (1987, 18). What counts as adequate paraphrase in one writing situation might not be adequate in another.

SUMMARY

Summary sits just outside the live discussion. While it doesn't offer the immediate back-and-forth exchange of direct quotation or the specificity of paraphrase, summary does provide the deep understanding of a writer's contributions that justifies why that writer was invited to join the conversation in the first place.

Developing a habit of effective summary writing is one of the best ways to become an informed writer. I used to think summary writing was a low-level activity analogous to a book report. And then I started reading my students' summaries instead of just checking them for completion. There's nothing easy about trying to capture the truth of a whole work. "Good summary writing," Bazerman says, "requires careful attention to the meaning and shape of the entire text," cautioning that "much meaning can be distorted or lost by too rushed a summary" (1995, 77).

Of the three ways to cite the words of other writers that I discuss in this chapter—quote, paraphrase, and summarize—summary is the most cognitively demanding and requires the broadest skill set. It also requires the most advanced ability to practice integrative thinking: the capacity to make connections, synthesize ideas, create wholes out of multiple parts, and draw conclusions by combining information (see AAC&U's Integrative Learning VALUE Rubric).

Students need opportunities to practice this demanding intellectual work. If they're always given a synopsis of their readings (or they have a habit of finding synopses online), students don't have the chance to develop their own skill in summarizing. Preloaded essential questions can also limit students' ability to listen with an open mind and do their own thinking. Sometimes those essential questions can even steer students toward the closest cliché syndrome (Graff and Birkenstein 2014, 198)—a superficial and forced reading of a text that doesn't account for its internal complexities. If we tell students to find something in the text,

> Summary writing is often part of the behind-the-scenes preparation that goes into developing a researched-argument essay. It can also be an effective citation choice if a writer wants to note the significance of a work as a whole.

they're probably going to find it—regardless of whether or not their own analysis of the evidence tells them it's there.

In the sections that follow, I share ways to help students practice quoting, paraphrasing, summarizing, and synthesizing the words of other writers as part of their responsibilities as conversation hosts.

Synthesizing Sources and Integrative Thinking

To synthesize the ideas of multiple writers is to make one writer "dance with" another writer, as Rabinowitz puts it so memorably in *Before Reading* (1987, 11). We put writers into conversation with each other, thereby broadening our own and our reader's understanding of the subject. Writing is a social act, and source-based writing is much richer and livelier when the sources actually socialize with each other.

Synthesis is different from citation—a point lost when "synthesis essays" are taught as a genre of school writing characterized by the use of sources. Using sources is not the same as responding to sources and relating them to each other. The value of synthesis is that it provides a deeper, more comprehensive understanding of the subject or question at issue by bringing together divergent and partial perspectives into a collective whole.

When I saw my students' early attempts at synthesis, I had to go back to my writing prompt to make sure I hadn't written, "Pick one quote from each source and explain that quote in its own paragraph." Because that's what most of my students did. No, my directions clearly asked students to synthesize multiple sources on the subject. As learners new to this task, however, they were reading *synthesize* as "find and use quotations" instead of "interpret and integrate multiple sources." Beginners tend to substitute an easier task for a more complex one, and it is far easier to sprinkle an essay with quotations than to work to fully comprehend, negotiate, and respond to the various viewpoints in an academic conversation.

Knowing this, I now try to provide extra support at the outset while also offering students a clear sense of where we're going. Students need to know that the goal isn't just to make their writing look like synthesis but to engage in the critical reading, listening, and thinking practices that facilitate actual synthesis—that is, the bringing together of different perspectives into a cohesive whole that accounts for the complexity of its parts. Not so easy. But so worthwhile.

Synthesis accomplishes multiple rhetorical and intellectual purposes:

- It contributes to the development of a writer's ideas.
- It establishes the context for the argument.
- It describes the ongoing conversation.
- It promotes depth and breadth of understanding.

Synthesis requires students to go beyond summarizing to analyze and make connections among multiple sources. When writers use one source to respond to or illuminate what another source says, that's a form of synthesis. This is a way of putting sources into dialogue with each other, as in the following example (see my prompt on nerd identity in Appendix Y):

> While some people define nerds by their personality traits—for example, "practical" (Nugent) or "awkward" (Serwer)—other people define nerds by their interests, such as "vector calculus," "minesweeper," "comics," and "Glee Club" (Yankovic).

Synthesis can also be used to identify one's own contributions to the discussion. Here's how linguist Mary Bucholtz effects this move in an article she wrote on nerd identity for a scholarly audience (1999):

> **Although previous researchers** maintain that nerd identity is non-identity or deficient identity, **I will show** that in fact nerds, like Jocks and Burnouts, to a great extent consciously choose and display their identities through language and other social practices. And **where other scholars** seem to equate nerdiness with social death, **I propose** that nerds in U.S. high schools are not socially isolated misfits but competent members of a distinctive and oppositionally defined community of practice" ("Why Be Normal? Language and Identity Practices in a Community of Nerd Girls," 211).

Notice how Bucholtz situates herself within this ongoing conversation on language; she first summarizes the views of previous researchers before taking a contrasting position. Her language choices clearly follow the "they say/I say" pattern common to academic writing that Gerald Graff and Cathy Birkenstein describe in their popular book (2014, xxi):

- Although previous researchers maintain/I will show that in fact
- Where other scholars seem to equate/I propose

This positioning of oneself within the conversation is a large part of what we're asking students to do when they synthesize sources.

In entry-level synthesis, students often just use sources rather than synthesize them—that is, they drop citations from multiple sources into their papers without actually relating these sources to each other or integrating them into a collective understanding. This is the mimicry stage of learning that Meyer and Land describe in their work on threshold concepts (2006). Synthesis is a threshold concept. That means that we're going to have to do some extra concept building in addition to teaching the mechanics of this skill. If we know that our students typically start with superficial approximations of the skills we're working to teach them, we can offer them strategic support for moving to the next stage.

> If your students could use some extra help with synthesis, invite them to use a Venn diagram to compare and contrast sources.

We're not just teaching the mechanics of synthesis; we're teaching the concept of synthesis.

Strategies for Teaching Paraphrase and Synthesis

The examples in this next section again come from my unit on nerd identity. I pair Benjamin Nugent's *New York Times* article "Who's a Nerd, Anyway?" (2012) with works like Gary Soto's play *Nerdlandia* (1999) or Junot Diaz's Pultizer Prize-winning novel *The Brief Wondrous Life of Oscar Wao* (2007). Adam Serwer's *Washington Post* piece "What Color Is Your Superhero?" is also part of this text set. Pairing fiction with nonfiction helps students examine an issue through a range of genres and perspectives.

CHARTING CLAIMS ACROSS MULTIPLE TEXTS

This activity is adapted from the California State University's Expository Reading and Writing Curriculum. The purpose of this activity is to help students track and relate the claims of multiple writers engaged in the same conversation.

> As students draft their compositions, invite them to consider the following questions: What are the relationships between your sources? What's the relationship between your sources and your own argument?

> *Directions to Students:* As you read about the issue, keep track of the claims different writers make and how these claims relate to the views of other writers. Annotate each text, noting the author, genre, main ideas, and key examples. Then use the chart in Figure 4.6 to compare the texts. An example is shown in Figure 4.7.

TITLE AND AUTHOR	GENRE	QUESTION AT ISSUE	KEY CLAIMS	EXAMPLES AND/ OR QUOTATIONS

FIGURE 4.6

Charting claims across multiple texts

"Charting Claims Across Multiple Texts"

Directions to Students: As you read about the issue, keep track of the claims different writers make and how these claims relate to the views of other writers. Annotate each text, noting the author, genre, main ideas, and key examples. Then use the chart below to compare the texts.

Title and Author	Genre"	Question at Issue	Key Claims	Examples and/or Quotations
Who's a Nerd, Anyway? by Benjamin Nugent.	Fiction	How are Nerds seen in today's society? • 2 points of view in the text.	• Nerds are becoming normal, more mainstream • Being a nerd is more of a racial behavior.	• "... rappers who wear pocket protectors and write peans to computer routing devices, are in vogue, and TV networks continue to run shows with titles like "Beauty and the Geek" • "people who are considered nerds tend to act in ways that are, as she puts it, "hyperwhite""
Tracy L Cross Nerds & Geeks Society's Evolving Stereotypes of Our Students ny Gifts and Talents.	Scholarly Article	How has the term "nerd" and "geek" evolved through out the years	• Nerds actually bring benefits to society • Being a nerd has become more neutral	"... I am pleased that these terms are using their negative power. I think there will be many benefits as the terms get increasingly fleshed out and used more frequently."
How Dorks, Dweebs, Techies and Trekkies can save America by David Anderegg.	Fiction	How do we deal Prejudices?	• Prejudices are things that we feel	"One reason it's hard is that prejudices are ubiquitous and therefore hard to examine"

FIGURE 4.7
Student example of charting claims across multiple texts

You'll notice that this graphic organizer doesn't sort sources into camps. Synthesis, after all, is about bringing ideas together, about accounting for and responding to the multiple perspectives in a conversation. It's not about just dividing sources into pros vs. cons for an academic version of dodgeball.

PRACTICING PARAPHRASE AND SYNTHESIS

This activity is adapted from an activity by Nanda Warren. It is designed to help students move from paraphrase to synthesis. Read the directions that follow for "Practicing Paraphrase and Synthesis." Then consider the following questions: What does this activity ask students to do? What would your students find helpful and/or challenging?

Directions to Students: In this group activity, you'll be practicing both your paraphrase and synthesis skills.

STEP ONE: Read the quotations below and choose two that address related ideas. Discuss what each quotation means with your group members.

STEP TWO: Paste the two quotations you selected on your group poster. Leave room to write under each quotation.

STEP THREE: Under each quotation, write a paraphrase. Make sure your paraphrase fairly represents what the writer has said.

STEP FOUR: At the bottom of your poster, write a brief synthesis paragraph explaining the connection between the two quotations. Consider the extent to which the writers share views or concerns (e.g., Serwer suggests that . . . Cross addresses this issue when she says . . .).

- From journalist and author Adam Serwer: "The perennial image of the nerdy white suburban kid locked away in the basement with his boxes of comic books is no longer operative, because as America browns, the comic book audience is browning with it" (2009).

- From journalist Ann Zimmerman: "Serious career aspirations aren't the first thing most people associate with Barbie, the impossibly thin, high-heel-loving fashion doll" (2010).

- From psychologist David Anderegg: "Young adult urban hipsters embrace nerd/geek stereotypes and costumes because this is a way of distancing themselves from mainstream America. In this way, 'geek chic' is like 'man purses' and other manifestations of metrosexual fashion: hipsters embrace a stereotype-bending fashion statement as if to say, 'Look how far beyond all that I really am.' But man purses never caught on outside a few big cities, and 'geek chic' has a similar problem. Geek might be chic in Greenpoint, Brooklyn, but it is not chic in Des Moines, or Dayton, or, to my knowledge, Wichita" (2011, 50).

- From linguist Mary Bucholtz: "From the Columbine High School killers to Microsoft monopolist Bill Gates, the label nerd clearly has negative associations in American culture (especially when, as in these cases, it is used to explain highly antisocial behaviors). It is also, as such examples suggest, a cultural category that is both ideologically gendered (male) and racialized (white), although these dimensions are not always contextually foregrounded" (2001, 85).

- From education scholar Tracy L. Cross: "[In the 1980s], nerds were generally considered as socially inadequate, shy or overbearing, smart, and perhaps too smart as we learned later in our studies. Nerds were also perceived as being very focused on academic endeavors, physically weak, uninteresting, unnecessary to society, and ultimately undesirable. Generally speaking, all these things might be categorized under the heading of feeling abhorrent" (2005, 26).

Just getting to the heart of the matter can take some high-level thinking and discussion. One group of students, for instance, couldn't agree about the most important things the quotes they'd selected had in common. Felipe said both quotes had to do with fashion. But Adrianna insisted that what the two had in common was an emphasis on negative stereotypes. Moving from paraphrase to synthesis requires an advanced ability to identify and compare main ideas.

I conclude this activity by posing a metacognitive question: What did you have to *do* to get to the synthesis? Operationalizing this knowledge helps students to be more aware of their meaning-making strategies.

Here's what some of my students said:

> "We analyzed the quotes, found the key ideas and similarities of the quotes, and then combined them together to explain similar ideas."

> "To get to the synthesis, we had to read and analyze the articles thoroughly for a brief understanding of each author's main point."

> "We had to compare and contrast the quotes."

> Just as the form of a summary differs according to purpose and discipline, what it means to synthesize information varies across contexts.

QUOTE, PARAPHRASE, AND RESPOND

This activity is adapted from *Language Exploration and Awareness* by Larry Andrews (2006).

The purpose of this teacher-prepared formative assessment is to gauge students' developing ability to negotiate different voices. Choose a single text for this activity. Then create a list of ten to fifteen statements that include all of the following:

- direct quotations from the text (do not use quotation marks)
- paraphrases of the text's main ideas
- statements that are contrary to the text's main ideas

Directions to Students:

Part I. Place a check in the space beside each statement that is directly stated in the article.

Part II. Place a check in the space by each statement that adequately paraphrases the author's views. Your check means the author would agree with that statement.

Part III. Based on your understanding of the article, and considering what you've learned about the issue, place a check by each statement that you agree with.

The example that follows is based on the article "Narrative and Medicine" by Rita Charon (2004).

PART I (Direct Quotation): Place a check in the space beside each statement that is directly stated in the article.

1. More and more doctors write about their practices not in scientific reports but in narrative records of meaningful human interactions.

2. In turn, doctors have learned about therapeutic listening from practitioners of oral history, trauma studies, autobiography, and psychoanalysis.

3. Only in the telling is the suffering made evident.

4. Without the telling, not only treatment but suffering, too, might be fragmented.

5. Stories have the power to change how we see our world.

PART II (Paraphrase and Summary): Place a check in the space by each statement that adequately paraphrases or summarizes the author's views. Your check means the author would agree with that statement.

1. All human beings have a profound need to be heard and understood.

2. By developing narrative competence, health care professionals can become more attuned to patients' experiences, more reflective in their own practice, and more accurate in interpreting the stories patients tell of illness.

3. The ability to listen empathically (i.e., with empathy and understanding) comes naturally to most people.

4. Illness, no matter how minor, reminds us of our mortality and frailty.

5. When we read someone else's autobiography, we have an ethical obligation to try to understand the text from the writer's perspective.

PART III (Response): Based on your understanding of this article, and considering your prior knowledge and experiences, place a check beside each statement you can support. These are the statements you personally agree with. Be prepared to defend your answer.

1. Reading and writing about literature deepens our empathy for other people.

2. Listening to stories develops our ability to pay attention.

3. We can't help people if we don't listen to them.

4. Health care professionals have an ethical obligation to try to understand and appreciate the feelings and experiences of their patients and/or clients.

5. Effective diagnosis and treatment start with empathic listening.

THE PARAPHRASE TEST

Anytime your students write a paraphrase in class, you can invite them to put their understanding to the test. Ask the student to read their paraphrase aloud to their peers. Then ask the other students, "Is that a fair representation of what the writer said?"

STUDENT CLOSER

An easy way to build in additional opportunities for students to practice paraphrase and synthesis is to designate one student to be the "student closer" at the end of each class. The "closer" is responsible for keeping track of the key points made or insights discovered during the day's lesson and then synthesizing the takeaway learning into a closing statement (a few sentences is sufficient). In other words, the "closer" offers a group paraphrase of the class meeting. This routine also works nicely as a formative assessment. And I like that a student gets the last word.

As I share in *Teaching Arguments* (Fletcher 2015), ways of reading such as Peter Elbow's believing game and doubting game (i.e., reading with and against the grain) work best when they move readers toward a synthesis of multiple understandings. Paraphrase and summary are particular ways of knowing a text, but they are not the only way. We can also read from the view of the original readership and from our own cultural and historical perspectives, layering our attempt to understand the author's intentions with a heightened awareness of what might make those intentions problematic.

A Side Note on Block Quotations

Be honest: Do you ever skip reading block quotations (i.e., quotes roughly four lines or longer) in your students' writing? We might eyeball the quotation and note its function as support for a student's claim, but we don't really have time to read the quoted passage critically. And unless we've read the source ourselves, what can we really say about it? How do we know if a quote is taken out of context or doesn't represent a source's main ideas? We think, *OK, that's their evidence; now let me keep reading for their claims.* If you're like me you do, that is, at least you do if you haven't read the sources your students are writing about and have no real way of knowing if they're citing those sources accurately. My feedback time is limited enough. Why am I going to worry about what someone who's not even my student says?

For this reason: Because if I don't take my students' citations seriously, I'm not taking their reading seriously. That's why until I have a class in which 100 percent of my students are advanced readers (and that hasn't happened yet), I need to have carefully read at least something that they're writing about.

Signaling Who Is Saying What

Students often need help learning to recognize and use signal phrases that distinguish one writer's ideas from another's. The readings in my nerd identity unit, for instance, can present challenges to writers who are unsure about whose "voice" they want to cite in their essays. For instance, several of the texts include direct quotations from other sources that students may want to include as support for their own arguments. Not only do they need to know how to use internal quotations for this purpose, but they also need to know who is saying what. Just because a writer quotes a source doesn't mean he or she agrees with the source.

For example, in "Who's a Nerd, Anyway?" Nugent describes a study conducted by linguist Mary Bucholtz. Whereas Nugent is a journalist and Bucholtz is a scholar, both have written books about nerds, and Nugent is not merely reporting on Bucholtz's research; he also has some opinions on the topic. Thus, he has to do a careful job of signaling who is saying what in his article. Here's an example, with the signal phrases in bold:

> **Though Bucholtz uses** the term "hyperwhite" to describe nerd language in particular, **she claims** that the "symbolic resources of an extreme whiteness" can be used elsewhere. After all, 'trends in music, dance, fashion, sports and language in a variety of youth subcultures are often traceable to an African-American source,' but 'unlike the styles of cool European American students, in nerdiness, African-American culture and language [do] not play even a covert role.' **Certainly,** 'hyperwhite' **seems a good word** for the sartorial choices of paradigmatic nerds. While a stereotypical black youth, from the zoot-suit era through the bling years, wears flashy clothes, chosen for their aesthetic value, nerdy clothing is purely practical: pocket protectors, belt sheaths for gadgets, short shorts for excessive heat, etc. (Nugent 2012)

Sometimes Nugent lets Bucholtz speak directly for herself through direct quotations. Other times he comments on her conclusions, like when he says that her use of the term *hyperwhite* "certainly [. . .] seems a good word for the sartorial choices of paradigmatic nerds". Because Nugent is writing for a newspaper and not an academic journal, he also has to try to make Bucholtz's complicated ideas more accessible.

Newcomers to academic writing often struggle to signal who is saying what. Especially when students are first learning to paraphrase, they may not clearly distinguish between their source's voice and their own voice. For instance, in integrating someone else's words into their own claim, students sometimes cite a source in ways that signal their agreement with a view they don't really endorse.

This reminds me of the time I got caught nodding my head in response to a coworker's complaint about an administrator, a person I admired. I meant my head nod just to show that I was listening, but my coworker took my nod as agreement with her complaint, and excitedly said, "Oh, you don't like her either?" I had to do some quick backpedaling to correct the false impression I'd given.

If a student's framing or paraphrase of a source is ambiguous, I ask them: Is this your claim or the author's claim?

We also practice distinguishing different textual voices with another article we read, this one about Mattel's Computer Software Engineer Barbie Doll. The article, "Revenge of the Nerds: How Barbie Got Her Geek On" by Ann Zimmerman (2010), brings gender into the mix in an interesting way.

I ask students to review the following quotations in the context of the article before answering this question: Which sentences can safely be assumed to be the opinion of writer Ann Zimmerman?

> Signal words and phrases such as "after all," "indeed," "to be sure," "actually," and "in fact" are clues that writers are probably speaking for themselves rather than paraphrasing the ideas of another writer.

1. "Serious career aspirations aren't the first thing most people associate with Barbie, the impossibly thin, high-heel-loving fashion doll" (1).

2. "Regardless, Barbie remains enduringly popular among young girls" (2).

3. "There is a perception that an interest in math, science, and computers means being socially awkward and boring and sacrificing the opportunity to be creative and fun" (2).

4. "[. . .] Barbie's sparkly leggings and pink accessories 'were over the top'" (2).

Sources may dominate or drown out student writers' voices. If student writers only repeat what their sources say, they miss the opportunity to develop their own position.

Introducing Sources

Knowing who is saying what (and why it matters) is an important reader need. The future-focused *MLA Handbook* makes this point nicely. One of the goals of the revised *Handbook* is to help writers "provide their audiences with useful information about their sources" (2016, 1). The updated guidelines show a heightened awareness of the interactions between writers and their readers and of the function of academic work.

> Integrating the words of other writers into their own prose can be a challenge for students. Quotations that are less effectively integrated are signs that students need more help reading their own and others' writing rhetorically.

Less experienced academic writers tend to skip the crucial step of introducing their sources to their readers. Doing a little more prep work as host can help writers avoid the confusion caused by unattributed quotations or unidentified sources.

Using Model Language

One strategy to help students orchestrate voices from varied sources is to use models of introductory language, such as the sentence templates that follow. If you decide to use these kinds of templates with your students, let them know this is a starter strategy for learning academic language. Encourage students to experiment with their own methods for integrating the words and ideas of other writers. You may also want to remind students that they are practicing the conventions of academic writing and that journalists and creative writers use different strategies for introducing quotations.

Main ideas or central claims can be expressed through lead-ins or summary statements:

- The issue of [anti-nerd prejudice] can be viewed from several different perspectives.
- Experts disagree on the meaning of [the nerd stereotype in the twenty-first century].
- Educational researcher Tracy L. Cross argues that . . .
- According to Mary Bucholtz . . .

Contrary views can be signaled by adding transitional phrases:

- Whereas Cross sees the term nerd as having evolved into a neutral or even positive identity, Anderegg insists the stereotype still causes harm, especially among children.
- In contrast to the concern cartoonist Lucy Knisley expresses over male dominance of nerd culture, Leslie Simon, author of *Geek Girls Unite*, sees female nerds as "taking over the world."
- On the other hand, slam poet and self-identified "Nerd of Color" Bao Phi believes . . .

Students can now add their own voice to the mix:

- Although some argue for _____, others argue for _____. In my view . . .
- Though researchers disagree, clearly . . .

The following activity afford students an opportunity to practice positioning themselves in relation to another voice in the conversation.

RESPONDING TO THE VIEWS OF ANOTHER WRITER

Directions to Students: Use model academic language to practice responding to the following questions: Do you think the concept of a "girl nerd" is "more elastic and differentiated" as David Anderegg, author of *Nerds: How Dorks, Dweebs, Techies, and Trekkies Can Save America*, argues? And do you agree with Anderegg that the default definition of nerd is "always male" (2011, 48)?

- Like David Anderegg, I also see . . .
- My own experience confirms Anderegg's observation that . . .
- Anderegg claims . . . ; however, I find . . .
- While Anderegg's view might have been valid twenty years ago, in today's context I believe . . .

NOTE: Keep in mind that the conventions of academic writing change over time and across contexts.

Rhetorical Dimensions of Documentation Styles

Documentation conventions have rhetorical purposes and are a special feature of academic genres. While they signal membership in an academic community, they're more than just a secret handshake. They're there to facilitate the exchange of ideas by helping other scholars to read what you've written. The expectation is that readers who take a writer's ideas seriously will actually be looking up some of these sources for themselves.

Moreover, different citation styles represent different ways of engaging and interpreting texts. These are functional differences, not just cosmetic differences. The conventions of the American Psychological Association (APA) or MLA have more to do with how a text *works* than how it looks. Psychologists and literary critics need different tools because they perform different tasks. APA style prioritizes the publication year because it values currency, while that of the MLA places a humanistic focus on the author. Social scientists are interested in the data; humanists are interested in the conversation. Moreover, the APA and MLA are discourse communities, not sets of rules— that's why the "rules" in the style guides keep changing because the nature of the communities' work continues to change.

> Documentation conventions meet a real need, not just a social expectation; they help your readers engage the writers you've engaged.

MLA Style: Teaching Citation for Transfer

"They change it every year, so why should we even bother teaching it?"

"It's a drag to teach documentation."

"MLA style is dry stuff."

"I don't enjoy teaching MLA style, but my students have to know it for college."

The comments we hear about MLA style say a lot about the challenge of teaching documentation conventions, especially if we're trying to teach for transfer and engagement. We want exciting and purposeful learning experiences our students can apply across contexts, and MLA style is just so . . . exciting and purposeful. Really. I'm not kidding. I felt this way when I first started to use the 6th edition of the handbook in earnest back in 2001, and I feel this even more strongly after seeing the 8th and 9th editions. For me, the *MLA Handbook* is like one of those full-color *DK Eyewitness* travel guides with all the fascinating maps and illustrations: our personal guide through the world of academia.

After the publication of the 8th edition, I went from being a fan to a superfan. Allow me to explain my enthusiasm. MLA style helps you to find and understand what you want to know. It also helps you to make meaningful connections to your audience (by attending to reader needs for sources of information) and to the academic community you're joining (by positioning yourself in relation to the work of other writers).

And today's *MLA Handbook* is built for transfer. It now has an even stronger rhetorical focus. Students have to think like detectives and make choices about the citation information most relevant to their audience and context. The editors explain their rationale for these changes: "[…] now more than ever we need a system for documenting sources that begins with a few principles rather than a long list of rules" (2016, 1). They argue that a contemporary documentation style must be designed for adaptability since "in today's world, forms of communication proliferate, and publications migrate readily from one medium to another" (2016, 1).

Recent editions of the *MLA Handbook* thus offer a documentation style based on principles instead of publication format. To contend with the explosion of new source types—and those sources that can't be imagined yet—the *Handbook* offers the following guidelines for scholarly writing:

> Cite simple traits shared by most works.
>
> Remember that there is often more than one correct way to document a source.
>
> Make your documentation useful to readers. (2016, 3–4)

Style is also now less of an insider's code: Full words are spelled out, citations are reader-friendly, and a "DIY" approach is encouraged. MLA style's rhetorical revision makes the point that writers' choices impact readers' experiences.

All this leads to more portable and flexible competencies. Take a moment to read through the following statements from the 8th edition and see which ones relate to transfer of learning or rhetorical problem solving.

1. "Good writers understand why they create citations. The reasons include demonstrating the thoroughness of the writer's research, giving credit to original sources, and ensuring that readers can find the sources consulted in order to draw their own conclusions about the writer's argument" (2016, 4).

2. "[…] learning the conventions of a form of writing—those of the research essay, for instance—prepares the student to write not just in that form but in other ones as well" (2016, 5).

3. "Learning a documentation style, in other words, prepares a writer to be on the lookout for the conventions to which every professional field expects its members to adhere in their writing" (2016, 5).

4. "Armed with a few rules and an understanding of the basic principles, a writer can generate useful documentation of any work, in any publication format" (2016, 4).

If we have any doubt about the importance of conditional knowledge—knowing what to do when—the 8th edition of the *MLA Handbook* can set that doubt to rest. Students can no longer rely on a fixed system of citation. Instead, they are going to have to think rhetorically. They'll have to examine the available information, evaluate their readers' needs, and make their own choices.

I was thrilled to hear the following student tips shared by MLA editor Angela Gibson at a 2017 NCTE workshop:

"Act as a detective and interpreter"

"Use judgment and find work-arounds" (November 16, 2017, St. Louis)

Don't you just want to cheer? I love that the *MLA Handbook* is asking students to practice the critical thinking skills that will help them communicate effectively in a variety of scholarly contexts. For instance, when students in humanities classes wish to cite sources from a digital source, they have to search through a website for clues to the source's author and publisher and interpret those clues according to the core elements of the new MLA style.

While I won't try to re-create what the *MLA Handbook*, 8th edition and the MLA Style Center (https://style.mla.org) do so well—that is, teach students how to use MLA style—I do want to offer a quick example that illustrates the way the updated approach teaches rhetorical thinking.

Take a look at the screenshot shown in Figure 4.8 and see if you can identify the title of this digital source.

Rhetorical Grammar

FIGURE 4.8

Students need to practice their detective skills when identifying the title for a digital source.

What do you think? Do you take the title from the top of the webpage or from the embedded video? And how much of the title do your readers need to find this source themselves? When it comes to the tricky business of identifying titles, authors, or publishers for web pages, students will need to practice making judgments and finding work-arounds. All of the options shown in Figure 4.9 are viable ones.

GOOD	BETTER	BEST
"The CSU Expository Reading and Writing Course: Rhetorical Grammar for Expository Reading and Writing"	"Expository Reading and Writing Course: Rhetorical Grammar"	"Rhetorical Grammar for Expository Reading and Writing"

FIGURE 4.9
While there might be a "best" way to identify the title of a digital source, other choices can also be acceptable.

The *MLA Handbook* now helps students understand that while there might be a best choice, there are other possibilities. Different variations are acceptable. MLA style no longer tries to have an answer for everything. Writers have options, including options for citations. The new MLA style acknowledges the many grey areas of academic documentation practices while still honoring readers' needs for clarity.

This means that students don't need to memorize MLA style. In fact, memorization can be a problem when publication formats change. If we invest too much instructional time getting students to memorize rules, we run the risk of creating sticklers who will dismiss new innovations by declaring, "That's not how I learned it!"

It's more important that students know how to handle a new kind of source that isn't explicitly addressed in the *Handbook*. How do they do this? Much the same way they effect any act of transfer: compare and contrast contexts, study models, draw on principles, repurpose learning. MLA editorial staff member Angela Gibson calls the new MLA style a "DIY citation generator" (NCTE workshop, November 16, 2017).

Now here's where that transfer-focused and rhetorical thinking helps students see the exciting potential in these changes. Notice the difference between bounded framing and expansive framing when it comes to MLA style (see Figure 4.10).

BOUNDED FRAMING	EXPANSIVE FRAMING
"If you don't do this, you'll get a zero."	"If you don't do this, your reader won't be able to understand the context for your sources or engage those sources themselves."
"I don't know why it's this way. I don't make the rules."	"The Modern Language Association meets annually to present and critique research in the fields of language and literature. Learning MLA style prepares you to contribute to the shared knowledge of this kind of academic community."
"The only way to learn this is to do it over and over again."	"When you understand the underlying principles, you can adapt them to new purposes."
"You have to know this for college."	"Knowing this will help you engage productively in academic conversations."

FIGURE 4.10
Teaching citation for transfer

The last example in Figure 4.10 is a little tricky, right? Telling students that they have to know something for college seems transfer focused until you think about *why* they have to know it for college. What's the larger goal we're working toward? What kind of work will they be doing and why is that work important—to themselves, to the academic discipline, and to local and global communities?

For this reason, I'm not a fan of citation generators like EasyBib. We don't outsource our intellectual labor if that labor is essential to understanding how a field does its work.

The challenge, for me then, is helping students see what I find so exciting and interesting: not the rules, but their underlying principles and the living community of scholars those principles represent. I've found that we don't fully understand how to use MLA style until we actually *use* MLA style. Let me explain. Until we have to rely on MLA style to verify and find the information other writers have cited in their works, we don't fully appreciate how much MLA style is a matter of meeting audience need.

If your reader really does want to engage your sources, an inaccurate citation can cause a heap of frustration. It's like clicking on a handle mentioned in a tweet only to find the wrong profile. I once clicked on the username @NWP in a thread, thinking I'd be taken to the National Writing Project, but found myself looking at the profile of an amateur food critic instead.[5] We won't keep the conversation going if we send our readers down a dead end.

> If you want to teach your students the real meaning of "it depends," try teaching MLA style (Figure 4.11). Nothing develops conditional knowledge like trying to identify when a website is not a "container."

Ultimately, the goal is not just to have students become proficient in academic style; the goal is to have students engage productively in academic conversations and help others to do the same.

Framing Feedback for Transfer

We can help students develop conscious knowledge of the connections among audience, genre, and citation by offering feedback that references the rhetorical situation. Say a student writes a research paper that does not include any sources (it's been known to happen). Instead of giving directions such as "sources needed" or "please use evidence," we might offer the following kind of comment: "Since this is a researched-argument essay, your audience will expect you to provide evidence for your claims and to cite your sources." Or, better yet, we can invite the student to revisit the rhetorical situation to see what they can figure out about audience expectations and genre conventions.

----

5. *If you're curious to know the real Twitter handle for the National Writing Project, it's @writingproject.*

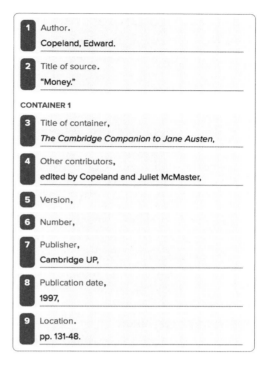

FIGURE 4.11

Generating a works-cited entry in MLA style

Grading Citations

Do you grade your students' citations? If so, what matters? What do citations do?

We can use citations to . . .

- generate a reading list for other scholars
- establish the scope and history of the conversation
- explore different perspectives
- provide validation or "proof" for a claim

When we evaluate students' documentation practices, we want to consider the extent to which their citation choices contribute to the productive exchange of ideas.

Obstacles to Understanding

Thus far, I've been sharing strategies for helping students productively interpret and integrate multiple voices and sources. I've been arguing that this ability requires rhetorical awareness, not just a mechanical set of citation skills. I now want to shift my focus to those behaviors that discourage dialogic communication.

What gets in the way of generating and engaging diverse perspectives? Approaches to academic work that expedite, rather than postpone, judgment. This kind of thinking is an obstacle to dialogue. Binary thinking, defensive listening, and lack of sincerity are all obstacles to dialogue. Combative forms of argumentation can also create "obstacles to *constructive* forms of advocacy, critique, and refutation" (Makau and Marty 2013, 12—emphasis in the original). Students are less likely to bring together different perspectives and problem-solving strategies if they believe there is only one right answer. As Zwiers and Crawford note, "One of the keys to effective negotiation is seeing the other person's perspective(s)" (2011, 82). In this final part of the chapter, I take a look at some of the practices that can interfere with students' ability to effectively and respectfully negotiate different viewpoints.

DEFENSIVE LISTENING

If my first priority as a teacher was student engagement, I'd probably teach *defensive* listening instead of nondefensive listening. I can get immediate buy-in from younger students by telling them I'm teaching them skills that will prevent other people from taking advantage of them. Getting students riled up is an easy way to put energy into a room. If you ask a class what's "wrong" with a "manipulative" advertisement or an article that uses a heavy dose of pathos, you'll probably get the enthusiastic answer: "Yeah! It's playing with our emotions!"

But I don't think a persistently defensive attitude serves students well either in college or their careers. Being on their guard for trickery isn't how we want students to approach academic or professional conversations. Students often enjoy being resistant readers, and resisting the authority of a text by looking for flaws and weaknesses is part of Peter Elbow's "doubting game" (1986, 264)—an important practice in critical reading (see Chapter 3). But there's a danger in habitually assuming the worst about other writers. A stubborn resistance to seeing the merits of a text or position doesn't promote a deep understanding of the issues or help diverse groups solve complex problems.

Imagine how challenging our classroom conversations would be if we *only* brought our doubting game skills to the discussion:

"You don't have any evidence for that claim!"

"That's a logical fallacy!"

"You're just using loaded language!"

"That's biased!"

We can't tap into our collective wisdom if we're not willing to learn from one another.

Playing the doubting game shouldn't be the first, last, or only thing we do with a text—or with a classmate's or colleague's comments.

AUTOMATIC REBUTTAL

Should we teach students to automatically rebut opposing views? How about this instead: Let's teach students to engage the reasoning; understand the reasoning; challenge or extend or complicate the reasoning, and when appropriate, perhaps rebut the reasoning. If we want collective decision making and civic participation not log jammed by partisan feuds, then we shouldn't teach rebuttal as the default response to diverse perspectives.

I've read hundreds of argument essays in which the next-to-last paragraph addresses a counterargument as a mere formality. These are the essays that say in the same breath, "While some people think [insert viewpoint here], these people are wrong." This kind of response opens the door to dialogic communication only to slam it in the other person's face.

Ethical responses to counterarguments start with a sincere attempt to understand another point of view *on its own terms*. Drawing on Makau and Marty's work (2013), I've learned to ask myself an important question: Do my responses to counterarguments capture the gist of what matters most to the people I'm citing?

THE STRAW MAN

The straw man is an imaginary opponent who has been fabricated for dubious purposes. One composition textbook describes a straw man as a claim "that exaggerates or misrepresents the opponents' position" (VanderMey et al. 2014, 301). If you've ever had your own views deflected by a straw man, you know how hurtful this can be. A straw man is an intentional misquotation. It obscures and distorts the views of those who genuinely hold alternative perspectives by giving voice to a fictitious naysayer instead.

I, unfortunately, had this experience when an administrator took issue with faculty resistance to a new policy she was implementing. She stated at a public meeting that those who opposed the new policy just had a "can't-do attitude" and didn't have faith in their own ability to effect positive change. I remember sitting there thinking sadly, "But that's not what we're saying." Rather than respond to the real concerns of stakeholders, this administrator invented an indefensible position that none of us actually held.

In student writing, I see this less as an attempt at deception or manipulation and more as a marker of a writer who is struggling to get going. Often, the straw man is the vehicle students use to tee up their argument. They need to start somewhere and why not with an overarching viewpoint that they can then either support or challenge? Opening with a commonly held view is a frequent move in academic writing. The problem occurs when the reported viewpoint (e.g., "People say . . .") isn't an authentic voice in the conversation students are engaging. The perspective doesn't come from anywhere other than the student's need to start their essay.

Conclusion: What's at Stake

When we teach for transfer, we carefully consider with what mindset and in what potential contexts our students will use what they've learned. Teaching for transfer means we don't just prepare students to succeed on a narrow range of school-based tasks; it means preparing them to flourish as contributing members of society.

In the wake of the violence and acrimony that characterized much of 2016, former presidents Barack Obama and George W. Bush made clear how essential empathic communication skills are to a thriving democracy. In speeches the two gave at an interfaith memorial service for five police officers killed in Dallas in July 2016, they described the challenges before us. "Faced with this violence," President Obama said, "we wonder if the divides of race in America can ever be bridged. We wonder if an African American community that feels unfairly targeted by police and police departments that feel unfairly maligned for doing their jobs, can ever understand each other's experience" (2016).

President Bush likewise described a country fractured by dissension: "At times, it seems like the forces pulling us apart are stronger than the forces binding us together. Argument turns too easily into animosity. Disagreement escalates too quickly into dehumanization. Too often we judge other groups by their worst examples, while judging ourselves by our best intentions" (2016).

But the two also expressed faith in our ability to transcend our differences. "At our best," Bush said, "we practice empathy, imagining ourselves in the lives and circumstances of others. This is the bridge across our nation's deepest divisions" (2016). Given this tremendous need for increased empathy, our work as English teachers is more important than ever.

The literacy skills involved in understanding and synthesizing the words of others are broadly applicable skills that help students appropriately adapt to new situations. These are also skills that benefit students personally—in their academic, professional, and private lives—and that benefit our communities and culture as a whole. Engaging in responsible citizenship depends on the ability to respectfully negotiate diverse voices and perspectives.

CHAPTER FIVE

Designing and Conducting Research

"My research made me realize I was asking the wrong question."

"I get stressed about it. I cry. Then I try to narrow things down."

"It looks like a rainbow of mess in the end."

—STUDENT COMMENTS ON THE RESEARCH PROCESS

W hen a Falcon 9 rocket exploded on the launch pad in Cape Canaveral, Florida, in September 2016, SpaceX CEO Elon Musk described the incident as a "difficult and complex failure" (*San Francisco Chronicle*, Sunday, September 11, 2016, D1). The fireball that destroyed the rocket and its payload—a communications satellite intended to increase Internet access in Africa— represented a major setback for SpaceX's research and development programs (Figure 5.1).

"Difficult and complex failure" also describes not a few of my own research projects. So, when I teach research as part of the writing process, I focus on the importance of problem solving. And I make the point that this work requires our most adaptive and flexible thinking, our highest tolerance for ambiguity, our best efforts to understand different perspectives, and our full embrace of failure. Because things are going to get a whole lot worse before they start to get better. There will be more than a few scorched launchpads before we find our way to the stars.

And this is the other big point I make to students: There's more than one right way to reach our goals. If ever a rule-based, formulaic approach was a hindrance to learning, it's in the case of the research project. A research project is nothing but a mess—at least

FIGURE 5.1
SpaceX launch pad at
Cape Canaveral, Florida

until the later stages. Trying to impose a predetermined formula on the research process is a surefire way to guarantee no real research gets done.

I once overheard a teacher implementing a new curriculum at a school say, "Oh good, we can finally get rid of the research project and teach something more interesting!" A research paper shouldn't be an annual endurance test for students and teachers. Research is the inquiry process by which all academic work gets done. It's the act of listening to the conversation, the answer to the question: *How do you know?* How do you know, for instance, that you can make a particular claim about a novel's theme? Design and conduct some research. Instead of presenting research papers as a rite of passage marked by tedium and arcane documentation conventions ("I suffered through this, and you have to, too!"), we can teach research as an integral process for all intellectual and creative endeavors.

> All writers conduct research. Whether they're researching a historical period, an author biography, consumer reports, a contemporary issue, or a literary theory, they're engaging in a process of discovery and integration, gathering the stuff of which texts are made.

Fostering a Disposition for Problem Solving

At the point in each semester when my students are writing research papers and I'm reading their drafts, I'm reminded how much research is a matter of working the problem. The questions students ask tell the story:

"What do I write about?"

"I can't find anything. What do I do now?"

"How do I get this to make sense?"

"I'm going in too many different directions! How do I focus?"

Students understandably feel stressed and overwhelmed when taking on a big research project. It's tempting to step in and make things easier for them. But the long-term payoff of a research project is what students learn from struggling through a series of challenges.

In fact, we don't just want students to cope with these challenges; we want them to revel in them. Research starts when we find an intriguing problem to investigate. In "Looking for Trouble: Finding Your Way into a Writing Assignment," Writing Center director Catherine Savini encourages students to "seek out difficulty" (2011, 52), that is, to find problems and questions worth pursuing. Savini elaborates, noting the transfer potential of this practice:

> All academic disciplines seek to impart in their students the ability to identify, mull over, and sometimes solve challenging problems. Not surprisingly, the benefits of a willingness and mental acuity to greet complex problems extend well beyond the classroom. (2011, 53)

Embracing complexity is a key to success in all areas of life.

This enthusiasm for trouble was readily apparent in an NPR story I heard about the team of scientists exploring the dwarf planet Pluto and its moon. When the team's spacecraft sent back unexpected and mysterious data on the planetary bodies' geologic activity, scientist Carly Howett was thrilled: "We keep looking at the data, and we don't understand it. And that's just—that's just the best feeling" (July 17, 2015). How great would it be if our students had the same response to confusion?

It could certainly boost their confidence. Understanding that confusion is actually a clue that we're on the trail of something good takes much of the self-doubt out of the research process. Like that pulsing blue dot on a Google map that marks the start of a journey, confusion tells us when we've found an important departure point—in other words, a problem worth pursuing.

One of the most revelatory insights we can share with students is that our depth of eventual understanding is equal to our depth of initial confusion. The more mixed up we are to start, the better chance we stand of ultimately arriving at a cohesive and nuanced conclusion.

> A disposition for problem solving helps students embrace the complexities of the research process.

The Design Process

The research paper is probably the most misunderstood genre in ELA instruction. I think the reason for this is because many students see the product but not the process. Too often, students focus on the conventions of the genre without understanding the lengthy process of discovery and integration that produces that final piece of writing—that what they're ultimately supposed to be writing about is all that evidence they've gathered and analyzed and all those observations they've made. They become preoccupied with things like MLA style or having enough sources or meeting a page count, and they don't take the time to actually read and process all those sources. What the research paper *looks* like becomes more important than what it says.

I see this most clearly in the case of research papers full of random and irrelevant quotations or with works cited lists where none of the sources were actually cited in the paper. I don't know that I've ever read an insincere or plagiarized personal narrative in my English classes, but I've read many research papers that had little to do with what their authors actually thought. Students sometimes seem to treat a research paper like those old compulsory figures in Olympic ice skating, in which everybody has to carve the same tedious pattern on the ice to show they've mastered requisite skills.

If we want students to approach research as creative problem solving—and not a boring duplication of a required form—then we need to make the intellectual labor that goes into the final product more visible to students. Design thinking helps us do this.

In the STEM fields, the design process is an iterative process for making decisions about resources, data collection, workflow, prototype development, testing, and trouble shooting. It's a feedback loop that makes a project more manageable and its outcome more successful. Research skills are made more transferrable when they include the ability to *design* a research process.

Try this: Share the following description of the engineering design process from sciencebuddies.org with your students and ask them how this description compares to the work they do in their English classes when they write a research paper. Use the table in Figure 5.2 to make these comparisons.

STEPS OF THE ENGINEERING DESIGN PROCESS	STEPS OF THE RESEARCH AND WRITING PROCESS
Define the problem	
Do background research	
Specify requirements	
Brainstorm solutions	
Choose the best solution	
Do development work	
Build a prototype	
Test and redesign	

FIGURE 5.2
The engineering design process

There are many different ways to make connections between the two processes. Figure 5.3 shows how one of my classes made the comparisons.

STEPS OF THE ENGINEERING DESIGN PROCESS	STEPS OF THE RESEARCH AND WRITING PROCESS
Define the problem	Identify a question at issue
Do background research	Start reading and taking notes
Specify requirements	Break down the prompt
Brainstorm solutions	Analyze evidence
Choose the best solution	Develop a tentative thesis
Do development work	Create an outline
Build a prototype	Write a draft
Test and redesign	Get feedback and revise

FIGURE 5.3
Comparing the writing process to design thinking

You might start by looking at your assignment directions for a research paper. The counterpart to "specify requirements" in an English class, for instance, might involve considering constraints, including audience, context, due date, and word count. "Define the problem" might include identifying the exigence. What I especially like about the language in the engineering design process is its transferability. It gives students a flexible and creative method for finding solutions to problems that they can use in many areas of their lives. Thinking about design additionally sets students up to think about *redesign* (when the first design doesn't quite work)—an important move for transfer.

> Approaching research through the design process helps students see that all extended inquiry involves trial and error.

In this chapter, I share ways we work through the research design process in my classes.

Defining the Problem

To help students define the problem they're investigating, I use an exercise I learned from *The Craft of Research* (Booth, Colomb, and Williams 1995). After doing some initial listening to the conversation to see what others are talking about, students complete the following template for creating a rationale in response to their own topic.

1. *Name your topic:*
   I am studying_____,

2. *Imply your question:*
   because I want to find out who/how/why _____,

3. *State the rationale for the question and the project:*
   in order to understand how/why/what _____. (1995, 43)

Taking the extra steps to identify a purpose motivates a research project with a sense of exigence. Booth, Colomb, and Williams tell students that taking this step "transform[s] your project from one that interests you to one that makes a bid to interest others, a project with a rationale explaining why it is important to ask your question at all" (1995, 43). By identifying our purpose, we also connect with our audience.

The example I share with students is the rationale I wrote for my own literary research: *I am studying male characters in Victorian fiction because I want to find out how writers represent their public and private identities in order to extend our understanding of 19th-century views of masculinity.*

Here's an example from a seventh-grade science project: *I am studying how people match faces to voices because I want to find out about stereotypes and biased opinions in order to better understand the world around us.*

> Teachers can provide guidance during the design process by asking open-ended questions: How's it going? What do you need to change? What were your reasons for this choice? How did it work for you?

Achieving Stasis

Students trained in rhetoric have an extra tool in their back pocket for defining a research problem: stasis theory. As you may recall from Chapter 3, stasis theory uses different types of questions—such as questions of fact, definition, quality, or policy—to locate the point of disagreement in a persuasive situation (Figure 5.4). A question of fact, for instance, investigates causes and effects of past events or the truth of an empirical claim, while a question of definition asks, "What is it?" and examines the key characteristics of the subject. A question of quality invites a judgment of good or bad qualities. And a question of policy asks what should be done in the future. The stases move students through a sequential inquiry process.

STASIS THEORY QUESTIONS	
Question of Fact	What happened? Does it exist? What are the causes and effects?
Question of Definition	What is it? How do we define it? What are the key characteristics?
Question of Quality	How do we evaluate it? Is it good or bad? Harmful or helpful?
Question of Policy	What should we do about it? What course of action should we take?

FIGURE 5.4
Stasis theory questions

Stasis theory helps us define a research problem by identifying what's at issue for the people involved and where they've already found common ground. We achieve stasis when we locate that pivot point in a conversation where some people say "yes" and others say "no" (Figure 5.5). That is, we agree on the question we want to ask but disagree about how to answer it.

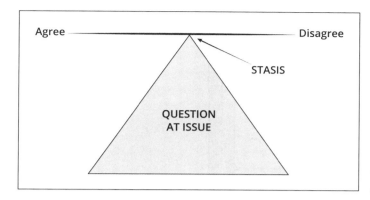

FIGURE 5.5
Achieving stasis

Stasis theory also helps students to think about whether the question at issue can be answered with the available evidence. Questions of fact can be especially hard to answer—something for students to think about before they take on that "Do the Illuminati still exist?" question as their research focus.

IDENTIFYING THE EXIGENCE BEHIND RESEARCH QUESTIONS

Directions to Students: Each of the following questions comes from a university report on the impact of faculty and student research. First, using stasis theory, identify the kind of question each research project asks. Then, brainstorm possible exigencies for each question. Use any sources of information you have to identify urgent, real-world needs that might motivate each research question.

from "UC Riverside 2013 Research Impacts, Office of the Chancellor"

1. Can we predict and prevent the onset of Alzheimer's?

2. How can we protect California's lucrative citrus industry?

3. What role do clouds play in climate warming?

In the context of a research project, finding a common focus can be a great help in making a project more manageable (Figure 5.6). In particular, knowing what you're *not* asking delimits the type of evidence and reasoning needed to support your position. Understanding, for instance, that neither parents, nor coaches, nor doctors contest the fact that youth tackle football has caused concussions in players younger than fourteen (a question of fact), narrows the issue to other kinds of questions: Should tackle football be prohibited (question of policy)? Is football still football without tackling (question of definition)? Are injuries something that should be avoided or accepted as a part of the game (question of quality)? We can take the question that's already been answered off the table since it's no longer at issue.

Both stasis theory and the concept of exigence direct our focus to what people are talking about and care about.

FIGURE 5.6
Stasis theory can help students find a focus for their research.

Understanding the Exigence

Defining the problem for an audience includes establishing the exigence—the thing that makes the research important. Students can dig deeper into the exigence motivating their research by exploring the following questions:

- Is there a particular event that sets up the exigence?

- How long has this issue been a problem? How many people does it affect?

- Why did you pick this topic?

- Do the examples and evidence you've gathered so far help to establish the problem or understand the problem?

- Does this evidence help you interpret data or understand the conversation?

When it comes time for students to write about their research findings, they need to be able to establish the exigence for their line of inquiry, to say, "Here's what happened (or is happening or might happen), and here's why it matters." Research that doesn't do this fails to have a real-world impact.

College admissions officers want to know how impactful applicants' research projects are. Stanford University, for instance, tells prospective students on their campus tours to highlight the real-word impact of any projects they describe in their application essays.

Did you research the importance of early childhood literacy and then create a summer reading program for local libraries in response to identified needs? Great! Then you're the kind of student we want to admit to our university, the Stanford tour guide told our group when I visited the campus with my niece a few summers ago. Asking about the impact and relevance of a particular line of inquiry is another way of asking about its exigence.

Building the Lab

An early step for all researchers is the process of setting up their "lab." Research is an ever-changing process. Each new research project needs a custom-built lab, a design process suited to the unique demands of the rhetorical situation the research engages. For researchers working in the field of literary studies, for example, that lab probably looks an awful lot like an office or corner of the library or a cluttered spot in the kitchen, but the idea is the same for all fields. Researchers need some kind of setup for making their work happen (Figure 5.7). Asking students to think about their research schedule and workspaces helps them to take themselves seriously as researchers.

FIGURE 5.7
Ed Rickett's marine biology lab on Cannery Row in Monterey, California

A RESEARCHER'S WORKSPACES

Directions to Students: Write a check mark by everything you need in each list in Figure 5.8 to design and conduct your research project.

AT HOME BASE	IN THE FIELD
Computer	Camera (phone)
Pens	Voice recorder (phone)
Calendar	Library card
MLA Handbook	Bus/subway pass
Notepad	Phone apps
Bookcase	Mentors/experts
Copier/scanner	Snacks
Tabletop for sorting materials	Student ID
Online file system	Permissions/release forms
Research process journal	Tablet or laptop

FIGURE 5.8
A researcher's workspaces

Note: Many students don't have a quiet or private space in which to work at home. In these situations, the classroom may be the best "home base" for their research materials.

A RESEARCHER'S SCHEDULE

Taking time at the start of a big project to create a schedule and project management plan is also part of setting up the "lab." Regardless of the time management tools they use (e.g., Google Calendar, smart phone calendar, student handbook, etc.), students need to know when and where they're putting in their hours on their research project. They also need to keep an eye on the phases of their project.

Directions to Students: Take time to set up your daily, weekly, and monthly (for extended projects) schedule for your research project. Make initial decisions regarding the following items:

1. On what days of the week will you read and write for your research project?

2. What time of day will you work?

3. When will you meet with other writers or researchers?

4. When will you meet with your teacher or mentor?

5. What is your timeline for doing background research and gathering your initial evidence?

6. What is your timeline for analyzing your evidence?

7. What is your timeline for drafting your research paper?

8. What is your timeline for revising your paper and conducting more research as needed?

9. What's your final deadline?

10. How will you keep track of how much time you put into your project and what you accomplish?

Talk over your scheduling decisions with a partner or small group. Be prepared to make adjustments as needed.

Collecting Evidence

If students ask, "Is my thesis OK?," I say, "I don't know. What evidence do you have?" And if they say, "I don't have any evidence yet," then I say, "Then why are you working on a thesis?" Academic arguments start with evidence. And to make claims about the evidence, we have to find the evidence. We have to collect, sort, and interpret the data points before we can draw conclusions. That's research.

> In addition to more traditional academic research projects, project-based learning, genius hours, and participatory action research are all ways to engage students in extended inquiry.

Another way to describe the research process is that we make a mess and then clean it up. Confusion and apprehension are appropriate psychic departure points for any big new project. So, I ask students, "Are you creating a big enough mess to clean up?" If you're not overwhelmed, I tell them, you need to do more research. Making a big research mess requires that students maintain an open mind and high tolerance for frustration. Research *doesn't* make sense at this stage. It's not supposed to. If you can see where you're going at the data gathering stage, then you've probably already rigged the results.

> Reading, writing, experiments, interviews, observations, and discussion are all forms of data collection.

Making a Mess

We make a mess by gathering a ton of evidence—like way more than we'll end up using in the research paper. This can be a bitter pill for students to swallow. One seventh grader I worked with said research is hard "because a lot of the stuff you read isn't helpful and none of the websites say what you want." Yep.

In addition to primary and secondary sources, evidence collection includes students' own ideas about the texts and topic. All those reading annotations, quick-writes, rhetorical analyses, graphic organizers, surveys, responses to discussion questions, double-entry journals, and vocabulary activities that took place during the rhetorical reading process now get dumped into the data pool. This is one of the most important acts of transfer students learn: the transfer from reading strategies to writing strategies.

During the exploratory stage of research, we cast our net to the inky (or digital) unknown and hope we catch something that will feed our curiosity. At this point, all's fish that comes to the net. We're learning what is and what is not relevant and important to the conversation we're joining. The bigger the data set, the more potential dots we can connect.

Keep in mind that students may need help making decisions about their process for collecting evidence. How are they actually storing the data they gather? In word files, on index cards, in notes on a smart phone, in a Google doc, in a journal? Regardless of the kind of research they're conducting, students need to build a data collection system that will allow them to sort and code information down the road. Ask your students what they plan to do.

Reading for Research

The texts we're reading are a big part of the mess we surround ourselves with during a research project. I remember being invited to the home of Michelle Barrette, a Marxist scholar at Queen Mary, University of London, and snooping around her house with the other graduate students, simply amazed at the number of books she was reading concurrently. Piles of books with marked pages lined her desk or lay open on tables, all evidently in immediate use.

Attaining critical mass (or critical mess, as the case may be) in a research project is key to bringing an idea to maturity. You've got to get enough bulk going for the project to develop its own gravitational pull, so you think about it when you're walking about, doing the dishes, talking to friends. The reading, writing, and thinking finally stay with you beyond the desk time you put in. I suspect this is what those too-good-to-be-true guides about writing your novel or dissertation in fifteen minutes a day are really after: critical mass. As with anything affected by the laws of inertia, the more stuff to move, the more powerful the forward momentum once it finally gets going.

Even at the college level, students still want to know how many sources they have to read for a research project, and my students become frustrated when I dodge this question. "It depends," I say when they ask if ten sources are enough for an eight-page paper. They don't like that my rubrics don't quantify a set number of references or citations needed for a paper to be considered "well supported by a variety of scholarly sources representing a range of views." Well-supported. Range. Variety. These are intentionally fuzzy terms. I ask students, "What kinds of sources are you using?" A single 200-page monograph is going to take longer to read and may offer more depth than several short articles.

How much does a writer need to read to be well prepared to contribute to the conversation? That's the question I want my students to consider as they create their reading lists.

For younger students, that critical mass can often be attained through a combination of reading and first-hand experience. I think of the science fair, history day, and community service projects my own children completed in middle school. Each of these projects included an extensive research component. Because the projects also involved many hours of hands-on experience doing things like testing plants for starch or volunteering at a local animal shelter, the students were able to present their findings with impressive confidence. They understood their subject at a deep level and knew exactly what they wanted to say about it.

> Arguments need to be about something. The better the understanding of the content, the better the argument.

Creating a Reading List

The following activity helps students think through how they might create a reading list for their research project.

WHO ARE YOU READING?

Directions to Students: Imagine you are a friend of the author of one of the sources you're reading for your research project, and the two of you are catching up over a cup of coffee. You've been chatting about your lives for a while when the conversation turns to books. You ask your friend, "What are you reading these days?" What does he or she say? Use clues from the author's writings to answer this question. What other writers does your friend mention in his or her own work? What topics is your friend interested in? Who else is writing about this topic at this time? What writers are listed in your friend's footnotes, bibliography, or works cited? Write your answer from your friend's point of view in the space below.

TWITTER FOLLOWERS

A variation on the "Who Are You Reading?" activity that students can try after they've generated a reading list is to have students speculate (or actually research) which writers would or do follow which other writers on the list. This can also be done with entries in a works cited list after a research paper is drafted to identify the connections among various sources.

Directions to Students: Who on your reading list or works cited list would follow whom on Twitter? For each name, identify the three other writers on your list who would most likely follow that writer on Twitter. Make your decisions based on common interests and experiences you believe the writers share.

Research is guided inquiry, and we're largely guided by the other writers we read. One of the best strategies I've learned for getting unstuck in a research project is to create a reading list from the references in one of my favorite sources. As long as students have found one source they really like, they can draft off the good work of that writer by reading the sources the writer read.

BACK COVER BLURBS

As an alternative to a literature review or annotated bibliography, you could have your students write "back cover blurbs" for some of the books they're reading for their research project. This activity works well as a group project.

Directions to Students: Imagine your group of four has been selected to read and review one of the books on your reading list. Prepare some short, insightful comments that the publisher can include on the book's back cover. Your remarks should help to "sell" the book to potential readers by capturing their interest and showcasing one or two of the book's best features. Write two or three well-crafted sentences highlighting the book's best "selling points."

An extra tip: Keeping tabs on what students are *doing* with the research that they've spent days online or at the library gathering is important. Kids can't write in response to the views of other writers if they don't understand what they've read.

TRAWLING WORKS CITED

Trawling through works cited lists in favorite books or articles is a great way to add more titles to a reading list. This strategy is a bit like scholarly speed dating. You do a quick scan of the people in the room, so you can zoom in and engage the folks who share your interests.

RECOMMENDED READINGS

Students can think about the special help mentors offer by considering the importance of reading recommendations.

> *Directions to Students:* Look again at the sources you've listed as your references for your research project. Then answer the following questions in a quick-write. Were any of these sources recommended to you by a teacher, librarian, parent, or classmate? If so, how do you view these recommended sources in relation to titles you just stumbled across in your research? What are you learning about the importance of getting help from mentors and experts?

> *Directions to Students:* Discuss the following questions with a partner. If you only had time to read one source, would you choose a recommended source or one you found on your own? Why? Is there a difference? What do book recommendations tell us about the nature of an academic conversation?

Engaging Primary and Secondary Sources

A research paper is a good opportunity to take students beyond the "I say" of an individual perspective to the "they say, I say" of academic argumentation.[1] Engaging sources turns a monologue into a conversation. If students tell us, "I've said what I have to say," and they're still short on development and support, we can tell them to go get some more "they say." Their "I say" may be out of proportion to their "they say." When we're writing a research paper, we can't meet our length requirement by just adding more of our own opinions once we've used up all our sources.

One of my students, Cori, brilliantly compared secondary sources to the "zoom out" feature in Google Maps. Primary sources give us an up-close look. But secondary sources are needed to situate that view in its full context.

- - - - - - - - - - - - - - - - - -

1. *See Gerald Graff and Cathy Birkenstein's book* They Say, I Say *(2014).*

How do we help students distinguish primary from secondary sources? This is another one of those "it depends" situations because classification depends on the line of inquiry and the way in which the source is being used rather than an intrinsic quality in the source itself. In general, a primary source can be any "raw" data that is not mediated by the interpretation of another scholar. The same text, moreover, can function as both a primary and a secondary source, depending on the research question.

See, for example, the following description of Dee Brown's book *Bury My Heart at Wounded Knee: An Indian History of the American West* in the California English Language Arts/English Language Development Framework:

> [*Bury My Heart at Wounded Knee*] is an historical informational text that describes the experiences of American Indian people from their own perspectives during the second half of the nineteenth century. For the unit on the U.S. Civil Rights movement, this book is considered a primary source as it was published in 1970 at a time of increasing American Indian activism, and it addresses the civil rights of Native Americans. The book weaves together many primary and secondary source documents from the 19th century. (For studying westward expansion in the late 19th century itself, the book is considered a secondary source.) (http://www.cde.ca.gov/ci/rl/cf /documents/elaeldvignettescollection.pdf)

> Primary sources are the "raw materials" of research. Secondary sources are reports of other researchers' findings. Whether a particular source is primary or secondary can depend on the research question.

Evaluating Sources

In a rhetorical approach, evaluating sources goes beyond establishing the source's credibility. We also consider the value of the source's contribution to the conversation—that is, the extent to which it offers a meaningful response to the question at issue. And, of course, what counts as a meaningful response depends on the values of the discourse community and the contributions that others have already made.

Sometimes the source is credible, but the content is not relevant. In the early stages of exploratory reading, we try to keep an open mind and see potential connections, but at some point, we have to recognize if a source really isn't in conversation with the other sources we've dumped in the data pool. Then we have to ask ourselves: Does it add something new? Or confuse the issue? Outliers aren't always irrelevant, but if a source is asking and answering different questions from the other sources we've read, we need to evaluate whether or not it makes sense to expand the parameters of the discussion to include a new angle. If the writing task is fairly brief and focused, the answer's probably "no."

Of course, establishing the relevance of the sources we cite is one of our responsibilities as a writer. Sometimes we need to convince a skeptical audience that a seemingly irrelevant source is the key to a new and surprising understanding of the issue. Diversity of perspectives is important.

The following questions from *So What? The Writer's Argument* can help students evaluate the significance and credibility of sources:

- Who wrote this? What makes them credible?

- What are the authors trying to achieve?

- How do they support their claims?

- Is anyone profiting from this? Who? How might money-making efforts influence the content?

- When was this written?

- Will this still be here next month? (Schick and Schubert 2014, 88)

The CRAAP Test, a strategy developed at Chico State University, can also be a helpful tool. While I'd prefer that students spend their time learning principles and practices rather than acronyms, the CRAAP Test identifies important considerations for evaluating sources:

- Currency: *The timeliness of the information.*
  - When was the information published or posted?
  - Has the information been revised or updated?
  - Does your topic require current information, or will older sources work as well?
  - Are the links functional?

- Relevance: *The importance of the information for your needs.*
  - Does the information relate to your topic or answer your question?
  - Who is the intended audience?
  - Is the information at an appropriate level (i.e., not too elementary or advanced for your needs)?
  - Have you looked at a variety of sources before determining this is the one you will use?
  - Would you be comfortable citing this source in your research paper?

- Authority: *The source of the information.*
  - Who is the author / publisher / source / sponsor?
  - What are the author's credentials or organizational affiliations?

- Is the author qualified to write on the topic?

- Is there contact information, such as a publisher or email address?

- Does the URL reveal anything about the author or source (examples: .com .edu .gov .org .net)?

- Accuracy: *The reliability, truthfulness and correctness of the content.*

  - Where does the information come from?

  - Is the information supported by evidence?

  - Has the information been reviewed or refereed?

  - Can you verify any of the information in another source or from personal knowledge?

  - Are there spelling, grammar, or typographical errors?

- Purpose: *The reason the information exists.*

  - What is the purpose of the information? Is it to inform, teach, sell, entertain, or persuade?

  - Do the authors / sponsors make their intentions or purpose clear?

  - Are there political, ideological, cultural, religious, institutional, or personal biases?

    (https://library.csuchico.edu/help/source-or-information-good)

When my students cite "scholarly" sources that feature inaccurate information or unsupported claims, I have to ask myself what principles they've developed about academic conversations. That form is more important than content? That completing the task is more important than contributing to the conversation? Such cases are a good opportunity for formative assessment for learning, especially for cultivating students' attitudes and beliefs about research.

> Credible sources start with scholarly search tools and solid mentor texts.

"Don't you have anything shorter?"

At a campus workshop I attended, I was surprised to hear our librarians say that one of their biggest challenges was persuading students to choose sources based on significance and relevance rather than length. One librarian shared how she'd helped a student find a six-page article for a research project only to have the student ask if she had anything shorter. We don't want students to reject a source just because it's difficult to read. If we're going to teach students to evaluate sources critically and rhetorically, we also need to help them grapple with challenging texts.

Analyzing Sources

Tom Morton, coauthor of the popular book *The Big Six: Historical Thinking Concepts* (Seixas and Morton 2012), offers an especially useful guide for analyzing sources. He outlines several intellectual moves students can practice as they work with textual evidence.

Making Inferences:

- What does this document tell you?
- What might you infer from it?
- What does this (detail) suggest?
- Although it doesn't say so, what might we infer from (detail)?

Investigate Corroborating Evidence:

- What is similar about these two sources?
- What can you see the same in this picture as in source X?
- What evidence in this source is similar to that in other sources?
- Does this source confirm what you have already learned?
- Does it extend it?
- Or does it challenge other evidence?

Selecting the Most Relevant Sources:

- Why is this source important?
- Why did you choose these sources?
- Why is the evidence in this source convincing?

Morton also offers sentence prompts to guide students in answering the following questions:

For inferences:

From (detail) we can infer that . . .

This (detail) suggests that . . .

It doesn't say so, but . . . is probably the case, because (detail) . . .

For corroboration:

If you compare these two pictures . . .

This source supports the evidence of . . .

Source X goes even further than source Y in showing that . . .

Source X contradicts the evidence of Source Y in suggesting that . . .

These pictures show different effects of . . .

For relevance:

This source is important because . . .

The value of this letter is . . .

I chose these two pictures to show different . . .

The evidence of this source is convincing because . . .

(http://historicalthinking.ca/historical-thinking-concept-templates)

While the above questions were developed to promote historical thinking, I find them tremendously useful for all kinds of textual analysis, including literary analysis. Thinking about how one piece of evidence corroborates or complicates another piece is important intellectual work in all academic disciplines.

See the website for the Historical Thinking Project for more great ideas: http://historicalthinking.ca/

Finding Mentors

Real-world researchers consult their colleagues and mentors throughout the research process. They form writers' groups, talk to experts, and meet with their advisors, editors, or teachers. All these activities keep a project going through the research, develop, test, and redesign process. Asking the same question of multiple people, especially procedural questions about how writers or researchers do their work, is an especially good habit for students to develop. I used to think of this as spreading my ignorance around, but I now see this as an earnest attempt to gather multiple data points. My conversations with all those mentors became a kind of scatterplot of my attempts at understanding.

Tech twist: If you really want to make the research process visible to your students, ask your students to use Google's My Maps to plot the physical locations of their writers' group meetings, interviews with experts, and conferences with teachers and mentors. Mapping their research process can help students see their research journey.

Cleaning Up the Mess

How do we know when to stop making a mess? Students occasionally get caught up in the pleasures of research and in low-stakes textual browsing and evidence gathering and forget about the end product. Sometimes a research project becomes almost a hobby, and students will collect everything they can find on video games or anime or baseball or whatever, regardless of its relevance to their line of inquiry. We also can sometimes fall into the danger of gathering evidence past our ability to create coherence. I've seen high school juniors working on their year-long research projects and college seniors in my capstone courses create data sets that were almost too big to manage.

Other times we want to rush through the early stages of inquiry even if we have more time because it feels so good to finally get out of the mess. However, if we start coding our data too soon, we lose the advantage of being able to see trends and patterns we couldn't see before we started our research. The evidence we've gathered should tell a story we didn't already know.

When students have a longer time horizon for their project, we can coach them to be patient while living in this state of intellectual confusion. Some writing just takes as long as it takes. For younger writers and researchers, it can be helpful to have some firm checkpoints in place, so that students know when it's time to move on.

PROCESS QUICK-WRITE

Directions to Students: Once you've decided that you have in fact gathered enough evidence to begin classifying data by categories, take a few minutes to consider your options before you start sorting. What are your organizational choices at this moment? What different stories does your research tell? What is your audience most interested in? Answer these questions in a quick-write.

Organizing Evidence

Organizing evidence is a matter of identifying different types of relationships. When we sort and code evidence, we're building a network of ideas. This takes time and patience. One colleague I talked with described his experience painstakingly coding (or labeling) evidence in a 100-page transcript; this organizational task took at least as long as the original data collection. What follows are some of my favorite strategies for cleaning up a research mess by identifying key patterns and making connections between important ideas. By the way, these are the same techniques I use to organize evidence for my own writing projects.

1. *List, Group, Label* (Taba 1967): Always my go-to classification strategy. Students physically sort terms, concepts, or pieces of evidence into different groups according to their similarities and then assign each group a label that makes sense to them. This can be done on chart paper, with index cards or sticky notes, or by using an app like Google Jamboard (see Figure 5.9).

2. *Motif Sorting*: Identifying and sorting reoccurring images, characters, or events is a good way to find meaningful patterns in literature. What are the different threads of meaning in a text? Which ones are you going to follow? How do they relate to each other? Classifying textual evidence according to motifs can help students identify important ideas and themes.

3. *Key Word Banks*: To help students see the anchor terms of their research—those terms that will give their readers a framework for understanding their argument—students can create a key word bank. The repeated words give the research a focus. The key words can be used in searching databases and as signal words in students' research papers. I encourage students to generate a list of key words from their research notes and the labels they generate for List, Group, Label, or other coding activities. Key words help students identify trends in their

thinking. Students create a "key word bank" by brainstorming synonyms for their key words that they can then use in their thesis and claims. Students can also use a wordle (www .wordle.net) to find their most frequently mentioned terms. The bigger the word in the wordle, the more times it's mentioned in the text.

4. *Margin Coding*: This activity is a form of annotation. If your students have collected their evidence in a single document or notebook, they can identify trends in their evidence by labeling each piece of data in the margin. The "insert comment" function works well in electronic documents. Similar pieces of evidence get the same margin code (e.g., "effects of concussions" or "gender stereotypes").

5. *Index Card Sorting*: Old-school but a classic. I think I first learned this technique from Peter Elbow's *Writing without Teachers* (1998) many years ago, but I still find it a more efficient and powerful way to *sort* evidence than the digital methods I use today. It's just a hassle to create and store all those index cards. Shoeboxes. Lots of shoeboxes.

6. *Sticker Coding*: One for the crafty set. Using stickers to sort and label individual pieces of print evidence offers students an introduction to qualitative research (Figure 5.10). The evidence can be on index cards or in notebooks, but it needs to be on a physical document for this activity to work. This is another good one for your hands-on or visual learners. Identifying what each sticker represents is a big part of the brainwork students do. Have students create a key showing what each sticker represents (e.g., "smiley face represents domestic idealism"). Using emojis with digital data is a good tech twist.

 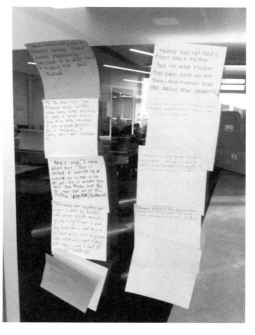

FIGURE 5.9

Students sorting textual evidence from *The Curious Incident of the Dog in the Night-Time* using List, Group, Label

FIGURE 5.10
Organizing evidence through sticker coding

Finding the Story

Once students have chunked information into meaningful categories or patterns, they can extend their thinking about the significance of those related ideas by increasing the altitude of their data analysis. Going up a level of generality helps students see the big picture. Thomas Newkirk reminds us in *Minds Made for Stories* (2014) that all readers need a sense of *plot*—that is, of anticipation and resolution—to sustain their interest in a text. The activities that follow move students toward finding the organizing plot of their research story.

1. Traditional outline: This is what many of my colleagues tell me they do; they still start a research paper by making an outline and loading it with content. I do worry that conventional outlines can impinge on the composing process. As long as students let the outline emerge organically from the process of analyzing and classifying their evidence, a traditional outline with headings and subheadings can provide a helpful structure for many students.

2. Research storyboard: Students who like sketch notes may enjoy this strategy. Instead of using only phrases or sentences to tell a research story, students can present their findings

through a panel of images. These could be original drawings or clipart. Encourage students who take this approach to sequence their images so that they build toward a compelling conclusion.

3. Descriptive outline: In addition to a full sentence or scratch outline, students can build another layer of complexity onto their research story by noting the effect or function of each of their findings. In other words, what do these findings do? What kind of contribution do they make to the conversation? What kind of impact will they have? See Appendix T for an example.

4. Abstract: Writing a brief 200-word abstract helps students identify the emerging purpose, claims, and methods of their work-in-progress. It might seem a bit odd to write an abstract for a paper that hasn't been written yet, but I know from personal experience that this is probably what most graduate students do. You see a call for proposals, hatch an idea, write that abstract, get accepted to the conference, and then six months later scramble to recall what on earth you had in mind as you write the actual paper you're going to present. Heck, I know of papers that have been written on the plane on the way to the event. But the abstract provided a road map for the completed paper.

5. Concept map (this idea comes from my colleague, David Reichard): Give students a large piece of paper on which to create their map. Instruct students to write their research topic at the center of the map and then build out subtopics from this central topic (like a cluster). Ask students to link topics and subtopics with lines and write *action verbs* on those lines that capture the relationships between the concepts. After mapping the concepts, students write research questions raised by the connections among topics on the margins of the map.

An additional strategy that I use with younger writers is identifying hashtags for research trends.

RESEARCH HASHTAGS

Directions to Students: What trends or big ideas do you see recurring throughout your research notes? If you were posting about your research topic on social media (which may, in fact, be the case), what hashtags would you use to organize your content? And in what order would they appear in a conversation? Create a list of five hashtags for the big ideas that are trending in your research, focusing on the data that you've personally analyzed, and sequencing them in order of appearance.

MAKING AN IMPORTANT BOOK

Do you know Margaret Wise Brown's *The Important Book*, first published in 1949? If you come from a family of elementary teachers, like I do, you probably do. Or you may have encountered Brown's writing as a parent. Brown authored more than 100 children's books, including *Runaway Bunny* and *Goodnight Moon*.

Elementary teachers have made brilliant use of Brown's structure in *The Important Book* to teach key concepts about units of study (see Figure 5.11). For instance, students

FIGURE 5.11
A page from *The Important Book*
by Margaret Wise Brown

studying the Amazon Rainforest might create the following Important Book in imitation of Brown's original style:

> The important thing about the Amazon Rainforest is biodiversity.
>
> Rainfall, habit destruction, and endangered species are also important.
>
> But the important thing about the Amazon Rainforest is biodiversity.

In my high school English classes, I used this strategy to help my students identify and remember key features of intellectual movements, such as romanticism, Transcendentalism, and modernism. Here's one we created for Transcendentalism.

> The important thing about Transcendentalism is spirit.
>
> Nature, self-reliance, and creativity are also important.
>
> But the important thing about Transcendentalism is spirit.

The value of this strategy is in the way it helps students focus on memorable main ideas. For students contending with a mountain of research data, creating an Important Book can be a way to synthesize and prioritize their most significant findings. (Just be sure students understand this exercise is about identifying a focus—and not about setting up a five-paragraph essay.)

Directions to Students: Create an Important Book for your research topic, synthesizing your most significant research findings so far. Identify one main idea that you see as the most important takeaway from all your research. Then identify three supporting ideas that are also important. Use the template below to create an Important Book.

The important thing about _____ is _____.

_____, _____, and _____ are also important.

But the important thing about _____ is _____.

Helping Students Own the Inquiry Process

Students have greater control over their inquiry process when they document their process in a research journal. Like the engineering design process, the process of writing a research paper is integrative and recursive. We try something, go back a step, tinker a bit, and try again. We're reading and rereading as we're writing and rewriting. Capturing this process in a research journal makes this intellectual labor visible.

Metacognitive journal prompts, such as the ones that follow, can help students notice the adaptive thinking that comes with working the design process.

- How would you describe your research process?
- What challenges have you encountered?
- What modifications have you made in response to these challenges?
- How is your writing supporting your reading?
- How is your reading supporting your writing?
- Do you need to write more? Read more? Both?

Writing about their process empowers students to try multiple designs to find out what works and what doesn't.

Students need conscious procedural knowledge they can carry with them into other contexts. That means that as teachers we're going to have to stand back and let students make some process decisions for themselves. While I might put an interesting resource or example in front of a student and say, "I wonder what you can do with that?," I try not to do more than invite students to make connections. I've learned that students have to make the connections themselves to see the connections.

Guiding questions, like those that follow, can take students further down the path of discovery.

- How else can you see it?
- What might be the reasons for that?
- What are the implications?
- How can you test that idea?

Asking a question or just saying "Interesting—keep going!" prevents me from stepping in too soon and shutting down students' ideas.

Annotated Outline

Students like models, and while I'm reluctant to show students model research paper outlines that can constrain their own thinking, I'm also aware that my students get tired of me saying "It depends" whenever they ask a question about how they should organize their work. They want some guidance on how they can bring order to the chaos I've encouraged them to create. My strategy for dealing with this tension has been to invite students to analyze and critique a sample research paper outline.

Directions to Students: Annotate the following sample research paper outline, noting the rhetorical function of each section. What does each section do? What is its purpose? Then respond to the quick-write below.

Sample Research Paper Outline

I. Introduction
  a. Problem
  b. Question
  c. Rationale
  d. Thesis
II. Context (secondary sources; "They Say")
  a. Historical/cultural background
  b. Summaries of the work of other scholars (literature review)
III. Case study (primary sources; "I Say")
  a. Close readings of primary sources
  b. Personal observations and examples
  c. First-hand interviews
IV. Research findings
  a. Synthesis of secondary and primary sources
  b. Analysis of evidence
V. Implications
  a. Cultural, historical, and/or social significance
  b. Purpose and intended outcomes
  c. Policy recommendations

VI. Conclusion
    a. What?
    b. So what?
    c. Now what?

Quick-write: Do you see yourself needing these same kinds of sections in your own research paper? Why or why not?

Draft outlines are also a good place for students to start thinking about how they're going to integrate and synthesize all the evidence they've gathered, including citations from primary and secondary sources, and their own observations, experiences, and personal examples when relevant. A draft outline can be a test of whether or not students actually have a research paper in the works or if they're writing in another genre instead.

I remember the "research paper" I received that turned out to be seven pages of personal examples of lying. Another student wrote six pages on her experience as a swimmer, ignoring the written conversation she was supposed to be engaging for her research. I had to tell these students that while they'd made a good start, they hadn't yet written a research paper because there were no other voices besides their own in their essay. They'd written a monologue instead of joining an academic conversation.

Research as an Act of Integration

When we teach research skills for transfer, we promote integrative thinking by encouraging students to apply relevant inquiry methods they've learned in other subject areas, like science or history, to their work in our English classes. Research is itself an act of integration: the bringing together of different views, data points, and methods to find a workable solution to a problem.

For example, students can draw on methods for historical research in their work with sources and evidence. Historians tend to ask two big questions about a potential source: (1) Is it significant? and (2) Is it creditable?

The Historical Thinking Project recommends considering the following questions about sources:

- What type of source is it?

- Who authored/created it?

- When and why was it created?

- Who was the intended audience?

- What historical events were occurring when it was created?

- How does the point of view/position shape the source?

These questions are highly rhetorical in nature. Seeing the connections between academic fields helps students transfer their learning across contexts.

Checklist for Knowing When You're "Done"

If you ask students if they're done with their research project, they'll probably say, "I am *so* done." Like stick-a-fork-in-me done because by the time students get to this point, they'll be fried. But they should also feel tremendously proud of what they've accomplished. I offer students a checklist for knowing when they're finished. If they can answer "yes" to all of the following questions, then they have indeed experienced the full research process.

__Did you gather more evidence than you could use?

__Did you read more sources than you cited?

__Did you write more pages than you included in your final draft?

__Did you annotate the sources you read?

__Did you write idea chunks, free writes, journal entries, and maybe an annotated bibliography?

__Did you adjust or redesign your research process as needed?

__Did you get help from mentors and colleagues?

__Did you experience healthy confusion and productive struggle?

__Do you have enough high-quality evidence to make your claims?

__Do you know the important insights your data reveal?

Congratulations! It's time to take a deep breath and celebrate all that you and your students have achieved.

Conclusion: Working the Process

Teaching for transfer doesn't mean we're just teaching skills that our students will use in the future, as in, "Remember what I'm teaching you about MLA style because you're going to have to do this in your college writing class." It means helping students understand that *they're* going to have to look for their own opportunities to apply their learning and that, in most cases, they'll have to adjust what they've learned to make it fit the new situation. Developing a spirit of transfer means developing a mindset for making connections.

In the case of research skills, a spirit of transfer offers double payoffs; it helps students adapt and apply those skills down the road, and it helps them make connections in the present moment. A research paper is, furthermore, a great opportunity to develop project design and management skills (including planning for trial and error) and to cultivate habits of mind such as curiosity and persistence. These are skills and attitudes that can help students succeed in a variety of settings as they seek answers to worthwhile questions.

I spend a lot of time thinking about how students perceive themselves in academic culture, especially in situations where "not fitting in" can cause students to drop out of school. If we let our students know that all writers struggle with research—and, in fact, that struggle is desirable and productive—then they're less likely to interpret their own struggles as a sign that they don't belong or they're not smart enough. They can approach the messy confusion and glorious failures of research with the resilience of a learner who expects and welcomes difficulties, who has confidence in the efficacy of working the process because the process has worked for them.

> The big idea to teach is that research is inquiry. Research doesn't just live in the genre of the research paper.

Reasoning from Evidence

Shared judgment constitutes human beings' best hope for having a sound basis from which to act reasonably and mindfully.

—EDWARD P. J. CORBETT AND ROSA A. EBERLY

Writing as Reasoning

John T. Gage calls writing "a search for reasons" (2001, 5). It's in the act of developing a written argument that we really begin to connect the dots that we've collected, forging links among ideas as we reason our way to a conclusion. "The serious attempt to compose your thoughts in writing," Gage says, "will often lead you to the very important discovery of what you think and *why* you think it" (2001, 5) (emphasis added). Students aren't likely to make these discoveries if we give them predetermined essay structures that do the thinking for them.

There's also an important difference between teaching students to provide support for their claims and teaching students to reason from evidence. The previous chapter explored some of the many ways evidence can be gathered through extended inquiry. In this chapter, I drill down into the specifics of what writers do with all that evidence. Evidence-based reasoning is reasoning *from* evidence *to* claims. This includes analyzing and evaluating data, unpacking assumptions (or warrants), identifying backing, drawing conclusions, and recognizing the limits of our understanding.

Above all, I want to make a case for the importance of reasoning *rhetorically*, or reasoning with an awareness of audience, purpose, genre, and context. Without this focus, exercises in logic might help students pass a geometry quiz, but they're unlikely to contribute much to students' collaborative problem-solving abilities. As Edward P. J. Corbett and Rosa A. Eberly write in *The Elements of Reasoning*, "Reasoning, by itself, will not get the potatoes peeled" (2000, 1). It takes humans in communication with other humans to accomplish real work in the world.

Argument Starts with Inquiry

Authentic, impactful arguments start with inquiry. I worry about some of the scaffolds I've seen that teach students to imitate the form of an argument without fully enacting the process of inquiry-based argumentation. Without commensurate support for inquiry work and critical thinking, scaffolds for teaching students how to write claims supported with evidence and reasons can too easily become the kind of "trivialized" writing instruction (Applebee and Langer 2013, 181) that interferes with students' growth as independent learners. Such superficial approaches teach toward mimicry not mastery.

I have to admit, when I give workshops on this topic, I feel like I'm asking for a lot. I think this is an indication of how far some forms of argument instruction have strayed from inquiry. If students have already spent weeks on a science project or community service project, it's not hard for them to talk about how they know what they know or how their thinking has changed along the way. They don't need to do extra prep for this kind of reflection because they can speak from deep, experiential knowledge. But if students haven't done extended inquiry work—if they've just been given a formula for producing a claim with evidence and reasons—then having to surface their assumptions and ways of knowing can feel like extra and unnecessary labor. It's when argument is uncoupled from inquiry and dialogue that the deeper work with assumptions, backing, and qualifiers starts to feel too aspirational.

> In academic contexts, arguments emerge from disciplinary ways of knowing.

When I think of the serious challenges we face today, however, of how acrimonious much of our public discourse is, I feel more strongly than ever that we can't just be teaching students to replicate the surface features of argumentation. Going through the motions isn't enough. We need to give students the space, frameworks, and support to really care about understanding the issues and themselves at a deep level.

Naw . . . Well, Maybe

The process of authentic critical reasoning often ignites through a potent mix of curiosity and doubt. We start with an intriguing idea—like whether or not mercury in the ocean can return to land as fog—and then our inner skeptic starts voicing all the reasons this can't be so. If you've tried Peter Elbow's "doubting game" (see Chapter 3), a method for reading against the grain of a text, you'll notice that this is the same line of thinking we take up when we deliberately try to resist the authority of a text in an effort to achieve critical distance. This is also the kind of thinking that values evidence-based reasoning.

So, we set up our lab, collect data, and test our thinking. What then to do with the data we've collected? We work to reason from our evidence, drawing conclusions about what the data mean and why our findings are significant (or not). Students benefit from receiving extended support in critical reasoning. Just as newcomers to academic conversations often need help understanding *why* we interpret and integrate multiple sources in academic writing (see Chapter 4), newcomers to evidence-based reasoning need help seeing the intellectual operations that allow writers to draw defensible conclusions from evidence.

Models of inquiry-based reasoning in action can make this intellectual work visible to students. Here's a good one: How about the decades-long experiment in Siberia that sought to turn foxes into dogs? Behold . . . the Russian domesticated fox (see Figure 6.1).

FIGURE 6.1
The Russian domesticated fox

You want one, right?

The end result of the experiment was an uber cute, so-fluffy-I-could-die, tame fox that would probably break the Internet if it ever became widely available for adoption. But it's the critical inquiry process—the evidence-based reasoning—that I want my students to fall in love with.

An article in *Scientific American* describes how the experiment began in 1958 when a group of genetic researchers set out to recreate the evolutionary process that transformed wolves into dogs (Trut and Dugatkin 2017). The scientists used another canid species, the fox, and tested the animals daily for friendliness to humans. Those that showed the least fear and aggression were chosen for the special breeding program.

As generation after generation of foxes was selectively bred for sociability with humans, something interesting started to happen. Around generations four and five, some fox kits started to wag their tails. Generation six, however, was the game changer. This special batch liked humans so much they whimpered for attention like dogs and answered to their names. The wild animals were becoming loving pets (Trut and Dugatkin 2017, 75).

But the researchers needed more proof that the kinder, gentler foxes were a result of genetics, not some other variable. So they developed another test: an embryo from a tame mother fox was implanted in the womb of an aggressive female. The tame foxes also became surrogates for embryos from the aggressive foxes. The result? Nature was far stronger than nurture. The researchers found that the "pups behaved like their genetic mothers, not their surrogate mothers." Their conclusion: "Tameness and aggression toward humans thus appeared to be genetic traits" (Trut and Dugatkin 2017, 72).

I share this kind of research story with my students to spotlight the process of reasoned inquiry. Breaking this model down through an Interrupted Reading—in which students and teacher stop after reading a line or two of the text to discuss what they notice—can help students develop their own procedural knowledge. As we discuss the text, my job is to describe what my students are doing and to ask probing questions. Examining inquiry models from a variety of disciplines can help students understand the ways different scholars reason from evidence to claims.

See if you think the following activity would also help your students to reason like scientists.

EXAMINING A MODEL OF REASONED INQUIRY: INTERRUPTED READING

Directions to Students: You'll be reading a few sentences at a time from the article "How to Build a Dog" by Lyudmila Trut and Lee Alan Dugatkin. Each sentence or group of sentences will be displayed on its own PowerPoint or Google slide to focus your attention. A different student will read each slide aloud to the class. As you read each slide, consider the following questions:

- What words or ideas seem especially interesting and important?
- What do you notice about the design of the researchers' experiment? What was their process?
- What questions were they trying to answer? What data did they collect?
- How did they test their thinking?
- What assumptions did they make? What general principles were they following?
- What was the source of their expertise?
- What conclusions did they draw?

After each slide, stop and discuss your observations and questions together as a class. Take a few minutes before you start the Interrupted Reading to silently preview the article, so you get the gist of the researchers' experiment.

As you'll see in the following transcript from one of my classes, an Interrupted Reading can become a kind of collaborative Think Aloud. You may want to give your students time to read the full article before beginning this activity.

Slide 1: "The animal runs toward me, its curly tail wagging and its loving eyes full of joy. It jumps into my arms and nuzzles my face, like a dog."

Me: What do you notice?

Taylor: Loving eyes full of joy. Jumps into my arms. The author uses a lot of description.

Kashanti: It says, *"like* a dog."

Me: Why might that be important?

Kashanti: It's telling you it's not a dog, but it's acting like a dog.

Ashlyn: And to show how civilized it is.

Me: What else do you notice?

Julia: The word *nuzzle* makes it sound like the animal likes to cuddle.

Oscar: It says, "the animal." It doesn't say "fox" or "dog."

Me: You're noticing a significant stylistic choice. When we read rhetorically, we pay special attention to how sentences begin and end. So, what does this choice do?

Kursi: Makes it seem like the animal is a mystery. We don't know the species.

Slide 2: *"But it is not a dog. It is a fox—a fox that looks and behaves much like a dog."*

Me: What's significant here? What are you seeing?

Jesus: It reminds me of the saying if it looks like a duck and quacks like a duck, it's a duck.

Kashanti: It's like the introduction to the research. You're starting to get the thesis.

Me: What language signals that start for you?

Kashanti: "It is a fox." Then she goes on to explain it's a fox that acts like a dog. You can tell she's going to compare foxes to dogs.

Oscar: She repeats the words *fox* and *dog*.

Me: What about the punctuation?

Jessenya: There's a double dash.

Me: What does that double dash, or em dash, do?

Isabella: Kind of gives it its own point or moment. It sets up this dramatic revelation.

Me: You're seeing its function. It announces the special subject of inquiry.

Slide 3: *"The animal and its close relatives are the result of 58 generations of selective breeding, performed in an attempt to discover in general the secrets of domestication and in particular how humans may have transformed wolves into the first dogs."*

Me: Let's unpack this. What do you notice?

Jenny: I'm not sure.

Me: OK, what words seem important?

Jenny: *Transformed.*

Me: What does *transformed* mean?

Jenny: Changed into something else.

Me: What else do you see?

Isabella: I notice "in general" and "in particular." There are two parts to their research—how domestication works overall and how dogs evolved from wolves.

Me: I like how you're noticing the argument structure. They're investigating two research questions, right? What kind of questions are these?

Taylor: About how something happened. Factual questions.

Adrian: They're going to explain how animals were domesticated.

Me: Good observation. Anything to add?

Michael: I notice they're still saying "the animal" and the study involved 58 generations.

Me: What does that do?

Michael: It shows that the animal is in a category of its own. It also shows how much work they did if they studied 58 generations of foxes. How much time is in between the generations?

Me: Not sure . . . maybe a year? Anyone know? What else did you notice?

Adrian: They used selective breeding as their method.

Erin: So, they're choosing the traits they want the next generation to have.

Me: That's the design of their study. What's their purpose?

Fernando: They say they want to discover the secrets of domestication.

Me: OK, at this point I'm going to ask you to make an inference to identify the researchers' hypothesis. Keep in mind a hypothesis is a claim about how something works.

Jessica: They're trying to verify if humans created dogs. And if tameness is genetic.

Kursi: That's what they're saying—that domestication is controlled by genetics.

Me: That's a helpful connection. So what ideas are they testing?

Jessica: That humans influenced domestication through selective breeding.

Me: What else do they need to know to answer their question?

Erin: If maybe tameness could be passed on other ways.

Slide 4: "Generation after generation, we would selectively breed those foxes that interacted in the most positive ways with humans."

> **Me:** What did the researchers do to try to answer their question of fact? What was the actual design of the study?
>
> **Ariel:** They went into the cages with the foxes and saw whether they were afraid of people. So they identified the animals that were less aggressive.
>
> **Me:** And what was the next step?
>
> **Jessica:** The animals that stayed calm were bred for that trait.
>
> **Oscar:** Later, they also used surrogates to see if genetics were the reason for the foxes' tameness.

Slide 5: "He had come to think the defining characteristic of domestication was tameness."

> **Me:** How do the researchers define *tameness*?
>
> **Oscar:** Being friendly to people. Not being scared of people.
>
> **Me:** What assumption did the researchers make about *tameness*?
>
> **Alejandra:** That this is the most important quality. This is what makes an animal domesticated.
>
> **Michael:** It's not enough that animals live with humans. They also have to be friendly to humans. Not all animals in captivity are domesticated.
>
> **Kashanti:** There's also an assumption that genetics influence behavior.
>
> **Me:** What reasoning process do you see the researchers using? How are they thinking about their subject? What are they trying to do?
>
> **Jessica:** They're also trying to define and classify things because they're saying that these are tame animals now.

Doing this kind of process study offered several insights. We noticed how the researchers defined key terms, tested their ideas, analyzed evidence, and asked follow-up questions. We also noticed how they based their conclusions on their professional expertise (along with some unspoken assumptions). The experiment itself became our mentor text for how to reason within a specific disciplinary context.

I've long believed in the importance of teaching the writing process. Initiatives like the Next Generation Science Standards are now helping me think more about how I teach the reasoning process. Apprenticing students in "essential disciplinary experiences" (Applebee and Langer 2013, 183) is key to developing their expertise in academic argumentation. If you choose to do this activity with your own students, try framing the Interrupted Reading with a special focus on the process of reasoned inquiry.

Teaching Reasoning in the Context of Writing

You can support students in developing their own flexible processes for reasoning from evidence by targeting key aspects of this brainwork. In the sections that follow, I offer practical ideas for teaching students how to analyze and evaluate evidence, develop a claim, justify their thinking, and understand the sources and limits of different ways of knowing. You'll notice these are the same transferrable skills the Russian scientists used to test their theory of domestication.

As I've shared, I'm primarily coming at this work from the perspective of teaching reasoning through writing, or more to the point, of teaching writing as reasoning. There are many courses and resources on formal logic that I think can be helpful, but, in my experience, students struggle to transfer their learning from exercises in logic to their academic writing. Like grammar, logic can't be effectively taught without meaningful content and context.

I need to repeat that this is challenging work. Both students and teachers have a habit of substituting easier tasks for more difficult ones in this area. Students do this because evidence-based reasoning is new to them. And teachers do this because our workload makes it hard to give all our students individualized critiques of their arguments. It's easier for students to cite a direct quotation than to explain their thinking, and it's easier for teachers to check that evidence has been used than to analyze a student's full line of reasoning.

But if we don't make the time and effort to do this challenging intellectual work together, we're not helping our students to grow beyond their surface understandings. We've taught them the basics of making claims and using evidence, but we're not pursuing deeper learning.

> Oversimplification is the novice's survival strategy. If we can reduce something that's highly complex to something simple, we feel like we've got things under control. The problem is that we then think we understand something when we don't.
>
> The process of reasoned inquiry can't be reduced to a checklist or fill-in-the-blank worksheet.

Developing Students' Critical Reasoning Skills

Think back to some of those key questions from the Interrupted Reading of "How to Build a Dog":

- What was the research process?
- What questions were the researchers trying to answer? What data did they collect?
- How did they test their thinking?

- What assumptions did they make? What general principles were they following?
- What was the source of their expertise?
- What conclusions did they draw?

Applying these same questions to students' writing can reveal the extent to which they've enacted their own process of reasoned inquiry . . . and can point us toward our next steps as teachers.

Let's imagine you're reading over my shoulder for a moment as I consider how to respond to a student's claims about Mary Shelley's *Frankenstein* in a literary analysis essay. You'll see my reader reactions in brackets. These are the kinds of questions I pose to students when we confer about their written arguments. This is also the kind of dialogue I want students to learn to have with themselves and their peers as they develop their critical reasoning skills.

What follows is an excerpt from the body paragraphs of the student's essay:

The gothic theme seemed to be unintentional [**Why do you think the gothic elements were unintentional? On what are you basing this?**] but it appears that Shelley's novel had minor themes such as cruelty and revenge. A quote from the book shows Victor's anger: "The tortures of hell are too mild a vengeance for thy crimes." Shelley potentially included such religious elements in her novel because she herself faced them [**Do you have evidence that supports this idea? Have you read a biography of Mary Shelley?**] but she could have potentially been showing the negative sides to the traditional views on punishment. [**How can you test this idea? What do others say?**] Adding to the earlier mentioned section on the Age of Reason, with the times changing so rapidly around her, Shelley could have been longing for the old traditional ways [**Where do you see this in the novel? What evidence are you drawing on?**] or she simply could have been highlighting the fact that the values that the Age of Reason was leaving behind weren't all that traditionalists believed it to be. [**How can you test this theory? What kind of inquiry process is needed?**]

In the end, *Frankenstein* was a novel that had many elements of the writer's personal life [**What is your evidence for this claim?**] and how the early 19th century was affecting society's views on religion and traditionalism. The Age of Reason most likely played a huge part in why and how Shelley shaped her novel. [**How did you arrive at this conclusion? Can you offer more concrete proof of this? What kind of historical evidence have you examined?**]

What do you see as the next steps in this student's growth? What kind of support would you offer to nurture her development as a critical thinker? When I confer with students about their early drafts, we often spend more time talking about their inquiry and reasoning process than the form of their writing. My most frequent questions are these:

- How do you know?
- What kind of evidence is needed to support these claims?
- What kinds of claims *can* you make about the evidence you've gathered and analyzed?

I try to ask questions during writing conferences that will help students reflect on their process rather than just red tagging shoddy claims. If we're approaching argument as inquiry, an unsupported claim is a reminder to go back and listen to the conversation more carefully and gather some more evidence. It's not a requisition to find evidence to support *that* specific claim.

If students have learned to play the doubting game, it can be easier for them to hear these kinds of critical questions about their own work—and to anticipate the kinds of questions their readers may ask. I want to stretch students' thinking, not shut it down. My goal is to move beyond me asking "How do you know?" to students asking themselves "How do I know?"

Before we take a look at how to help students think critically about their claims, I'd like you to think about where claims come from: the analysis and evaluation of evidence.

> Providing more support for process work moves students further along the continuum from novice to expert.

Analyzing Evidence

When my kids were in elementary school, I made a glorious discovery: I could buy myself several hours of summer quiet by giving Dryden and Ellerie one of those Highlights Top Secret Adventures kits. The detective kits included evidence packets filled with everything from suspect profiles to maps to local histories. Thoroughly engrossed in the task of piecing together the various clues needed to solve the mystery, my kids would shut themselves in a bedroom for a full morning, leaving me free to tackle to my to-do list in peace. What made these kits so engaging was the richness of the evidence they contained.

Deeply engaging with evidence develops expertise. One way I like to make the process of evidence analysis more visible to students is an activity I borrowed from Harry Noden's *Image Grammar* called "Examining the Contents of the Mystery Purse" (2011, 52). In my version, we use bags rather than purses, but the idea is the same.

EXAMINING THE CONTENTS OF THE MYSTERY BAG

Directions to Teachers:

1. *Bring several bags of various styles and sizes to class (e.g., purses, backpacks, tote bags, diaper bags). You can purchase these from stores like Goodwill or use bags you find around your home.*

2. *Fill each bag with a range of mysterious personal items that might generate discussion.*

3. *Divide the class into small groups.*

4. *Instruct each group to examine the contents of their mystery bag and to draw conclusions about the bag's owner based on the evidence the bag contains (Figure 6.2). A spokesperson will present the group's findings to the class. (Adapted from* Image Grammar *by Harry Noden 2011, 52.)*

FIGURE 6.2
Examining the contents of the mystery bag

After using this activity as a warm-up, you can swap out the personal items in the bags for textual evidence you've gathered from course readings and ask students to repeat the activity, this time drawing conclusions from direct quotations and paraphrases. For instance, you can fill a mystery bag with quotations from a novel or a set of scholarly articles you're reading together. Groups now have to construct the story the textual evidence tells. This works best if the quotations and paraphrases are printed on individual slips of paper that students can examine and sort.

> Evidence produces and justifies a claim.

The follow-up activity gives students extra practice sorting relevant from irrelevant information. While they still have to deal with outliers—those pieces of textual evidence that don't seem to fit the general pattern—they don't have to use everything that they find. You can extend students' thinking by asking questions about the significance of individual pieces of evidence: How relevant is this piece of evidence? How important is it?

CREATING AN EVIDENCE PACKAGE

Ultimately, students need to curate their own evidence packets. Some evidence writers will generate themselves: annotations, quick-writes, observations, personal experiences. Other evidence may be gathered through a formal research process (see Chapter 5).

Deep knowledge of the value of evidence comes from the inquiry work. If a student asks, "How am I going to use this?" about a piece of evidence she's gathered, I toss the question back to her: "Good question. How *are* you going to use that?"

The experience of analyzing or assembling an intriguing evidence package also moves students beyond the perennial question of how many sources they have to use for an essay. Although I never grow tired of saying "It depends," I do offer students some advice I picked up from my business colleagues on writing winning proposals: Don't put all your eggs in one basket. Put a convincing evidence package together. Don't make one reason or example do all the work of convincing your audience for you. If your audience doesn't buy your main source or reason or example, and you don't offer other ways to help readers see your point of view, they're probably not going to buy your argument.

The following activity affords students the opportunity to assemble an evidence package. I use Mark Haddon's 2003 novel, *The Curious Incident of the Dog in the Night-Time* for this activity, but you can adapt this for a text your students read. This strategy works especially well with full-length literary works.

> *Directions to Students:* Working in a group of three or four students, create an evidence package—that is, a collection of quotations, examples, and paraphrases—related to one of the following topics in *The Curious Incident of the Dog in the Night-Time*: gender, love, lying, growing up, stereotypes, or visual images. Choose the topic you'd like to investigate as a group. Once you've assembled your evidence, discuss the questions that follow with your group members:
>
> - What trends do you see in the evidence?
> - Given the assembled evidence, what conclusions can you draw?
> - What story does the evidence tell?
> - What are the other stories the novel tells? Why is this important?

The bigger the data pool, the more opportunities we have to identify significant patterns and make meaningful connections.

> The types of evidence and claims used and valued vary according to the rhetorical situation.

Valuing and Evaluating Evidence

Two plus decades of teaching writing have taught me this: Me saying "use evidence" isn't enough to get my students to use evidence. Without the expansive framing that helps students understand the principles and values underlying evidence-based reasoning, my directives can just sound like nitpicky teacher nagging.

Let's say a student has produced a draft of a research paper or literary analysis that doesn't yet include any citations, and you want to help this student learn to incorporate direct quotations as evidence for their claims. What kind of thinking do the teacher comments or questions shown in Figure 6.3 promote?

OPTION A	OPTION B
Use direct quotations.	What evidence informs these claims? How do you plan to engage the views of other writers? What other texts are part of this conversation?

FIGURE 6.3
Framing for transfer

The kind of approach we take (prescriptive or rhetorical) and the kind of framing we provide (bounded or expansive) impact the intellectual work we ask students to do.

Students need help knowing what counts as evidence in different academic contexts and how to collect it. Even more importantly, students need to know why all academic disciplines value evidence-based reasoning.

In an era where fake news can spread like wildfire, cultivating a shared belief in the value of evidence and inquiry is more important than ever. Physicist-turned-billionaire Yuri Milner made this point at the 2016 Breakthrough Prize gala, a Hollywood-style event honoring achievements in science and mathematics research. Implicitly invoking transfer theory, Milner told reporters that "we will all benefit, collectively, from applying scientific method to everything. Those methods involve rigorous fact-checking and intellectual honesty. The more we spread those values, the better off we will be" (*San Francisco Chronicle*, Sunday, December 18, 2016). Our profession is certainly doing its part.

But we can cultivate these values even more directly by calling out the transfer potential of the skills and habits of mind students develop in our classes. Along with fostering a disposition for problem solving, when we teach inquiry for transfer, we also develop our students' appreciation of evidence-based reasoning. These are habits of mind we want students to carry into their future lives.

Evaluating Evidence Rhetorically

A deeper understanding of reasoning includes the knowledge that the significance and availability of evidence varies according to context. Citing Aristotle's claim that rhetoric is a tool for discovering the best *available* proofs, rhetoricians Sharon Crowley and Debra Hawhee note that ". . . proofs are made available by the interactions of human beings who find themselves in particular sets of circumstances" (2009, 48).

Thinking rhetorically about evidence enhances students' adaptability. What counts as evidence in a particular field? Which of the following, for instance, typically comprise part of an evidence package for a humanities research project?

examples	testimony	letters
illustrations	case law	meeting minutes
hypothetical examples	photographic evidence	public records
statistics	interviews	first-hand observations
measurements	direct quotations	

Now let's change the context. Which of these would you expect to see in a social science project? A science project? What counts as evidence in a biology class differs significantly from what counts as evidence in a literature class—for reasons directly related to audience and purpose. We see these same distinctions in professional settings. The differences between the evidence needed to process an insurance claim and the evidence needed to determine school board policy arise from how data is used in each context.

> Encourage students to explain how their evidence helped them to develop their ideas.

I make the point about different audiences valuing different types of evidence by sharing one of my favorite posters from the January 2017 Women's March in Washington, D.C.: "What do we want? Evidence-based science! When do we want it? After peer review!"

How much and what kind of evidence a writer provides depends on the audience. A scientist who is giving a presentation to fellow scientists will need to assemble a different kind of evidence package from the scientist who will be talking to nonscientists.

Moving from Evidence to Claims

Students can't be expected to know or do what they can't see. And the first thing that beginners typically see is just a surface appearance, not what goes on behind the scenes. A beginner's approach to reasoning thus often involves dropping a few pieces of evidence, such as direct quotations or statistics, into a paragraph and then writing a few statements about that evidence. The connections between the evidence and the claims are often underdeveloped and unarticulated. What's frequently missing from the process at this stage is the back-and-forth discussion, testing, low-stakes writing, and corroboration work that help a writer move from evidence to claim.

We need to show students that there's an order of operations in evidence-based reasoning: that is, that we draw conclusions *after* we collect, analyze, and evaluate evidence. If we try to work from a claim back to evidence, we significantly diminish the likelihood of reaching an informed and reasonable conclusion. As one of my students said, "If I start with a thesis, I tend to only look for sources that support my thesis."

This skill applies across contexts. Writing on research methods in the social sciences, for instance, professors Gordon Morris Bakken and Brenda Farrington note that "moving from evidence to interpretation is the most creative, yet challenging, task of the historian" (1999, 67). This is also the most challenging task of the literary critic. And the biologist. And so on. All of us in academia, students and faculty, must make interpretive arguments about the evidence we've collected and analyzed in our respective fields.

Organizing ideas—that is, finding relationships between ideas and a narrative thread that connects them—is part of how we reason from evidence. Reasoning is pattern finding. That's why predetermined organizational structures can sometimes limit our ability to reason through the evidence. If one schema has already been imposed on our vision (e.g., the reason-reason-counterargument outline or a cause-and-effect text structure), it makes it hard for us to see other possibilities. However, if students have developed multiple methods for organizing evidence, then they can look for patterns with an open and creative mind.

I'll share a few sentence starters with my students to get them going:

The common element of all these things is _____.

These ideas are related because _____.

The important connection here is _____.

This can be a transformative practice for students. Anna, one of my first-year college students, wrote the following reflection:

> When I map out my ideas, I am able to see the trends that might help me gather my information. However, the technique of gathering my evidence before making my claim is something new that I am trying to do. I struggled on trying it because I am so used to making my claim and finding the evidence to support my claim which is a bit easier. I believe I did an okay job because this kind of task was something that I had never done before which made it a bit more challenging.

The Problem with Shortcuts

If students can write a claim supported with evidence and reasons, why worry about the "extras" not measured by high-stakes tests? Why worry about whether or not they can unpack their assumptions, engage in extended inquiry, respond to the cares and concerns of others, or critically examine the source of their way of thinking? For this reason: Because teaching students shortcuts to reasoning that bypass dialogue, inquiry, and reflection not only interferes with their ability to solve problems but may also increase the amount of conflict and injustice in the world. Such shortcuts can also discourage students from drawing on their lived experiences and sharing their hard-earned insights. If teachers or high-stakes tests don't ask students what they really think and why they think it, students learn to just go through the motions of argumentation in school.

Developing and Supporting a Full Line of Reasoning

Developing and supporting a full line of reasoning involves more than just the use of evidence. We reach a conclusion because we've gone somewhere in our thinking. Our evidence is our starting point. Our reasons and justifications, a bridge. Our claim is the understanding we reach by doing this inquiry work.

Many teachers use ideas from philosopher Stephen Toulmin to teach students about these different components of arguments. I also find Toulmin's work useful, especially as it relates to dialogue and inquiry. For me, the important takeaway from Toulmin is the way his model helps writers anticipate audience reactions and engage in disciplinary ways of thinking.

Michael W. Smith and Jon-Philip Imbrenda offer a clear summary of Toulmin's model in *Developing Writers of Argument: Tools and Rules That Sharpen Student Reasoning*:

1. Claim (what you're arguing for)

2. Data (the evidence you use)

3. Warrant (an explanation of the principles that link the data to the claim) (2018, location 756)

When I teach these elements to my students, I like to list "data" first so that students start with inquiry, but the basic components are the same ones Toulmin describes in *The Uses of Argument* ([1958] 2003). I use Toulmin's concept of "backing," too, for reasons that I'll explain in a bit. Smith and Imbrenda's student-friendly explanations puts this kind of reasoning within reach of younger writers. The Toulmin model of argumentation is useful when it helps students to be more rigorous and responsive in their thinking.

Toulmin's model is dialogic. It enacts an imagined conversation between a rhetor and their audience in which the audience accepts or challenges the rhetor's argument based on their own assumptions, beliefs, and ways of knowing. Rhetorician John Edlund (2018) explains the process this way:

> When a claim is made, and questioned, the assertor will produce data or evidence. If the evidence is challenged, not in terms of its facticity, but in terms of its relevance, a warrant will be produced to connect data and claim. If the warrant is challenged, the assertor refers to a body of knowledge, a system of principles or accepted wisdom, or disciplinary practices, to give backing to the warrant.

The model thus helps students to reason rhetorically—that is, with an awareness of how audience and context impact the structure and validity of arguments.

Because Toulmin's system was created as a tool for analyzing arguments, rather than creating them, I like to use his questions primarily during peer review and revision. Those "How do you know?" and "What makes you say so?" questions are great to ask during a rhetorical analysis of a rough draft.

Let's look at claims and warrants (or justifications) more closely.

> Novices tend to fixate on the parts of an argument rather than the process of argumentation.

Going Beyond Fact vs. Claim

A claim is an answer to a question at issue. It might express a belief about our world or how we should live in it or make any other kind of debatable assertion that cries out for support. There is nothing debatable or undebatable, but disagreement makes it so. Questions of fact can be debatable and, indeed, often are debated in academic settings. How old is the Grand Canyon? What's causing childhood obesity? The answers to these questions aren't "facts" we can take for granted because scholars disagree about the answers. Even statistics can be debatable if there is disagreement about how the numbers were reached. How do we know if a question is at issue? We listen to the conversation. If other writers and scholars are asking the same question and arriving at different answers, it's debatable. If nobody's talking about it, it's not at issue (yet). If everyone agrees, it's a commonplace.

Instead of trying to teach students the difference between facts and claims—a difference that will get fuzzy fast in a college classroom where factual claims are daily bread—I find it more helpful to distinguish between data and claims. The claim could be a statement of fact as long as it's at issue. "The planets rotate around the sun" is an example of a factual claim that was once, but is no longer, debated in intellectual circles. The question of a heliocentric solar system is no longer at issue.

> We teach the components of arguments to help students discern and deploy different components of thinking.

Understanding Warrants: How Did You Get to That Idea?

Understanding warrants can help students chart the connection between evidence and claims. A warrant can be an underlying rule, definition, principle, or belief. Toulmin says that a warrant is needed in cases in which our task is to show that "the step to the original claim or conclusion is an appropriate and legitimate one" (2003, 90). Describing warrants as "bridges" (91), Toulmin explains that a warrant authorizes the connection between the "starting point" (91)—i.e., the data—and the conclusion. In other words, warrants justify how an argument moves from point to point. If an audience wants to know how you reached a particular conclusion, you can trace your thinking by surfacing your warrants.

A warrant entitles you to draw a conclusion from the data. Can we justify taking this step in our reasoning? Is this step warranted? We commit ourselves to implicit assumptions by the claims we make. Sometimes, we're not even aware of the steps we've taken in our argument or of the underlying principles these steps invoke. If our audience sees a problem with our ideological commitments—but we don't—we could find ourselves basing our argument on a faulty warrant, that is, an underlying assumption that our audience doesn't share with us.

Say a person claims that we should reduce the social safety net because doing so will motivate people to find a way out of poverty. Here the warrant is explicit (the "because" clause). But what if the audience believes that reducing the social safety net will lead to more homelessness and food insecurity? And that these conditions are demotivating? Assuming that your audience shares your beliefs when they don't is the kind of faulty reasoning that can cause real harm to deliberations and relationships. If community members don't share the same beliefs, that's something that needs to be addressed at the outset, not ignored.

Reasoning rhetorically demands (or warrants) that we consider our audience's beliefs, values, and assumptions, as well as our own, in building our arguments. As Smith and Imbrenda note, "[. . .] effective arguments also require the audience or interlocutor to accept the bigger assumptions underlying our claims and data" (2018, location 509).

You might try introducing your students to the concept of a warrant by having them generate their own understanding from some examples. Here's a quick activity.

WHAT DO WE MEAN BY A *WARRANT*?

Directions to Students: Read each of the following statements. Then rewrite the statements in your own words using alternatives to the term "warrant." Finally, use the examples and your sentence revisions to explain what it means when something is "warranted."

1. The initial promising results of the study warrant further research.
2. My aunt's unusual behavior warrants close observation.
3. Your criticism of my outstanding work is totally unwarranted.

Spinning out the different parts of speech in this word family can also give students a deeper—and more widely applicable—understanding of this concept. "Warrant" isn't just jargon in Toulmin's model of argumentation. It's lots of things students are already familiar with.

Warrant (noun)

Warrant (verb)

Warranted (adjective)

Unwarranted (adjective)

Warrants in the Wild

To make this point, I show my students examples of "warrants in the wild"[1] I've collected from real-world texts. Here are a few:

- From a financial advice column for senior citizens: "If the sister had been correct in thinking he was not safe at home . . . the decision to move him to a facility may have been warranted" (Horvath, 2018).

- - - - - - - - - - - - - - - - - -

1. See Donalyn Miller's wonderful book Reading in the Wild (2014) for ways to help students develop authentic and independent reading lives. The phrase "in the wild" refers to literacy practices that aren't constrained to the captive audience of the classroom.

- From a newspaper article on the investigation into Donald Trump's ties to Russia: "They're admitting to enough that warrants scrutiny" (*Monterey County Herald*, Tuesday, May 8, 2018).

- From Sheridan Blau's 2017 NCTE presentation on close reading (Section D34, "The Problem and Promise of Close Reading," Friday, November 17, 2017): "Is how you are thinking/feeling warranted by the text?"

- From a newsletter for humanities professionals: "Crisis rhetoric about the humanities isn't new. But is it warranted?" (MLA Career Alert, June 2018)

> Deeper reasoning involves understanding how different assumptions lead to different conclusions.

These examples can give students a more concrete and authentic understanding of this concept in its natural settings.

Faulty Warrants

My son made this request while watching a 49ers game: "Since it's game day and the commercials say it's not game day without a Coke, can I have a Diet Coke?" I told him I didn't accept his reasoning, but that, yes, he could have a soda as a treat—not a necessity. (Sometimes it's hard to be an English teacher's kid.)

Basing a claim on a premise that the audience doesn't accept (in this case, "It's not game day without a Coke") is a faulty warrant. A faulty warrant is one of those logical fallacies that I pay attention to because of its rhetorical and ethical implications. Pinning a claim on a warrant your audience doesn't share is a failure to attend to audience beliefs and values. Without a shared sense of the principles authorizing an argument, rhetor and audience can't engage in productive discussion.

Thinking Rhetorically About Warrants

Not all rhetorical situations call for arguments with explicit warrants. How do writers know when they need to articulate the general principles linking their data to their claims? By analyzing the audience and anticipating the questions it might raise in response to the writer's claims. If their audience shares or accepts a writer's underlying assumptions, explicit warrants aren't needed. Making our reasoning visible can often strengthen our arguments—and help newcomers to academic argumentation develop reasoning skills—but the necessity and effectiveness of clearly calling out a warrant depends on what the audience values and believes.

In some cases, exposing those hidden values and beliefs is the whole point of an argument. Robin DiAngelo's powerful book *White Fragility: Why It's So Hard for White People to Talk About Racism* makes a direct case for the importance of surfacing underlying assumptions in conversations about race. By examining the foundations of racial inequality, she argues, white people can overcome the defensiveness that prevents them from acknowledging their participation in racism. Drawing on her work as an antiracist educator and consultant, DiAngelo notes several common assumptions authorizing white

CHAPTER SIX: REASONING FROM EVIDENCE

people's claims that they're not racist, including a definition of a racist as a bad person (which means a good person cannot support racism) and the ideology of individualism (which says we can freely choose what we believe instead of being socialized into particular views) (2018, 85). Note how DiAngelo unpacks the connections between evidence and claim in the following example:

> . . . in a conversation about racism, when white people say they work in a diverse environment or that they have people of color in their family, they are giving me their evidence that they are not racist. If this is their evidence, how are they defining racism? In other words, what underlying system of meaning leads them to make that claim? If working near people of color is the evidence that distinguishes them from a racist, then evidently a racist cannot work near people of color. This claim rests on a definition of racism as *conscious intolerance* . . . (79)

Getting at the hidden definitions, beliefs, and principles upon which our claims rest is critical inquiry work. DiAngelo uses the image of a pier stretching over the water to illustrate the hidden structure of the claims she analyzes: "In the same way that a pier sits on submerged pillars that are not immediately visible, the beliefs supporting our racial claims are hidden from our view. To topple the pier, we need to access and uproot the pillars" (2018, 79). This is what an understanding of warrants can help us do.

> Toulmin's model is useful for helping students explain their ideas. A warrant can be a key tenet or belief that underpins a claim.

The value of the Toulmin model is not in the superficial structure it provides but in the deeper reasoning process it reveals.

Questions to Help Students Connect Data to Claims (adapted from Stephen Toulmin 2003):

Why do you think that?

What makes you say so?

How did you get to that idea?

What ideas or definitions does this claim depend on?

Unpacking Assumptions

For some reason that probably has to do with human frailty, it seems to be easier to unpack the assumptions behind other writers' claims than to examine the assumptions we implicitly make ourselves. We'd rather take the speck out of someone else's argument than remove the log from our own.

The following activity helps students to surface and examine their own assumptions.

ANTICIPATION/REACTION GUIDES

We can give students more practice with this kind of thinking by inviting them to analyze the assumptions they make in responding to Anticipation/Reaction Guide statements (Readence, Bean, and Baldwin 2004). In this two-part survey, students decide if they agree or disagree with a list of statements both before and after reading a text.

Anticipation/Reaction Guides let students test out their provisional thinking. Just as when they play the believing game and doubting game, students are trying on tentative perspectives for size prior to a full analysis of a text or topic. It's important that these kinds of activities be framed with this understanding. We need to explain to students that this thinking is exploratory and that we're not practicing how to make snap judgments based on little evidence. Students are already pretty good at taking a stance on an issue. They can use some help, however, developing an informed position that respectfully engages the multiple stances others have taken on the issue.

If you've used this literacy strategy before—and especially if you've written intentionally ambiguous statements for your own Anticipation/Reaction Guides—you've probably seen your students struggle to work out their stance on a particular statement. The example that follows comes from my unit on lying.

Directions to Students: Read each statement below. Then, in column one, write a plus sign if you agree with the statement, a minus sign if you disagree, and a question mark if you are unsure about your opinion. There are no right answers.

After you have read the text, reread the statements and indicate your reactions in column two.

Column ONE	Column TWO		
_____	_____	1.	All human beings tell lies.
_____	_____	2.	It is easier to deceive ourselves than to deceive others.
_____	_____	3.	Numbers don't lie.
_____	_____	4.	Words are more harmful than deeds.
_____	_____	5.	We can never know the whole truth.
_____	_____	6.	No lie is justifiable.
_____	_____	7.	We have the right to decide what truths we reveal about ourselves.
_____	_____	8.	Liars can't be trusted.

I like to facilitate Anticipation/Reaction Guides as the "Take a Stand" activity in which I label one side of the classroom "Agree" and the other side "Disagree." I then read select statements aloud, and students must stand by the wall indicating their position. Each time students take a stand on a statement, three volunteers from each side get to explain their views, with the side with the fewest students sharing first. Students can change sides if they're persuaded by another view.

Initial reactions often involve a look of confusion and a desire to hedge. "What do you mean by a *liar*?" they ask me. I tell them they have to figure that out for themselves. They say, "Well, it depends" and linger in the middle of the room.

Unpacking their rationale for their responses on the Anticipation/Reaction Guide can help students see the intellectual operations they had to perform before deciding on their opinion. These include the following:

- Defining key terms
- Establishing an underlying principle
- Noting their own exceptions or qualifications
- Determining their value hierarchy

This is the same brainwork that creates warrants for arguments. Noting the conditions of their belief (the exceptions and qualifications) is a way to authorize the connection between the claim ("I believe this . . .") and whatever evidence the students can think of that led them to that belief. The warrant then includes the conditions under which that belief is tenable ("I believe this if we're defining lying as . . ." or "I believe this if we're not including cases of . . ."). Explaining the rationale for their responses can also uncover assumptions they had to make in deciding on their stance ("I believe this based on the assumption that . . ."), including the way they've chosen to define key terms.

As stasis theory makes clear, a question of definition is an important point of disagreement in many academic arguments. We often have to define our terms before we can analyze or evaluate them precisely because there are so many different meanings to contend with—and each meaning carries its own assumptions and ways of knowing. If this seems like a tall order for high school students, consider this: How can we evaluate the "truth" of a text like *The Things They Carried* if we don't define the term "truth" first? Asking students, "What do you mean by that term?" gets them to unpack their own thinking.

> Warrants are underlying principles or assumptions.

This ability to uncover and critically examine assumptions is one of the most important reasoning and communication skills we can develop in students. As Josina Makau and Debian Marty write in *Cooperative Argumentation*, "We seldom, if ever, explicitly state

> Encourage students to ask themselves: "If I make this claim based on this evidence, what principles or assumptions am I committing myself to?"

or present all that we intend to communicate. Yet communication can only work well if readers and listeners either consciously or unconsciously fill in the blanks by providing the missing assumptions" (2001, 132).

Model Language for Calling Out Warrants

I sometimes provide language to help students reason like scholars by identifying possible warrants and evidence for their claims. Here are a few sentence stems I've used:

> To counter the author's argument, one could provide . . .
>
> My work is premised on . . .
>
> My argument is based on . . .
>
> My research is inspired by . . .
>
> Guided by . . . , I . . .
>
> I draw on . . .
>
> Drawing on . . . , I . . .
>
> Given the . . .
>
> The belief that _____ supports the assertion that . . .
>
> I'm defining X as . . .
>
> I can say this because . . .
>
> This claim depends on . . .

Model language, like model questions, should deepen students' thinking, not do the thinking for them. We want students to reason like scholars, not just imitate their writing.

Understanding Backing: What's the Context for This Way of Thinking?

Backing refers to a type of reasoning or thinking specific to a particular context—in other words, a way of knowing. The authors of *Argumentation and Critical Decision Making* define backing as "any support (specific instances, statistics, testimony, values, or credibility) that provides more specific data for the grounds or warrant" (Rieke, Sillars, and Peterson 2005, 100). In academic contexts, backing includes disciplinary research methods (e.g., scientific method) and theoretical frameworks (e.g., postcolonial theory).

While in Toulmin's model backing doesn't need to be provided unless the audience demands further support for the argument, academic writing frequently assumes that backing is needed. In fact, this is partly the purpose of a literature review: to identify where a way of thinking comes from. Notice how the following sentence from the introductory essay to *Understanding Writing Transfer* names its backing:

> Writing transfer research builds on broader studies in educational psychology and related fields on transfer of learning, and many of the terms used to describe writing transfer are borrowed from these other realms. (Moore and Bass 2017, 2)

This statement calls out the scope and depth of the expertise on which the writer's work is based.

If the backing is missing from an argument—and the audience calls for it—and the rhetor doesn't know how to provide it, chances are it's the disciplinary research methods or theoretical framework that's missing. Think, for instance, of a person who is not in the health care profession who insists their father's cancer was caused by drinking diet cola. How could this person respond to a doctor who challenges this claim? If you don't know how causality is established in medical research, you can't provide backing for the diet-soda-causes-cancer argument that the medical community would accept (although you might be able to persuade other audiences).

Until we've worked really hard to know something, we can't fully appreciate the limits of our understanding. Sustained inquiry changes how we view knowledge. After pursuing a question through hours of research, reading, observation, and testing, we start to sense that the question may be more difficult to answer than we first thought. The bigger the data pool, the more ambiguity and complexity we have to contend with.

Backing isn't just needed for persuading resistant audiences; it represents the expert knowledge needed to solve problems effectively. Deep, context-specific learning is going to get us closer to a solution than just a lightly held opinion.

If we're teaching the structure of formal reasoning (i.e., data, claim, warrant) without a deep appreciation for inquiry and subject matter expertise, we're not preparing students to solve real-world problems. Without this framing, the transfer from syllogistic reasoning to something like a town hall meeting on land use will be a bridge too far.

When I hear people call journalists liars, for instance, I think of the students I know who are working really hard to become journalists. And of the professors I know who are working really hard to help those students. And of the professional journalists I know who work really hard to get the story right. What does a deep understanding of journalism and media look like? Here's a snapshot from my university's course catalog, for starters:

HCOM 307: Social Impact of Mass Media

HCOM 310: Free Speech and Responsibility

HCOM 316: Media Ethics

HCOM 319: Global Communication and Culture

HCOM 387: Media Production Lab

HCOM 388: Investigative Reporting

HCOM 411: Media Law and Policy

The intellectual and practical investment required to develop expertise as a journalist is not slight. Understanding the difference between superficial and expert learning changes how we evaluate the quality of claims. Backing is depth of knowledge. Claims that can't be supported by backing—whether called for by the audience or not—confuse the issue instead of contributing to a solution.

> Deep learning includes understanding how knowledge is produced, validated, disseminated, challenged, and changed.

What does it take to really know something? How do we know what we know? What does it take to make claims with an informed awareness of the limitations of our knowledge? These are the questions backing can answer.

UNDERSTANDING THE IMPORTANCE OF BACKING: COMPARING SUPERFICIAL TO DEEP KNOWLEDGE

Directions to Students: This activity asks you to write and compare two quick-writes, each on its own topic. As you follow the steps below, think about the importance of *backing*—or assurances of how we know what we know—in academic arguments (see Stephen Toulmin's *The Uses of Argument* for more on backing).

STEP ONE: Write for three minutes on the importance of something that you haven't studied in depth. Choose one of the topics below:

- The printing press

- Crop rotation

- Canine obedience training

- Space exploration

STEP TWO: Analyze your language choices and the effects of those choices. What do you notice? Turn and talk to a partner.

STEP THREE: Now list four subjects that you know a great deal about. Then choose one item from the list you generated and write about that subject for three minutes. Now what do you notice about your language choices and the effects of those choices? What conclusions can you draw from these observations? Talk to your partner again.

CLAIM AND BACKING T-CHART

Directions to Students: Use the T-chart shown in Figure 6.4 to record several claims from a draft of your argument essay. Then, in the right column, explain how you know what you claim to know in each of the assertions listed in the left column (see Figure 6.5). What inquiry work, subject matter knowledge, and/or special training or experiences authorize you to make each claim?

CLAIM	I KNOW THIS BECAUSE . . .

FIGURE 6.4

Claim and backing T-chart

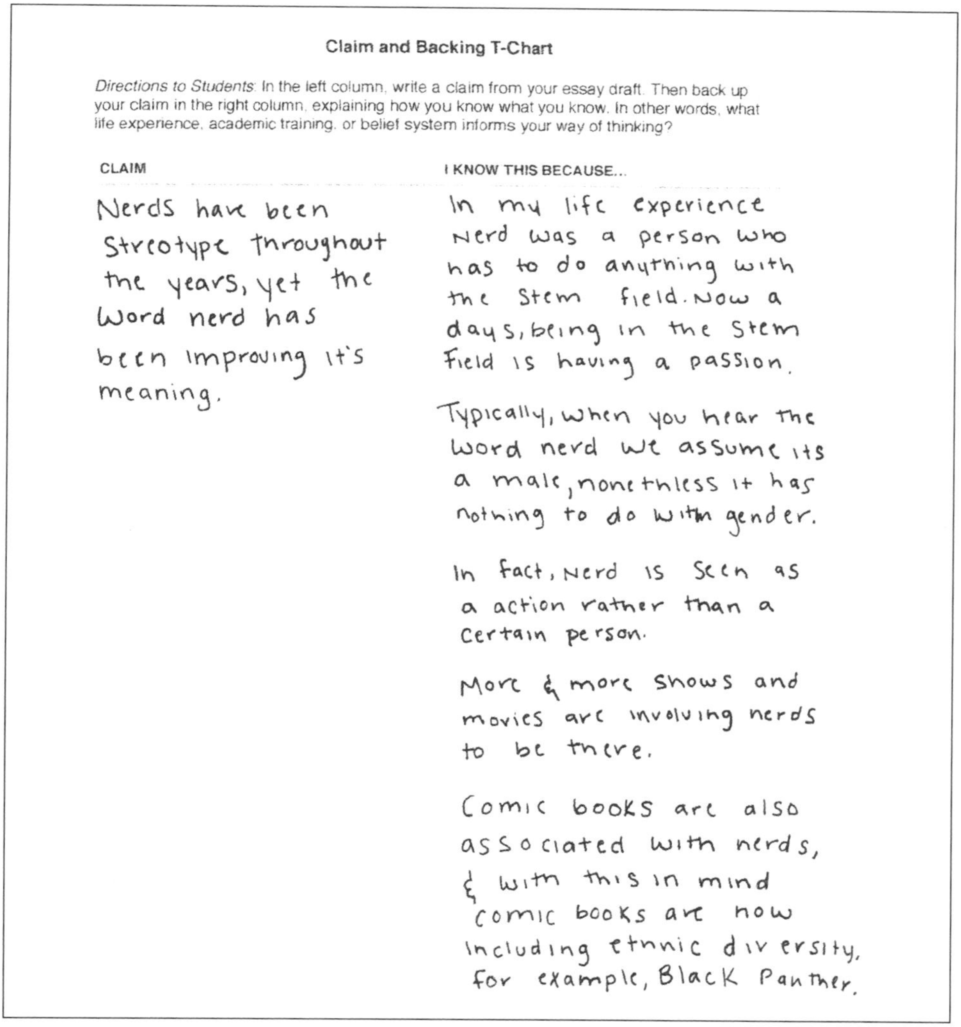

Claim and Backing T-Chart

Directions to Students: In the left column, write a claim from your essay draft. Then back up your claim in the right column, explaining how you know what you know. In other words, what life experience, academic training, or belief system informs your way of thinking?

CLAIM	I KNOW THIS BECAUSE...
Nerds have been Streotype throughout the years, yet the word nerd has been improving it's meaning.	In my life experience Nerd was a person who has to do anything with the Stem field. Now a days, being in the Stem field is having a passion. Typically, when you hear the word nerd we assume its a male, nonethless it has nothing to do with gender. In fact, Nerd is Seen as a action rather than a certain person. More & more shows and movies are involving nerds to be there. Comic books are also associated with nerds, & with this in mind comic books are now including ethnic diversity, for example, Black Panther.

FIGURE 6.5

Student sample of claim and backing T-chart

LANGUAGE FOR SURFACING WAYS OF KNOWING

If your students could benefit from additional support for articulating and drawing on backing for their claims, you can share the following templates with them:

I know this because my education has taught me _____

My knowledge of _____ comes from _____

My research into _____ has prepared me to understand _____

My belief in _____ shapes my understanding of _____

From my culture, I have learned that _____

Try asking students: "Why do you believe that?" "What in your background or personal history contributes to that belief?"

TAKE A STAND AND TELL YOUR STORY

To help students know themselves and others better, I've experimented with how I facilitate discussion around Anticipation/Reaction Guide Statements. While I like having students explain why they agree or disagree with particular statements, I've found that it can be even more powerful to have students explain their story rather than their stance. Thus, instead of offering a rationale (or warrant) for their position on an issue, students reflect on and share where their way of thinking comes from (their backing). Engaging ways of knowing facilitates perspective taking and understanding.

Directions to Students: First, read each statement. Then decide whether you agree, disagree, or are unsure about your opinion. After completing your responses, choose one statement to discuss with a partner or small group. Instead of explaining your position on this statement, tell your story of who you are. What experiences have shaped how you see this issue? Why does this issue matter to you? What's your personal history with this issue? How do your particular beliefs and perspectives influence your thinking?

FOUR SQUARE REASONING

This next graphic organizer can be used to brainstorm ideas during prewriting or to analyze a draft during peer review and revision.

Directions to Students: Examine a line of reasoning you are developing by responding to the questions in the boxes shown in Figure 6.6. Figure 6.7 shows a student example.

When I look back on my teaching life, I notice that the times I told students, "You need to know this for the test," were those times when I didn't know myself why students would need to know something beyond a test. I'm sure I used this stick the first few times I taught iambic pentameter or MLA style. Because I didn't have a deep understanding of the principles

Jennifer Fletcher, CSU Monterey Bay

Four Square Reasoning

Data: What is your evidence?	**Claim**: What does the evidence suggest?
Warrant: Why do you think this?	**Backing**: Where does this way of thinking come from?

Quick-write: How do you expect your audience to react to your claim? Will they accept it? Challenge it? Explain your response.

FIGURE 6.6

Four square reasoning

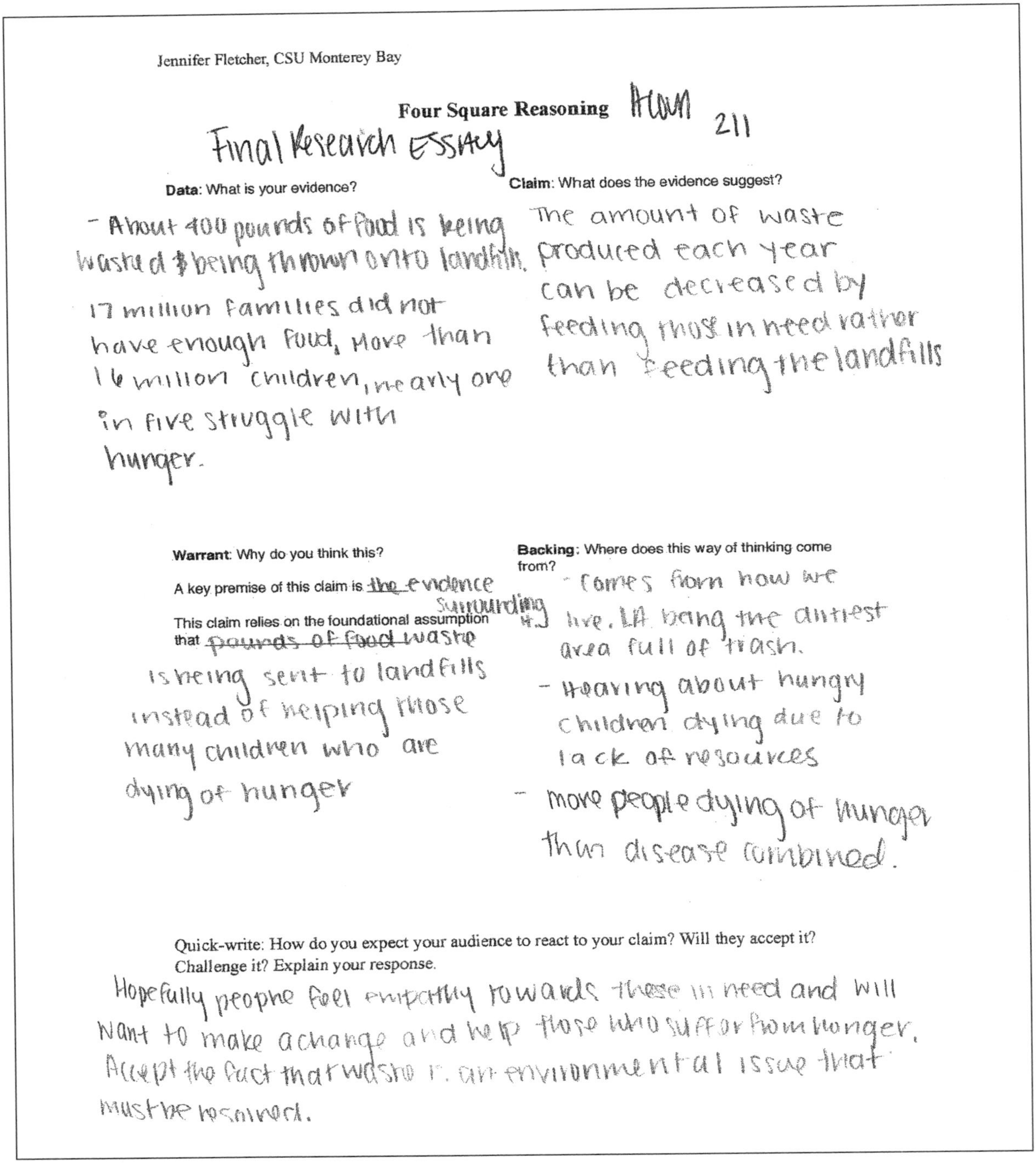

Jennifer Fletcher, CSU Monterey Bay

Four Square Reasoning Acam 211

Final Research ESSAY

Data: What is your evidence?

- About 400 pounds of Food is being wasted & being thrown onto landfills.

17 million families did not have enough food, More than 16 million children, nearly one in five struggle with hunger.

Claim: What does the evidence suggest?

The amount of waste produced each year can be decreased by feeding those in need rather than feeding the landfills

Warrant: Why do you think this?

A key premise of this claim is the evidence surrounding #3

This claim relies on the foundational assumption that pounds of food waste is being sent to landfills instead of helping those many children who are dying of hunger

Backing: Where does this way of thinking come from?

- Comes from how we live. LA being the dirtiest area full of trash.

- Hearing about hungry children dying due to lack of resources

- more people dying of hunger than disease combined.

Quick-write: How do you expect your audience to react to your claim? Will they accept it? Challenge it? Explain your response.

Hopefully people feel empathy towards those in need and will want to make a change and help those who suffer from hunger. Accept the fact that waste is an environmental issue that must be resolved.

FIGURE 6.7

Student sample of four square reasoning

behind poetic meter or documentation conventions, I'd double down on enforcing the practice. Depth of knowledge liberates students and teachers from the bind of compliance.

Justifying Claims

Backing, whether called for by the rhetorical situation or not, prepares us to justify our claims. Asking for elaboration and clarification surfaces the processes students used to arrive at their conclusions—or points the way toward an inquiry process that hasn't yet been practiced.

SEMANTIC MAP: ELABORATION AND CLARIFICATION

In *Academic Conversations: Classroom Talk That Fosters Critical Thinking and Content Understandings*, Jeff Zwiers and Marie Crawford recommend that teachers use semantic maps to help students elaborate on their ideas. Different branches could include "examples, applications, details, questions, and anything else that supports the idea" (2011, 84). Zwiers and Crawford offer several questions for teachers or peers to ask students that can further develop and clarify their thinking:

Can you elaborate on . . .?

What do you mean by . . .?

Can you tell me more about . . .?

What makes you think that . . .?

Can you clarify the part about . . .?

Can you be more specific . . .?

How so . . .?

How (or why) is that important?

I'd love to hear more about . . .

I wonder if . . .

Can you unpack that for me?

I am a little confused about the part . . . (2011, 32).

Directions to Students (adapted from *Academic Conversations* by Zwiers and Crawford 2011): Choose one claim from your argument essay to analyze for this activity. Write that claim in the center of your semantic map. Draw branches out from the center for each of the following: examples, details, applications, questions, and other perspectives. Add to your map by brainstorming ideas for each of these areas.

When you're finished, share your semantic map with a partner. Talk about any elaboration or clarification you think your claim needs.

Using this approach, I had my students create a semantic map of one of their key claims from their argument essays (Figure 6.8).

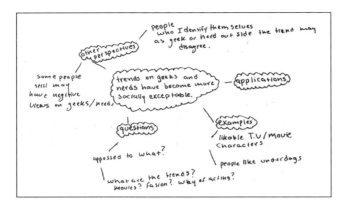

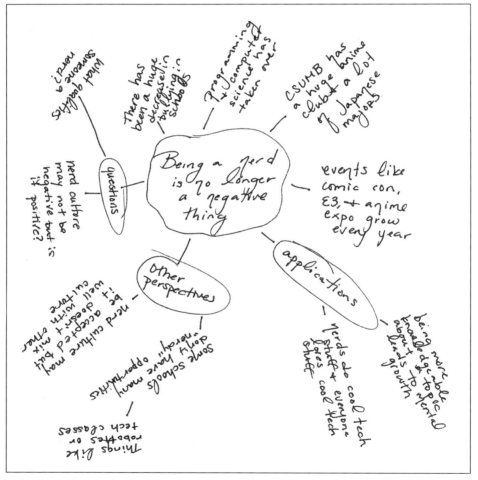

FIGURE 6.8
Student samples of a semantic map of a claim

This kind of elaboration and clarification is a form of critical reasoning. Often students will tell me during writing conferences that their underdeveloped essays just need a few more examples. I tell them, "You don't just need more examples; you need more reasoning." (I try to say this kindly.) I imagine this is a familiar problem to you. One student told me candidly, "I had to do a lot of fluffing to get to the page count." Readers don't want fluff; we want thinking. While fluff may certainly be part of what we all generate during the early stages of composing, students short on development are often better served directing their energy back toward their inquiry process rather than on filling up a blank page or screen.

> Elaboration isn't just adding an extra sentence or two of commentary; it's developing a carefully considered chain of reasoning.

QUESTIONS FOR JUSTIFYING CLAIMS

The following are additional questions that can help students justify their reasoning:

Can you explain the relevance of this information?

Why is that the case?

What are other possible interpretations?

What are other possible data sets?

Is there additional evidence that could change how you see this?

What's your conclusion?

Why do you think that?

Why is this evidence important?

What do other sources say?

The best way I've found to help students think through these questions is a writing conference. See Brian Kissel's book *When Writers Drive the Workshop* (2017) for a helpful guide to conferring.

Revising Claims

Students sometimes initially make illogical claims because writing is hard. They become focused on the form of expression instead of the thinking being expressed. This is a normal part of the process. I appreciate the way the National Writing Project's C3W Program recommends supporting "the recursive development of claims that emerge and evolve through reading and writing" (Friedrich, Bear, and Fox 2018)—an astute acknowledgment of the way our claims progress from dodgy to compelling as we work the inquiry process.

In revising claims, a good starting place is to look for inconsistencies between evidence and assertions. For instance, one of my students claimed in an argument on immigration policy that immigrants sometimes caused harm to U.S. workers by taking their jobs; however, this student then cited from a study saying immigration leads to labor specialization which increases productivity. In this case, a closer examination of the evidence led the writer to revise her claim. The student's revised claim used the old claim to set up a rebuttal: "While some people think that immigrants steal American jobs, the evidence suggests that immigration benefits American workers by increasing specialization and productivity."

In each of the examples shown in Figure 6.9, consider how the peer or teacher feedback can promote the recursive development of claims.

CLAIM	PEER OR TEACHER FEEDBACK
Gun control leads to increased crime and tyranny.	What do you need to do to establish cause and effect?
Most of Shakespeare's plays use the tactic of deception.	How many of Shakespeare's plays do you need to read to make this claim? Consider qualifying or modifying your claim if you have limited evidence.
The play gives the impression that Romeo and Juliet will live happily ever after.	What is your evidence for this claim? What does the Prologue say?
In California, it is a requirement that all students complete two years of English to graduate from high school.	How do you know? How confident are you about the validity of this claim?

FIGURE 6.9
Providing feedback on students' draft claims

Qualification: Recognizing the Limits of Our Understanding

There is great transfer value in the ability to recognize the limits of our understanding. In professional settings, a ready "I don't know" can sometimes be the most welcome answer you can give. Far better to acknowledge the unknown than to bluff your way forward on incomplete or misleading data. Colleagues who conceal what they don't know impede the work of the group. Being candid about our limitations also promotes healthy interpersonal relationships and more equitable communities.

In argument writing, a *qualifier* is an "explicit reference to the degree of force which our data confer on our claim in virtue of our warrant" (Toulmin 2003, 93). A qualifier signals how far we are willing to commit ourselves to a claim. Qualification is thus the act of saying "I'll go this far but no farther," as indicated by modifiers such as *probably*, *possibly*, and *perhaps*. Quantifiers such as *many*, *few*, and *some* can also be qualifiers.

We sometimes teach the idea of qualification in argumentation as a kind of defensive armor that protects our logic from attacks by opponents. If we qualify our claims, the thinking goes, we can lower the burden of proof. But there's another way to approach qualification that has greater value for students' future lives. Instead of thinking of qualification as a defensive strategy, we can view it as an invitation for others to share their expertise.

A mature understanding of this aspect of argumentation includes a recognition of positionality—the extent to which our own identity and experiences constrain our view of the world. In "How Does Your Positionality Impact Your Epistemology?" David Takacs identifies the ability to understand how we know what we know—including how who we are shapes what we know—as a key to lifelong learning (2003, 27). That learning both empowers and disempowers students, Takacs says, as they come to recognize the uniqueness of their expertise while also questioning the "correctness" of their position (29).

These can be heady ideas for younger students. Novices tend to interpret the recommendation to limit or qualify a claim as "be specific"—an interpretation that stops short of the heightened self-awareness and reflection we're seeking in teaching students to think critically about the social construction of knowledge. As Takacs writes, acknowledging "that one's positionality can bias one's epistemology . . . is itself a leap for many people, one that can help make us more open to the world's possibilities" (2003, 28). By recognizing the limits of my own experience, I become more willing to step aside when someone else is better positioned to speak to aspects of the issue I'm not qualified to address.

This move makes more space for other perspectives. For example, as a white woman who teaches works of literature that address racial oppression, I'm aware of how my own experience with white privilege biases my view of the world. As a result, I work on being a listener and facilitator during classroom conversations on race. This is a time for me to stand back and make room for students to take control of the class discussion. Bringing in guest speakers and other textual voices are additional ways to promote a shared understanding of a text or topic based on multiple sources of expertise.

> A deep understanding of qualification includes the ability to ask oneself, "Who am I in this situation?"

Acknowledging what I don't know can sometimes be the most important contribution I can make to the conversation.

Making Judgments About Degree of Certainty

After students have analyzed and evaluated the evidence they've collected and started writing their drafts, we can encourage them to think about the degree of confidence they have in the claims they are making. What can they say they know with a fair amount of certainty, what do they sort of know, and where are the gaps in their knowledge? This brainwork helps students recognize when they need to qualify claims or acknowledge hypothetical or speculative thinking and when they can take a stance with conviction. This also helps students see when they need to do more research.

For instance, one of my students, Becca, claimed in an early draft of her paper on U.S. immigration policy that "we don't allow anyone to enter our country now." This was a good claim to put to the confidence test. As part of her rhetorical analysis of her draft, Becca considered the following questions:

- How confident are you about this claim?
- Will your audience challenge your assertion?
- How conclusive is your evidence?
- How thorough was your inquiry process?

I like to have students complete an activity called "What I Know I Really Know, What I Sort of Know, What I Know I Need to Know" (adapted from Leila Christenbury) after composing their first draft, when they're better prepared to assess their reasoning after working to express their ideas in writing. A student example of the completed chart is shown in Figure 6.10.

> Reasoning is a recursive process. Lockstep approaches rarely yield exciting insights or writing.

I also invite students to rank their confidence in the defensibility and reasonableness of specific claims on a scale of 1 to 5. The claim analysis graphic organizer (Figure 6.11) is another way to do this.

Transitions such as *therefore* or *consequently* raise the bar for substantiating a claim. If a student asserts that something happens "as a result" or "in consequence" of something else, they need to provide convincing support. The following transitions, or signal words, call for a high degree of certainty on the part of the writer:

> The goals of a rhetorical approach are growth and agency. The goal of a prescriptive approach is compliance.

- It follows
- Thus
- As a result
- Consequently
- Therefore
- In consequence

When your students use these academic words in their writing, ask them to test their thinking with those all-important questions: Are you sure? How do you know? What's your evidence? If their evidence is not conclusive, they might need to use a different transition or qualify their assertion.

> Encourage students to think of how they can limit their claims in terms of people, places, or things (much thanks to Dutch Henry at Seattle College for this tip!).

Argument Essay #2   HCOM 211

What I Know I Really Know, What I Sort of Know, What I Know I Need to Know
3-Column Chart

Directions to Students: Use the 3-column chart below to assess the degree of confidence you have in the argument you are making. Which claims do you strongly believe to be valid (what you really know)? Which claims are a little fuzzy or doubtful (what you sort of know)? What gaps do you see in your knowledge (what you need to know)? Consider views, sources, or perspectives you haven't yet engaged for this last column.

What I Know I Really Know	What I Sort of Know	What I Know I Need to Know
I know that children who are snatched away from their families suffer from mental health problems	•These children don't recieve Medical attention	What does this say for these childrens future?
• Immigrants who are deported find it difficult to accustom to the unfamiliar environment	•These people end up homeless, jobless, and hungry. (desperate)	• How many people that are deported end up like this?
• The US aren't taking reasonable and appropriate action to this issue by putting innocent children in cages at the detention centers.	• These children are at risk of suffering from trauma and anxiety	• What is being done about the mental health of these innocent children.

FIGURE 6.10

Student sample of "What I Know I Really Know, What I Sort of Know, What I Know I Need to Know" (adapted from Leila Christenbury's *Making the Journey*, 2000)

Claim Analysis

Writer's claim:
What does the writer say?

~~Best~~ fast fashion ~~effects~~ consumer culture
and ecosystems. → contributes.

Genre:
blog → brochure

Audience:
mothers + college students

Evidence:
List the data provided that informs the claim.

— "since individually identity continually evolves, and requires a materially referential re-imagining of self to do so, we hypothesize that actual..." (Taylor, Francis online).

Justification:
Describe the writer's reasoning (e.g., assumptions, principles, elaboration, definitions, clarification).

— I was not aware of everything that contributed to consumerism and how fast fashion may contribute to consumer culture.

Backing:
Describe the source of this way of thinking (e.g., academic discipline, life experience, philosophy).

— After the 1930's, a consumer culture grew and this involved society's critics, which led to the mass production of cheap clothing and cheap labor.

Degree of Confidence:
Rate the degree of confidence the writer seems to have in the validity of the claim.

1	2	3	4	5
low				high

(4 circled)

Quickwrite: How convincing is this claim? To what extent does the writer draw on reasonable and sufficient support for the claim? To what extent is the claim warranted or justified? Is the line of reasoning appropriate to the genre and audience? Explain.

The claim is convincing but there needs to be more evidence to back up the claim. The claim is justified but there is room for improvement. The genre may not be the best outlet for mothers so the brochure would be better.

FIGURE 6.11

Claim analysis

Conclusion: Teaching for Transfer and Agency

Writing instruction gives teachers a uniquely direct and focused opportunity to develop our students' reasoning abilities. By teaching reasoning rhetorically—and in the context of students' own writing—we introduce an element of critical thinking that is sometimes missing from, well, critical thinking. Making sense involves more than just supporting claims with reasons and examples. If we're not carefully considering our purpose and audience, or deeply engaging in dialogue and inquiry, we're ignoring the social dynamics and subject matter expertise that impact how meaning is constructed and negotiated in real-world situations.

Our students have important work to do in the world. We can prepare them for the challenges ahead through writing instruction that develops the critical reasoning skills that lead to informed, effective, and ethical responses to twenty-first-century problems.

CHAPTER SEVEN

Making Choices About Genre and Structure

[A Writer] cannot begin to fill up a blank page without making assumptions about the readers' beliefs, knowledge, and familiarity with conventions.

—PETER J. RABINOWITZ

If the three most important things in real estate are "location, location, location," then the three most important things in written communication are "audience, audience, audience." I know this is supposed to be a chapter about teaching genre and structure, but bear with me for a moment. Teaching these elements of writing rhetorically involves enhancing students' ability to detect and respond to audience expectations and needs. Knowing *what* genre and structure choices to make *when* depends on an informed understanding of the choices target audiences find most appropriate and compelling.

This is why one-size-fits-all approaches to writing limit a writer's effectiveness. I get that students would like to just follow a simple formula that takes the stress and confusion out of writing. But I'm not going to give it to them because doing so would not be in their long-term best interests. Struggling with that perennial question of "How do I do this?" is part of the inquiry work writers do when assessing a new rhetorical situation. Do students feel frustrated and overwhelmed when they don't have a clear teacher-generated process or outline to follow? Yes. Is it productive for them to feel this way? Absolutely—especially if that anxiety is accompanied by peer and teacher reassurance that all writers feel this way.

We all struggle with the blank page or screen. But most writing situations in the postsecondary world—especially those in which the writer aims to take rhetorical action—don't come with a ready-made outline. We don't set students up for success by taking the guesswork out of writing; we set them up for success by preparing them to embrace the process of discovery and decision making needed to effectively respond to diverse rhetorical situations.

Success ought to mean more than just earning a proficient score on a high-stakes test (a writing situation in which formulas admittedly can sometimes serve students well). But if students *only* work on mastering an easy three-step process that helps them pass an exam, they're postponing their writerly frustration and confusion for a later day: that day when their college professor or employer asks them to produce a text they have no idea how to produce and to which the formula they've learned does not apply. It's a matter of pay now or pay later. And I'd rather have young students "pay" (i.e., struggle, stress, inquire) when they have the support and encouragement of a caring teacher to take some of the sting out of work that is inherently messy and complicated.

The Challenge

In choosing to teach rhetorical decision making, we're swimming against some powerful currents in our profession. In their landmark research on writing pedagogy in the United States, Arthur Applebee and Judith Langer paint a discouraging picture of dominant practices:

> . . . the actual writing that goes on in typical classrooms across the United States remains dominated by tasks in which the teacher does all the composing, and students are left only to fill in missing information, whether copying directly from a teacher's presentation, completing worksheets and chapter summaries, replicating highly formulaic essay structures keyed to high-stakes tests, or writing to "show they know" the particular information the teacher is seeking. (2013, 27)

For many students, writing instruction is largely a matter of following someone else's template or outline. Applebee and Langer blame this tendency to limit students' autonomy on reductive applications of the Common Core State Standards, especially as manifested in high-stakes testing (2013, 180). Such approaches foster a culture of dependence in which students look to teachers to tell them exactly what to say and do at each step of the writing process.

Our pedagogies have important implications for social justice. In *Culturally Responsive Teaching and the Brain*, Zaretta Hammond explains that "many culturally and linguistically diverse students are 'dependent learners' who don't get adequate support to facilitate their cognitive growth" (2015, 14). Characteristics of dependent learners include relying on the teacher to carry most of the cognitive load and not being able to complete a task without scaffolds (Hammond 2015). Such dependence is the result of pedagogies that fail to provide the choice and challenge needed to foster independence.

The challenge, Applebee and Langer note, is "to provide students with a rich under-standing of the rhetorical context" implicit in the kinds of writing tasks called for by the Common Core and to support students in developing "a flexible array of strategies for addressing a wide variety of audiences and specific purposes" (2013, 181). We need to remember that transfer isn't just about learning that can be applied to multiple contexts; it's about developing the deep procedural, conceptual, and conditional knowledge needed to *adapt* learning so that it can be *appropriately* applied to different contexts.

Helping Students Develop Their Own Decision-Making Process

A couple of students came to see me with a question about their senior research proj-ect. "We know this is a research project," one said, "but can we use personal stories as part of our evidence?" Since I'd already worked with these students quite a bit, I said, "Well, you know me pretty well. What do you think I'm going to say?" They both grinned, and one replied, "Figure it out yourself."

But then they grew serious again. "But really . . . how do we do that? How do we find out if we can use personal examples?" They tossed around a few ideas, including checking to see what a particular instructor wants, before finally landing on the big concepts we'd been working on all year: audience, purpose, genre, and occasion. We talked about how people who write for publication often use mentor texts, style guides, and submission checklists to answer these kinds of questions . . . and how some writing situations don't offer any guidelines aside from the dynamics of the rhetorical situation itself.

What struck me about this conversation was the difficulty of the goal we're pursuing. In teaching writing rhetorically, we're attempting no less than to help students develop their own theory of communication. A theory is an explanation for how something works. Students who understand how writing works in different contexts can use this knowledge to develop their own rhetorical decision-making process. That theoretical knowledge is the aim of college composition courses that use the Teaching for Transfer (TfT) model, like the course designed by Kathleen Blake Yancey and her colleagues at Florida State University.

Such deep learning calls for a balance between productive struggle and strategic sup-port. Making rhetorical choices is challenging work. With younger students especially, we might lighten the cognitive load—and provide a clear instructional focus—by making some choices for our students. For instance, we might choose a particular question for them to engage or we might ask them to follow a particular set of language conventions. But if we're making *all* the writing decisions for our students, we have to wonder what they're learning aside from how to follow someone else's directions.

Some of the choices writers must make about form and style involve specific features of genre and text structure. Take a look at Figure 7.1 and think about how often your students get to make their own decisions about these options. Choose the frequency rate that best describes your students' experiences.

Frequently = F   Sometimes = S   Rarely = R

GENRE CHOICES		STRUCTURE CHOICES	
Genre or form		Text structure (e.g., cause and effect, frame)	
Types of sentences		Beginnings/introductions	
Use or avoidance of figurative language		Inductive or deductive reasoning	
Formatting conventions		Transitions	
Documentation style (if required)		Twists or shifts	
Types of evidence/examples		Use or avoidance of narrative	
Medium		Endings/conclusions	
Level of diction		Repetition	

FIGURE 7.1
Genre and structure choices

Some of these options—like whether or not they can use a simile in their writing—are frequently within students' control. But others are rarely given over to students. Students need opportunities to practice rhetorical decision making. They also need the conditional knowledge that will help them make effective decisions. Making strategic choices about text structure, for instance, depends on knowing in what particular situations a structure such as "compare and contrast" is useful. The more choices students make for themselves, the more knowledge they gain of how writing works.

I like what Ericka Lindemann says about rhetoric, that "when we practice rhetoric, we make decisions about our subject, audience, point of view, purpose, and message" (2001, 40). The idea that writing is a craft has been a key principle in writing pedagogy since the early days of the process movement. Donald Graves explains that a craft "is a process of shaping material toward an end" (1983, 6)—a description that resonates with any writer who has labored to form a mess of notes into a composed text.

As we celebrate student freedom and agency, we also need to keep in mind that too many options on the table can be overwhelming for less experienced writers. Expert writers play with a wide variety of rhetorical moves. Student writers who are learning how to become experts benefit from having curated selections. We can offer students a focused tasting menu to start, knowing they'll eventually have access to the whole buffet.

> Students need conscious theoretical knowledge of how writing works (i.e., "writer's brain"), to effectively repurpose their learning in new settings.

Scaffolding Rhetorical Decision Making

Consider what kind of instructional support your students will need to make effective choices while composing different kinds of texts. How can you help students understand the array of meaning-making options they have as writers? How can you help them invent new strategies for reaching their target audience?

In scaffolding rhetorical decision making, you might decide to give your students focused support for one area of decision making. For instance, you could focus on helping students make organizational choices by zooming in on text structure, signal words, and shifts, and by practicing strategies such as descriptive outlining. Or you could focus on helping students make choices about language by analyzing word connotations and levels of diction.

Whatever scaffolds we use need to be in the service of students owning their own learning and writing processes. Graves made this point decades ago, noting that instruction needs to be centered on helping writers solve problems for themselves "otherwise, the child will see the teacher as the one in control of the writing process" (1983, 231).

The goal of this pedagogy is to help students develop their own theoretical understanding of how writing works.

FACILITATING RHETORICAL DECISION MAKING

One strategy I've used for facilitating rhetorical decision making is whole-class brainstorming that starts with the topic or question at issue. Let's say my students have been reading a series of articles on the rising costs of college and the problem of student debt, and it's now their turn to respond. What choices do they have for entering this national conversation?

FIGURE 7.2
Choosing an issue

We put the topic or question in the middle of a cluster (Figure 7.2).

We start with our purpose. "What do you want to do?" I ask. Imagine that the class decides its goal is to reduce student debt.

Then I ask students, "OK, who do you want to reach? Whose views or actions do you want to change? Who has a stake in this issue?"

We draw lines branching off from the main topic for *audience* and start brainstorming our options: students, parents, teachers, state legislators, members of congress, voters, universities, funders, and so on (Figure 7.3).

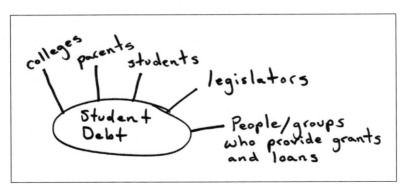

FIGURE 7.3
Identifying potential audiences and stakeholders

"All right," I say now, "who do we want to target as our primary audience? Who has the power to make a difference? What would they need to believe or feel to make this change? Let's pick a focus for our message—but keep in mind that other audiences may also hear what we have to say." Now we're setting priorities based on our purpose. This calls for some additional discussion and analysis. We also have to carefully consider where will this audience need the most convincing: That the problem exists? That they are the ones who can solve the problem? That the benefits outweigh the costs? That the solution will work?

Let's say we ultimately decide we want to pitch a policy argument toward state legislators. After all, they're the ones with the power to fund public institutions of higher education. So now we have to decide how to reach these good people. "What are our options for communicating with state legislators?" I ask. The wheels start turning again: tweets, open letters, op-ed pieces, advertisements, phone calls, emails, petitions, memes, position statements.

I draw more lines out from the cluster for *genre* (Figure 7.4).

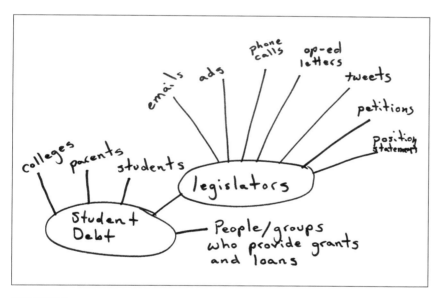

FIGURE 7.4
Exploring genre choices

Now students can choose their genre based on their audience and topic. Or they can decide to develop a full communication plan that takes advantage of multiple genres to achieve a desired purpose. Or they might create a multigenre text using the features of several genres. By exploring these kinds of choices with our students, we model situated, rhetorical decision making (Figure 7.5). This process makes clear to students that one decision is related to another . . . and that all these decisions are in the hands of the rhetor.

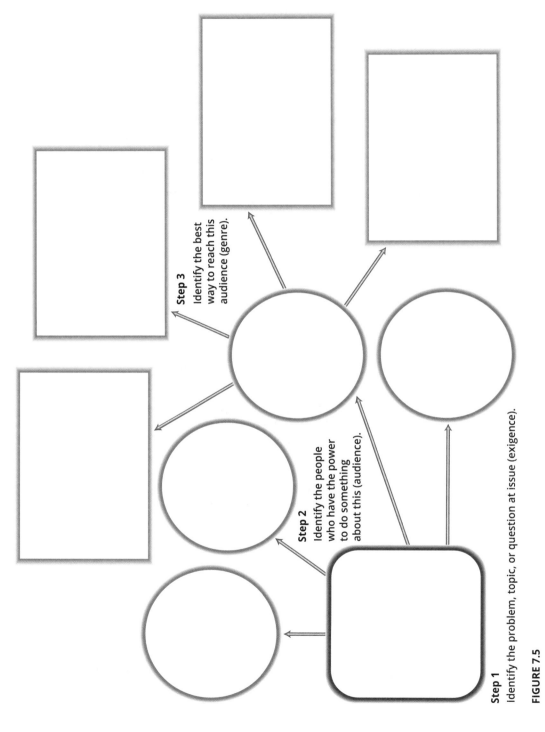

Step 3
Identify the best way to reach this audience (genre).

Step 2
Identify the people who have the power to do something about this (audience).

Step 1
Identify the problem, topic, or question at issue (exigence).

FIGURE 7.5

This graphic organizer offers a process for rhetorical decision making.

Figure 7.6 shows an example of how one of my classes practiced rhetorical decision making in response to the problem of food waste.

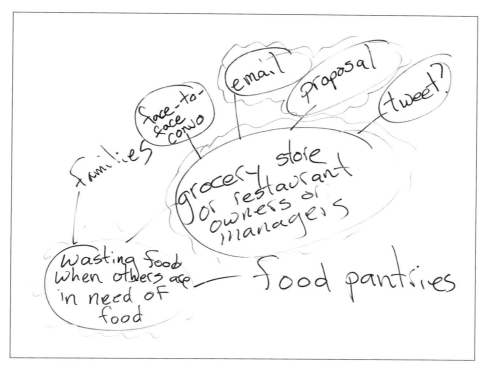

FIGURE 7.6

Class brainstorm on options for responding to the problem of food waste

Making Choices as You Write: It All Starts with Audience

Thinking about the audience is also helpful for those moment-by-moment decisions writers make as they compose texts. Any writerly consideration of genre and structure needs to start with what readers do with texts: how they notice different features, look for the expected, deal with the unexpected, and work to create their own coherent meaning. The National Council of Teachers of English makes this clear in its 2016 Position Statement on Professional Knowledge for the Teaching of Writing:

> [Readers] expect the style in a piece of writing to be appropriate to its genre and social situation. With that in mind, writers try to use these surface elements strategically, in order to present the identity, create the relationships, and express the ideas that suit their purpose.

When we facilitate rhetorical decision making, we empower students to make their own choices and contributions.

Think of that student in your classroom who keeps you honest, the one who will call you out if you mix up a due date or forget to post a resource you said you'd share. You know how that teacher interior monologue goes: "I better get this right, or [insert student name] will tell me I've messed up again." This same sense of accountability should also apply when writers are working to reach specific audiences.

Anticipating Your Audience's Reading Experience

When we talk about audience expectations, we're really making predictions about audience reactions. What's likely to get bounced back by an editor or teacher? What's likely to be praised? What might spark a wave of angry or enthusiastic reader emails or Web comments? What might prompt a reviewer to say in response to a magazine or journal submission, "revise and resubmit" or "accept without change"? Which sentences are most likely to be quoted by other writers, bolded by editors, or tweeted by readers? These are the considerations working writers have in their heads when they think about audience expectations.

Linda Flower describes reader-based prose—that is, writing that privileges the reader's needs over the writer's—as "a deliberate attempt to communicate something to a reader" (1979, 20). It does this, Flower says, by creating "a shared language and shared context between writer and reader" (20). What it doesn't do is a TMI rehearsal of the writing process, as in "When I first got this assignment, I wasn't really sure what to write" or "I was confused at first, but then I reread the directions." Unless, of course, that kind of backstory is germane to the writer's chosen purpose and genre, such as in the case of an I-Search project. As Flower notes, structure and style must be adapted to a reader (1979).

We know what it's like to read writing that doesn't communicate with others in mind—those texts that march ahead indifferent to reader response and experience, like a telemarketer who persists in reading from a script no matter how many times you say, "I'm not interested." That we-just-need-to-cover-this attitude rarely results in a meaningful reading experience.

Designing the User's Experience

In design theory, we see this same kind of rhetorical orientation toward audience in the idea of the user's experience. Today's designers are deeply interested in how people interact with the things they make. In *The Six Academic Writing Assignments: Designing the User's Journey*, Jim Burke (I'm assuming my audience already knows Jim's important work) explains how design thinking can help teachers create learning experiences that are "more effective, more engaging, more instructive" (2018, 3). One reason for this is because of the important role empathy plays in the design process. Successful designs start with a careful consideration of the user's experience. Burke describes this critical first stage:

> Empathize: Work to fully understand the experience of the user for whom you are designing. Do this through observation, interaction, and immersing yourself in their experiences. (2018, 5)

This idea has been transformative for design work. The famous story of the redesign of the map of the London Underground in 1938 by electrical draughtsman Harry Beck from a model based on traditional cartographic principles to one based on readability and function is a classic example. The old map of London's subway system (Figure 7.7a) was cluttered with extraneous information. Excessive geographic detail made the map difficult to understand. Beck realized that people traveling underground don't need to know how far apart one destination is from the next or what landmarks they might pass on the way. They just need to know where to change trains and when to get off at the right stop. So, he redesigned the map to focus on what matters to users: the connections and sequences (Figure 7.7b).

> Reader-based writing is user friendly; it privileges the reader's experience of the text above the writer's need to complete the task.

Beck's user-friendly subway schematic was a game changer; it freed future cartographers and designers from adhering to conventions or principles that interfere with the intended use of their products.

Writing as Social Practice: Considering Conventions and Constraints

The idea of the user's experience heightens writers' sensitivity to the constraints and conventions associated with particular rhetorical situations. Writing on the importance of reader expectations, Rabinowitz says, "The writer who wishes to be understood—even to be understood by a small group of readers—has to work within such conventional restraints" (1987, 24–25). There are limits on a writer's options. Once some choices have been made, new choices become available while others are no longer options, like a choose-your-own-adventure plot. Choices constrain and engender other choices.

Why are these ideas important for young writers to understand? Let me give you an example. If students see that by choosing to write a blog, they have raised their readers' expectations about the tone and style of language they'll use, they are more likely to write with their audience's needs in mind. A choice activates a set of conventions.

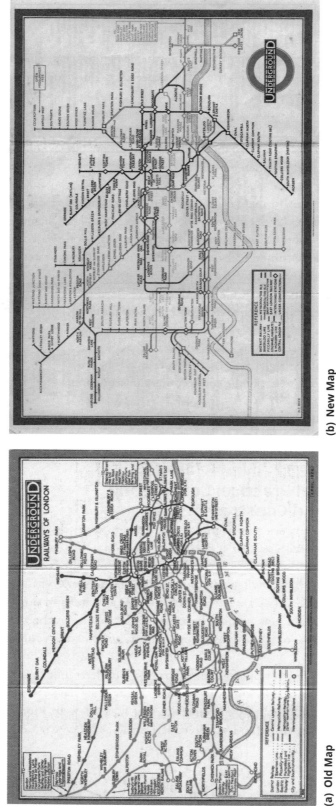

(a) Old Map

(b) New Map

FIGURE 7.7

The old map was confusing and cluttered. The new map was clear and aesthetically pleasing.

Look at Figure 7.8, and see if you can identify some additional aspects of writing that students might consider as they practice rhetorical decision making.

Making Choices as You Write

Content	Genre/Form	Language
Organization	Evidence	?
?	?	?

FIGURE 7.8
Expert writers make many decisions about form and style as they compose texts.

Now think about one of these choices in the context of a particular rhetorical situation, for example, the language used for a research paper in an undergraduate social science class. What language conventions and constraints will a writer in this situation need to deal with? Academic English, technical vocabulary, passive voice, and complex sentences probably come to mind.

Some writing tasks—especially standardized tests—choose the evidence (typically textual evidence) that students must use in their arguments. OK, then this is a situation in which some choices have already been made for students. That's a constraint of this rhetorical situation. What choices, what resources of thought and language, are still available to students under these conditions? There are several:

- Organizational patterns and structures
- Language conventions and forms of expression
- Claims and conclusions

Even a standardized test can be an occasion for students to choose the best words in the best order. And to see themselves as creative and independent writers. When we help students to approach all writing as decision making, we set them up for success in the many situations when all the decisions will be in their own hands.

In the sections that follow, I share ways to help students develop the principles and practices that will enable them to make effective choices about genre and structure.

Fostering a Deeper Understanding of Genre

I sometimes think of *genre* as the George Harrison of rhetorical situations: the quiet one who gets overshadowed by its flashier group members. We pay a lot of attention to audience, purpose, and context, but genre is every bit as important as these other elements and, in fact, is the component of rhetorical situations that offers the most support to novices. Through the study of mentor texts—and in particular, the genre features and functions of those texts—we learn how to communicate effectively in new discourse communities.

Genres are forms of rhetorical action. A genre can be thought of as typified response to a "recurrent rhetorical situation" (Miller 1984, 155). Composition scholar Charles Bazerman says that "genres are ways of doing things" (2013, 24). A lab report, for instance, is a way of developing a hypothesis, reviewing previous research, conducting scientific experiments, evaluating results, and communicating findings. This is what a lab report does.

Understanding genre as a way of doing things gives students all kinds of power. Instead of genre being a form to fill, genre becomes a strategy to deploy. In making choices about genre, student writers can ask themselves, "What do I want to do?" and "What's the best way to do that?"

Genres both contain and create acts of communication, dual capacities suggested by the etymology of this term. We use genres to classify forms of expression (think "genus" here) and to generate or "engender" them. For instance, publishers often have clear guidelines for what can be published under the label of a particular genre, like young adult romance, which differs significantly from adult romance. At the same time, a skilled writer can extend and exploit a genre's boundaries—or even originate a new genre. When we teach genre awareness as a habit of mind, we prepare students to be alert to changes in generic forms and audience expectations.

> Genres document the ways people have chosen to communicate with each other in particular settings for particular purposes.

Genre Analysis: Mentor Texts and Audience Expectations

Rather than teach students the conventions of a particular genre, our job, to use Anne Beaufort's words, is to teach students *to learn how to learn* the conventions of writing in new situations they will encounter" (2007, 15) (emphasis added). That's where the transfer value is. This is why the study of mentor texts is so important, especially when those texts are situated in specific rhetorical contexts.

GENRE ANALYSIS GRAPHIC ORGANIZER

A mentor text analysis gives students a useful framework for learning how to learn about new genres. I use the graphic organizer shown in Figure 7.9 to facilitate this work. See Appendix R for a blank version of the genre analysis graphic organizer.

Genre Analysis: Textbook

Mentor Texts:
List the titles of several texts that exemplify the key characteristics of this genre.
Prentice Hall Literature, McDougal Littell Science, and Houghton Mifflin Social Studies

Purpose:
To guide students through the key concepts and skills of an academic subject; to teach "facts"; to support classroom instruction

Organization:
How are texts in this genre generally structured (e.g., chronological order, compare and contrast, etc.)? Are there paragraphs, stanzas, dialogue, chapters, lists, headings, etc.? Do texts usually have a certain kind of beginning or end?

Table of contents, chapters, clear paragraphs, easy-to-find main ideas, end-of-chapter summaries and activities, numbering, labels, section headings and subheadings, overviews, glossary, and index

Language Choices:
Describe the kinds of words and sentences commonly used in this genre. Is the language typically formal or casual, simple or complex?

Standard academic English; diction is formal and professional with many words of Greek and Latin origin; sentences use transitions and signal words to help the reader understand the information; many abstract concept words; sentences often use appositives to define new terms; language that "tells" instead of "shows."

Writer's Ethos:
How do writers generally present themselves in this genre? What kind of "voice" do they typically use? Do you get to know the writer personally?

Textbook authors are experts in the subject who don't expect their readers to challenge their knowledge. The reader is seen as a "beginner" who needs help with introductory information. We usually don't get a sense of textbook authors' individual personalities because the books are written in a formal, objective style.

Special Features:
List any other conventions or stylistic choices that characterize this genre, including features like documentation style (e.g., MLA), figurative language, pictures, and rhetorical moves.

Captions under pictures, description, classification, charts, tables, graphs, window quotations, word glosses/definitions, illustrations, review questions, graphics, references and/or recommended readings

Context and Audience: In what situations is this type of writing typically used? Who typically reads this genre? Textbooks are used in classroom settings, especially in introductory courses where there is a lot of new information to learn. Older K12 and college students are the typical readers of textbooks. More advanced courses tend not to use textbooks.

FIGURE 7.9
The genre analysis graphic organizer can help students learn from the choices of other writers.

GENRE ANALYSIS: UNDERSTANDING AUDIENCE EXPECTATIONS

Students can also conduct a genre analysis by considering the user's experience. The following questions about audience expectations and interactions with a genre come from the California State University's Expository Reading and Writing Assignment Template:

- What kind of language does this audience expect?

- What kinds of information do they need and where do they expect to find it?

- How much detail do they expect?

- How do they expect to be addressed?

- How do they expect the writer to present him or herself?

- How will they use the document? (ERWC 3.0 Assignment Template)

Conducting these kinds of analyses develops students' understanding of how to make decisions about genre when they write.

DIY SUBMISSION CHECKLIST

Directions to Students: After studying a collection of mentor texts in the genre you'll be writing in, create your own submission checklist for your composition. This kind of DIY style guide is a good way to make sure you are responding to the demands of a rhetorical situation. Use the sample submission checklist provided by your teacher as a model (see the submission checklist from the *Journal of Adolescent and Adult Literacy* in Appendix V).

> Genre analysis helps students to read and write across contexts.

From Mimicry to Mastery

As students take more control over their own writing process, we can expect to see more mistakes. This can be especially true as students shift their reliance from teacher directives to mentor texts. Often, those first attempts to implement moves learned from a model get close but don't quite work. That's because novices tend to mimic the form of something without having a deep understanding of its purpose.

Let me give you an example. When my daughter first began to dance on pointe, I helped her sew the ribbons on her toe shoes by pinning the ribbons in the correct place for her. After doing this a few times, I told her she was on her own. "Just use one of the other pairs of toe shoes as your model," I said. So she took the first pair we'd sewn together, looked at it closely, pinned the ribbons where she thought they belonged, and sewed them on. That original pair of toe shoes was her mentor text. Figure 7.10 shows what she saw, and what she did (she's kindly given me permission to share these images).

> Even with the support of a mentor text, novices will still probably make a few wrong turns on the path to independence.

If you've danced on pointe yourself, you're probably noticing that the ribbons are too far forward in Figure 7.10b. The ribbons look OK to the casual eye, but they won't provide the ankle

FIGURE 7.10
The mentor text (a) and the imitation (b)

support a ballet dancer needs. My daughter was imitating the form of the mentor text without fully understanding its function.

It's easy to assume that students know what we know when they do what we do—because we've told them exactly what to do. We don't know what they know until we turn them loose to rely on their own learning.

Learning from models takes time and practice.

> We need to help students grapple with novel situations in ways that increase their independence and flexibility.

Revisiting Mentor Texts

I've seen this same kind of rookie mistake in my writing classes, which is why I now have students revisit their mentor texts after producing a text of their own in that genre. One of my culminating assignments invites students to take rhetorical action through one of two ways: a research project or an advocacy campaign. For the advocacy campaign, students can choose to write in any genre appropriate to their message, audience, and purpose. We conduct genre analyses of a variety of different texts as part of our prewriting, including newsletters, tweets, blogs, public service announcements, and an academic research paper. We also conduct audience analyses for particular genres.

One of my students chose the research paper option but had written a text that looked and functioned more like a newsletter. When we conferred, I pointed out some of the features I'd noticed of the text she had produced, such as her use of "you" to speak directly to her audience, her friendly tone, use of exclamation points and bullets, and inclusion of only one source. We then looked back at the mentor texts we'd studied and compared the student's writing to the published models.

"What do you notice?" I asked.

"That my paper looks a lot more like a newsletter than a research project," she said. We talked about how her rhetorical choices seemed to belong to a genre other than the one she was writing in. Then we looked back at her audience analysis to see what her supposed target audience seemed to care about and expect. Again, she seemed to have a different audience in mind from the readership for academic research. It was clear from our discussion that what she really wanted to do was write an accessible piece that could impact people's daily lives.

Finally, her eyes lit up, and she asked, "Can I write a newsletter instead?"

"Yes!" I told her. "This is your chance to choose the form of rhetorical action best suited to the purpose you want to accomplish."

Making Choices About Genre

Expert writers are skilled in making choices about genre. Many rhetorical situations afford writers the opportunity to choose the genre or genres that best suit their purposes. Other situations might constrain a writer to a particular genre (e.g., a cover letter for a job application) but still allow writers the opportunity to choose what features of that genre they wish to use or emphasize.

Sometimes the discourse community we're engaging has already made most of the decisions for us, and, unless we know how to break new rhetorical ground in that field, we're probably going to have to follow the established genre conventions. Sometimes we have a great deal of leeway; indeed, creativity and novelty may even be valued features of a genre.

Supporting students in making choices about genre fosters their growth and independence as writers. In that same research or advocacy project I mentioned earlier, I also have students reflect on their rationale for the genre choices they make. This is one of the ways I try to help surface their procedural and conceptual knowledge. Remember that Beaufort identifies genre knowledge as one of the knowledge domains expert writers draw on when they practice rhetorical problem solving (see Chapter 3). This expertise includes the "ability to understand that genres are context specific, complex, and recurring tools used to accomplish work central to a discourse community" (Slomp et al. 2018, 85).

Ulises, one of my first-year college students, considered a range of genre choices for his project on kelp forests before choosing his final product: a narrated photo essay that could be shared via social media. In the quick-writes that follow, Ulises explores options for communicating his findings.

Genre Quick-Write 1: Trifold Brochure

> "I believe that many people don't know much information about the kelp forest. In this approach I will be reaching adults living in the Monterey area. In the first page I'll have a picture of an otter to grab the audience's attention. Some of the subtitles may be, what's the kelp forest, who depends on the kelp forest, and why should we protect it. The language would be basic, and I'll add many pictures to keep the reader intrigued. The goal is to think about our environment. My voice would be of an advocate, trying to educate the importance of the topic."

Genre Quick-Write 2: Letter/Email to an Authority

> "During these times it seems like our government won't pay attention to climate change. I want to send a letter to Sacramento asking for our environment to be taken in consideration in California. I'll explain the importance of the kelp forest to the Monterey area. My hope is for them to fight for our environment. I yet to find a mentor text that satisfy the point I am trying to achieve. I'd organize the letter or email as formal as I can, making sure that there is absolutely no errors whatsoever. My language choice would be heavy, highly complex in order to persuade the reader the importance of the topic."

Ulises's second quick-write makes an important point that sometimes gets overlooked: Mentor texts for some rhetorical situations can be hard to find. If the text to be produced isn't intended for a public audience, other writers might not have easy access to it. In such cases, novices might need to find help from other sources.

Connecting Genre and Purpose

Finding the right mix of purpose, genre, and medium transforms a good idea into effective rhetorical action. National Book Award-winner Ta-Nehisi Coates writes of the publication of his essay "The Case for Reparations" in a 2014 issue of *The Atlantic* that it was "hearten[ing] to see the reparations argument make its way to people who'd never seriously considered it before" (*We Were Eight Years in Power* 2017, 161). Coates describes the attention the essay attracted as a result of its genre and medium—in this case, a highly regarded magazine:

> It was a lesson in what serious writing married to the right platform could actually achieve. The fact was that *The Atlantic* was regarded in a way other publications that had made the reparations argument before were not. *The Atlantic* was seen as serious and respectable. If it was putting an argument for reparations on the cover, reparations had to be considered. (161)

The paths writers choose to reach their audience (of those available to them) have a profound impact on the extent to which they successfully convey their message and achieve their purpose.

Surfacing these options and reflecting on their impact helps students develop conscious procedural knowledge. Jasmine, another one of my students, wrote about her process for choosing genres for her project on the cost of a college education. Her target audience was her peers. Notice how a sense of purpose guides her thinking. Notice, too, how Jasmine compares what each genre does (see the text in bold).

Jasmine's quick-write:

> [. . .] a powerpoint will be **less appealing** to a student then a flyer or
> a brochure. A brochure will **include more information** and pictures
> that students will always have at hand and can come back too at any
> time. As for a powerpoint, that is information given in the moment and
> information that one has to retain. So the idea of having to rhetorically
> persuade an audience through each genre was difficult to approach and
> to express in my genres. Also another challenge I faced was providing
> the information onto each genre. Either the information amount was
> **small or too impacted**. So in a brochure there is **more impacted**
> **information** then a flyer that has straight to the point information. [. . .]
> Although on a flyer it's **harder to get straight to the point** then as for
> a brochure. A brochure that **has more room and sections** to organize
> information then a flyer does.

By thinking through the functions of the different genres she was considering—a
PowerPoint, brochure, or flyer—Jasmine was practicing rhetorical decision making.
She ultimately chose a genre that would allow her to make a strong emotional impact
on her audience: a poem. Here's her argument in its final form:

Money Should Not Be the Problem

Students become brainwashed with the idea of getting an education.
Don't get me wrong an education is worth it but we come to a point of hesitation.
We begin to realize it's harder than just going to class and maintaining a four
point zero GPA.
Then we look again and realize that our financial aid was low.
Now what? We were motivated to continue our education and go to college.
Told that money was everywhere, but then again we had to have the knowledge.
Competing against the world for the perfect school; be able to attend
without worries.
Just to come to school and see friends are slowly forced to leave.
After a lifetime of hard work to create one's own profile, we get into a school.
To find out that some of us will fall into a pool of statistics.
Approximately only forty two percent of us are considered to graduate.
May ask why this is so low? We ask why the price is so high.
We are expected to perform well yet at the same time be able to pay for education.

Get a job but become a full time student or the financial aid help will be cut.
Making it harder for us to stay in class; leading to lack of study to get a good grade out of luck.
All because we have to find a way to stay in your education system.
Stress becomes a concern we don't realize is there.
The days get tougher, getting to a point where we think of plan A, B, and C.
Dropping out seems like the easiest fairest decision.
Realizing that the count of people we know is drastically declining.
We are so sickly brainwashed with the idea of an education's worth.
All we worked so hard for, just to come to sense that we have to drop out.
We are forced to go back home and settle for something less because we can't pay.
So you tell me; put yourself in these our worn out shoes, how should money not be our problem?

When Jasmine read her powerful poem aloud to our class, it was clear she'd struck a chord with her peers.

PROMPTS FOR QUICK-WRITES: MAKING CHOICES ABOUT GENRE

We can help students make thoughtful choices about genre by encouraging them to reflect on their decision-making process. Invite your students to respond to the prompts that follow.

> Making informed choices about genre requires paying attention to the conventions readers rely on as they construct meaning from a text.

1. What did you notice about the genre features and functions of your mentor texts? How might these observations influence your own choices about genre as you write?

2. How do you know how to communicate in different situations? What concepts or principles influence your communication choices? Describe your process for analyzing rhetorical situations and making rhetorical decisions.

> "How do you know?" and "What did you do?" are two of the best questions we can ask students.

Fostering a Deeper Understanding of Structure

Text structure impacts audience focus and reading experience. Through choices about structure, writers create a "hierarchy of attention and importance" (Rabinowitz 1987, 20). When deployed effectively, organizational choices help a reader follow the writer's thinking.

Organization is different from genre. A graduation speech and a researched argument essay for a humanities class may both use similar organizational strategies—narrative, cause and effect, a surprise shift, a frame structure for the intro and conclusion—but they are significantly different genres. We teach students to think strategically about genre as they're writing, so that they can apply their knowledge of mentor texts. They learn from writers who have made similar things (e.g., a graduation speech or researched argument essay), and they make choices about how they're going to organize these things by considering a variety of cross-genre strategies (e.g., text structures, transitions, logical progression of ideas, highlights).

A deeper understanding of text structure considers both the form and its function. We can study structure, Rabinowitz says, "not only in terms of concrete textual features but also in terms of the shared interpretive strategies by which readers make sense of them" (1987, 1). In other words, we can examine how structural features work—what they do to the reader's experience and what readers do with them.

A descriptive outline is a good strategy for analyzing the effects and functions of text structures.

DESCRIPTIVE OUTLINING

Descriptive outlining, or what some teachers may call "chunking" or "charting the text," creates a structural map of what each section of a text both *says* and *does* (see Figure 7.11). In *Reading Rhetorically*, John C. Bean, Virginia A. Chappell, and Alice M. Gillam (2014) explain that a descriptive outline attends "to both the content and function of paragraphs," thus emphasizing the "dual focus of rhetorical reading" (40–41). When we read rhetorically, we do more than just try to comprehend the writer's message; we're also analyzing the many moving parts of acts of communication that determine whether or not a message effectively reaches its audience and achieves its goal.

Directions to Students: After reading the text, draw a line after the introduction. Then draw a line above where you think the conclusion begins. Divide the remaining text into "chunks" or sections that seem to do specific work (e.g., offer a close-up view of the problem, establish the context for the issue).

SAYS	DOES
Message	Move
Content	Effect
Paraphrase	Function
Claim	Purpose

FIGURE 7.11
Charting the text

It's OK if students don't agree on the functional divisions. It's the mental operations performed in making these determinations that we're after. Ask students: Why is that chunk the way it is? What impact did the text structure have on your experience as a reader? As students share their response, ask if anyone else had this same experience as a reader.

Some essay planning tools make the structural choices for students. A good test of whether or not an essay organizer promotes rhetorical decision making is to create a descriptive outline of the organizer. Take the popular Intro-Reason-Reason-Counterargument-Conclusion essay organizer (see Figure 7.12).

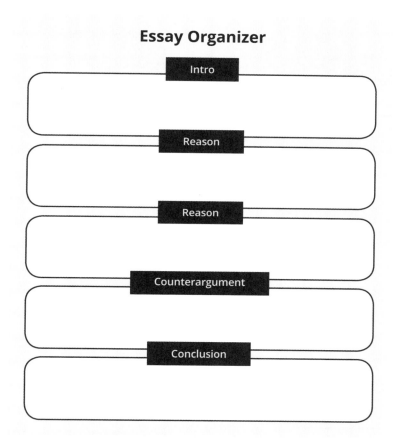

FIGURE 7.12

Some essay organizers make all the structural choices for students.

If students struggle to describe what each of their body paragraphs does—that is, how each paragraph impacts their audience and purpose—they're probably not thinking rhetorically. Remember, descriptive outlining looks at what writers are trying to do in each functional chunk in a composition. A student who can only describe the work of the paragraph on "Reason 2" as "explaining my second reason" isn't practicing a decision-making process that will help them successfully communicate in diverse contexts.

A descriptive outline of a mentor text can prepare students for using this strategy with their own writing (see the sample in Figure 7.13, on Andrew Lam's op-ed piece "Waste More, Want More"). Chapter 8 offers ways to use descriptive outlining as part of the peer review and revision process.

Descriptive Outlining of
"Waste More, Want More"

Adapted from *Reading Rhetorically* by John C. Bean, Virgina A. Chappel, and Alice M. Gillam

Paragraph[s]: 1–3

Says: We used to scavenge expired food from the trash bin at the supermarket where my brother worked when we first came to America.

Does: Shows the writer's personal experience with the vast amounts of edible food Americans waste; questions definition of "garbage"

Paragraph[s]: 4–6

Says: Americans persist in wasting more food than people in other countries despite the financial costs.

Does: Moves from personal example/individual case to broad cultural and historical trends; shows persistence of problem; appeals to American financial self-interest

Paragraph[s]: 7–10

Says: Wasteful habits have serious side effects, including large amounts of non-biodegradable garbage and diminishing natural resources.

Does: Links food waste to trash production (7–8); establishes exceptionality of Americans' consumption of resources and production of waste; lays grounds for making Americans responsible for change

Paragraph[s]: 11–12

Says: People used to value frugality, but now we favor consumption even though we're facing multiple environmental disasters as a result.

Does: Notes shifts in cultural values; shows disconnect between current values and current environmental problems; suggests need for values to be aligned to our current realities

Paragraph[s]: 13–16

Says: Americans are increasingly aware that our consumer-based economy is causing problems, but we find it hard to change.

Does: Blames Americans and their consumer economy for wasteful and unhealthy habits; accuses Americans of complacency

Paragraph[s]: 17

Says: The largest human-made structure on the planet today is the Eastern Great Garbage Patch.

Does: Presents a frightening image of the devastation caused by waste

Paragraph[s]: 18

Says: I was happy with the scavenged garbage I brought home in the 1970s, especially in comparison to the struggle for survival in Vietnam.

Does: Returns to the opening anecdote to draw a cultural contrast between American excess and war-time scarcity; prepares reader for final apocalyptic vision

Paragraph[s]: 19–21

Says: My family and I fully participate in American consumerism and have not resisted the lifestyle that's desired by people around the world.

Does: Concedes the attraction of American consumerism while noting its dangerous influence; suggests shared, global responsibility; implicates himself in the problem

Says: I saw two women scavenging garbage in Chinatown who reminded me of my past and humanity's potentially catastrophic future.

Does: Completes the frame structure by closing with a frightening warning

Main Argument: A consumer-based economy fueled by the American Dream has contributed to Americans being the most wasteful people on the planet. Because of its disproportional resource consumption and global influence, America plays a central role in environmental disasters and their potential remedy, but it doesn't bear sole responsibility.

FIGURE 7.13

Descriptive outline of a mentor text

The questions that follow offer students additional ways to think about text structure.

CONSIDERING THE STRUCTURE OF MENTOR TEXTS

Directions to Students: After reading and annotating a mentor text, take another look at how the text is organized. With a partner or small group, answer the following questions:

- What do you notice about the length of the text? Why does this matter?

- Does the writer use headings, titles, charts, images, or graphs? Why is this significant?

- Does the form of the text ever change? Why is this significant?

- Do you notice any unusual features? If so, what's their impact?

- Can you think of any other types of writing that have similar features to this text?

- Which moments in the text make the biggest impact? What do those moments tell us about what the writer is attempting to accomplish?

- How is the content organized? What comes first, next, last? What is the effect of this order on the reader?

- How does the organization help the reader follow the writer's thinking?

By now, you've probably noticed another benefit of a rhetorical approach: making strategic choices about structure as writers also makes students better readers. A deep sense of how structure directs a reader's attention helps students use these same structural clues to understand the main ideas in the texts they read.

Making Choices About Structure

I want to say again that I understand that there are short-term benefits to making structural choices for students. We give a student who previously struggled to generate *any* academic writing a step-by-step essay organizer, and the student suddenly completes full essays. This can feel deeply satisfying to both student and teacher. A passing mark in the grade book sure looks a whole lot better than a zero.

I also want to say that, when we're ready as teachers, we need to start thinking about moving the measure for success from just completing an assignment or even passing a class to long-term thriving. And that requires some different instructional decisions.

If we ask students, "Why are you using a five-paragraph structure for this essay?" and they can only answer, "Because you told me to," we aren't helping them develop a rationale for the choices they make as writers. They need their own operating system for communication. Throughout this book, I've invited you to consider how framing instruction for transfer supports students' growth and independence. See what you think of the two approaches to teaching text structure in Figure 7.14.

BOUNDED FRAMING	EXPANSIVE FRAMING
You need to know the structures of arguments for the 30-minute SAT essay.	Expert writers know how to choose effective text structures for a variety of rhetorical situations.
Essays that are not organized into paragraphs will receive a zero.	Choosing organizational structures that are appropriate to genre, content, purpose, and audience expectation is key to effective communication.
Each paragraph must include a claim, evidence, and elaboration for this assignment.	Consider your reader's needs and your rhetorical situation as you determine the length, content, and purpose of each paragraph.

FIGURE 7.14
Teaching text structure for transfer

Remember that bounded framing binds learning to a particular task, class, or grade, while expansive framing helps students to see the larger value and applications of what they're learning. In my efforts to provide expansive instructional framing for my own students, I've had to learn to pay more attention to the principles underlying my activities and assignments. I've also had to learn to be less directive in my feedback.

> In an inquiry-based approach, writing begins with the thinking rather than the form.

For instance, when I used to receive an academic essay that didn't have any paragraph organization or indentation, my approach to teaching text structure was to write, "Please organize your ideas into paragraphs" on the student's paper. These days, however, I try to pose questions to the writer instead:

- How does your organizational structure help you communicate your ideas and achieve your purpose?

- How are you guiding your reader through the story of your thinking?

- Think of the choices you are making about text structure. To what extent does a single paragraph help you convey your meaning and achieve your goals?

As writing professor E. Shelly Reid notes, paragraph length must "be managed rhetorically" (2011, 14) as part of the negotiation between writer's needs and reader's needs. This isn't something we can work out by following a decontextualized set of rules.

We may occasionally still decide to teach a paragraph structure such as the popular CEE method (claim, evidence, elaboration) because we find it helpful in meeting short-term goals, such as demonstrating proficiency on a test. What I'm asking is this: If we make this instructional choice, can we also teach underlying principles students can take with them that will help them communicate in new situations? And if we choose a paragraph structure for our students, can we open up space for students to make their own choices about other elements of composing?

We can acknowledge the realities of today while preparing students to face the contingencies of tomorrow.

Strategies for Organizing Texts

ANNOTATED IDEA CHUNKS

Many writers experience a stage of composing that's part outlining and part drafting. We write chunks of ideas—a few sentences here, a paragraph or two there—as we sketch out the general form of the text we're trying to create. Rick Hansen, Writing Program Director at Fresno State University, explains to students that "idea chunks are short pieces of writing . . . that attempt to capture an idea you have, find some support for that idea, and explain the importance of the idea" ("What's Next?", California State University 2013).

These snippets of writing can live in multiple places: separate word documents, writers' notebooks, quick-writes, emails, digital notes, etc. At this stage, it can be helpful to note what these different chunks or fragments are saying and doing, so that we can start to piece them together into a cohesive order.

I encourage students to work with hard copies of their idea chunks when possible, so that they can move the different sections around after they've annotated them.

> *Directions to Students:* "Idea chunks" are short pieces of writing that help you explore your thinking.
>
> STEP ONE: Start by gathering all the different pieces of writing you've generated for this task so far. Include any notes, journal entries, or quick-writes you think are relevant. If all your notes and idea chunks are in one electronic file, print this document so you can annotate it easily.
>
> STEP TWO: Annotate your idea chunks—those pieces of writing that capture one of the key points or ideas you are exploring. Label what the chunk is saying in the right margin and describe what that chunk is doing in the left margin. For example, does that chunk offer some insight into the historical or cultural context? Does it provide an alternative view? Does it establish the relevance or importance of the topic? Does it offer a close-up look at an example?
>
> STEP THREE: Arrange your idea chunks into an order that makes sense to you. Consider what each chunk is doing as you make decisions about organization.

I like the way working with idea chunks lets students experiment with a nonlinear approach to composition. While conventional outlines can be helpful, they can also be limiting. Sometimes the best ideas emerge through a roundabout process.

If we want to build our students' confidence as communicators and problem solvers, we need to support them in engaging communication problems, like how to organize an essay. Confidence comes from solving the problem of structure, not avoiding it altogether.

CREATING A VISUAL PRESENTATION OF A WRITTEN TEXT

To deepen their understanding of how their organizational choices move their audience through their argument, students can turn a written composition into a visual presentation. Public relations consultants often advise their clients to use pictures instead of words in their presentations. In *Why Bad Presentations Happen to Good Causes*, communications expert Andy Goodman notes that his own image-heavy PowerPoint presentations are intended to support his talk "not duplicate it" (2006, 15).

In addition to being a great way to engage and retain an audience's attention during a live presentation, this strategy can also offer writers surprising insights into the emotional and intellectual experience they've designed for their readers. Transforming text into images graphically portrays the journey the audience takes. And it gives the writer a ready-to-go slideshow when they have the chance to share their work publicly.

> *Directions to Students:* Create a slideshow of your composition using only visual images. Use a program such as PowerPoint, Keynote, or Google Slides for this task.

REFLECTING ON STRUCTURE CHOICES

> *Directions to Students:* Look at the different sections in your draft and notice what they're doing. Then respond to the following questions in a quick-write or pairs conversation:

- Are the choices you've made about structure helping your audience to understand your message? Why or why not?
- Does your structure address your audience's expectations for this form of writing?
- If your choices play with audience expectations for this genre, have you used other organizational and rhetorical strategies to keep your reader with you?

PROMPTS FOR QUICK-WRITES: MAKING CHOICES ABOUT STRUCTURE

The following questions invite students to reflect on the effects and purposes of the choices they've made about text structure:

- Why did you begin your essay this way?
- Why does this paragraph follow that paragraph?
- Why did you use this particular example here?
- Why did you conclude your essay this way? What do you hope to accomplish?

- Why did you choose this order for your ideas?

- How do the sections relate to each other?

We can also ask students to think about the strategies they use to organize different texts:

- How do you usually organize your essays?

- What strategies have you learned for organizing your writing?

- Which ones do you find most helpful? Why?

Being able to describe what they're doing when they're making choices helps students to make effective writing decisions in the future.

Playing with Structure and Genre Conventions

Learning experiences built around a redesign of an existing artifact can help students apply their strengths and see themselves as knowledge producers, rather than just knowledge consumers. Below are some ideas for doing this:

- Redesign a visual document, such as an event flyer.

- Redesign a website created for a public awareness campaign.

- Redesign a book cover for a novel or work of literary criticism (see Figure 7.15).

- Redesign the typesetting for a poem (i.e., change font style, size, page layout, images, and conduct rhetorical analysis of the original and the redesign).

- Redesign an author's web page.

- Redesign an artifact for a new medium (e.g., an email to a letter, a print story to a digital story).

Begin this activity by asking students: What are you designing this text to accomplish?

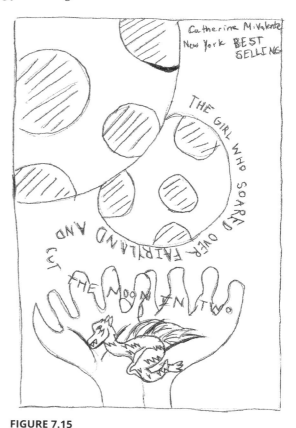

FIGURE 7.15
Redesigned book cover for *The Girl Who Soared Over Fairyland and Cut the Moon in Two*

> Transfer pursues a moving target: the unknown, untried task down the road.

Making Choices About Placement: Beginnings, Endings, and Turning Points

When I ask students in our Summer Bridge program what help they'd like with their writing, here's what they often say:

"How to start"

"How to transition from the introduction"

"How to transition to other topics"

"How to end an essay"

These responses show the students have excellent instincts as writers. They know that introductions, conclusions, and turning points are some of the most important moments in a composition, and they want to make the most of their opportunities to engage and retain their reader's interest.

As readers, we expect to find important information in key positions: openings and closings, for instance. Rabinowitz notes the critical impact of how writers begin and end sentences, paragraphs, and compositions:

> [. . .] such placement affects both concentration and scaffolding: our attention during the act of reading, will, in part, be concentrated on what we have found in these positions [i.e., first and last lines], and our sense of the text's meaning will be influenced by our assumption that the author expected us to end up with an interpretation that could account more fully for these details than for details elsewhere. (1987, 59)

And here I was giving students their opening lines as a new teacher! The "model" topic sentences I used to write for students[1] deprived them of the chance to focus their audience's attention on what *they* thought was important. I grabbed that special opening spot for myself like it was no big deal, so that my students didn't even have a sense of the opportunity they'd lost.

The activities that follow offer ways to support students in making their own choices about beginnings, endings, and turning points.

Making Choices About Introductions

"The beginning of all discourse," say rhetoricians Edward P. J. Corbett and Robert J. Connors, "is a topic, a question, a problem, an issue" (1999, 27). All writing emerges from some kind of problem or question. Starting with this understanding infuses a sense of purpose into students' choices about introductions.

----

1. *See my prescriptive prompt for "The Monkey's Paw" in the introduction to this book.*

COLLABORATIVE WRITING: OPENING LINES

One of the strategies I use to promote rhetorical decision making is to have students collaboratively write the opening sentence of a text for a particular rhetorical situation, such as a cover letter for a scholarship application. A shared Google doc works well for this activity (adapted from an activity developed by the writing faculty at California State University, Monterey Bay).

> *Directions to Teachers: Create or find a writing prompt that asks students to respond to an authentic rhetorical situation they are likely to face, such as writing a cover letter for a scholarship application. If possible, use the actual directions for a real writing task. Share the prompt with your students. Students will then work in small groups to collaboratively compose the first sentence of the text called for by the prompt. Distribute one large index card to each group. After using a Google doc to collaboratively compose their opening sentence, groups will copy the final version of that sentence onto one side of the index card. On the other side of the card, groups will write a metacognitive process statement about how they collaboratively composed their opening sentence, sharing the thinking that went on behind their choices.*
>
> *Collect the cards from the groups and share as many you can with the class. Compare opening sentences and ask students what they think works well. Critique what makes a good opening sentence for this particular rhetorical situation. Read the metacognitive process descriptions for the opening sentences the class identifies as particularly effective.*
>
> *Directions to Students:* Work together as a group to collaboratively write the opening sentence for the text. Use a shared Google doc to draft your sentence. Once all group members are satisfied with your opening sentence, copy that sentence onto one side of the index card you've been given. On the back of your card, write a description of the thinking and decision-making process your group used to compose your sentence. Consider the following questions:
>
> What are you trying to do with this sentence? What impact do you want this sentence to have on your reader?

The class discussion we have in response to the student examples gives me a chance to offer feedback on their choices. For instance, if a group decided to open with a famous quotation that feels sorta random, I might say, "Can you help me understand why this is important? Is there another opening move that needs to happen before or instead of this quote?" Asking students to explain their choices and describe their composing process further develops their ability to think rhetorically.

Making Choices About Conclusions

"Your conclusion should restate your thesis." That's the advice you received when you were a student, right? Tell your reader what you already told them? My first attempt to move my own students beyond this limited approach was to give them three questions to address in their conclusions instead: What? So what? Now what? The last two questions pointed students toward the significance and implications of their findings, which was an improvement on the old repeat-the-thesis approach.

But these days I find even these prompts a bit restrictive. They don't quite get at the underlying principles I want students to understand. I'm afraid if I ask students why they're addressing these questions, they'd say things like, "I don't know. I'm not the teacher."

What are the underlying principles we want students to understand about conclusions? What do conclusions do? And what do students need to understand about their audience, purpose, occasion, and genre in order to develop an effective exit strategy?

Just as we hope to make a compelling entrance with our introduction, we also want to make a memorable exit with our conclusion. I use one of Goodman's tips to presenters to help my student writers think about the connection between their introduction and conclusion. Goodman portrays the structure of a presentation as a continuum from Point A to Point B, with A being what the audience members "are thinking and feeling when they enter the room" and B being what the presenter wants them "to think, feel, and do when they leave" (2006, 19). A skilled speaker or writer knows how to take their audience on a journey from Point A to Point B.

I want to share a few more gold nuggets from Goodman:

- By the end of my presentation, what do I want them to have learned?
- By the end of my presentation, what do I want them to feel?
- By the end of my presentation, what do I want them to do? (2006, 19)

These planning questions for presenters can also help student writers make effective choices about conclusions.

DRAWING CONCLUSIONS

If students have used section headings in their composition, invite them to label their final section "Conclusions" instead of "Conclusion." Ask them what this change does to their thinking. How is drawing conclusions a different mental process from writing a conclusion? See the activity directions that follow. This activity works especially well with researched arguments.

Directions to Students: Create a heading for the final section of your composition that says "Conclusions." This could be the last chunk of your essay, final slide(s) of a presentation, last few seconds of a podcast, or concluding section of a document you've created. Then, in a five-minute quick-write, respond to these questions:

- What conclusions have you reached as a result of your inquiry process?
- Which of your conclusions are most important?

- To what extent do you think your audience will share these same conclusions with you by the time they've finished reading, viewing, or listening to the text you've created?

QUESTIONS TO ASK ABOUT CONCLUSIONS DURING WRITING CONFERENCES

1. You and your reader are about to part ways (at least for the time being). How can you bring closure to your shared experience?

2. As you say goodbye to your reader, what kind of lasting impression do you want to leave?

3. Does your conclusion need to make some kind of "ask"? If so, does this need to be explicit? Does your audience need additional information to do what you are asking them to do?

4. You had many different choices for how to end this piece of writing. Why did you want this to be your last sentence? Why did you want this to be your last word?

> Knowing how to do something is not the same as knowing why we do it. To transfer learning, we have to understand the principles behind the practice.

Making Choices About Focus: Rules of Notice

If I'm excited about something I've learned, it's a good bet I can get my students excited, too. Learning about Rabinowitz's rules of notice, configuration, and coherence was one of those "this is so cool!" experiences for me. My teacher brain knew I could put these ideas to good use. I admit I've been critical of rule-based approaches, but Rabinowitz's "rules" are descriptive, not prescriptive (more like interpretive guidelines than actual rules). And what Rabinowitz calls "rules," we now typically call "moves"[2]: rhetorical strategies like the use of titles, headings and subheadings, repetition, beginnings and endings, and transitions.

Rabinowitz's "rules of notice" can help writers make informed choices about form and style. He makes two points I find tremendously important:

1. [. . .] the stressed features in a text serve as a basic structure on which to build an interpretation.

2. Communication can exist only if author and receiver agree beforehand about what is worthy of notice. (1987, 53)

In this next section, I share strategies writers can use to tell their audience where to direct their attention.

Distinguishing Foreground from Background

In visual design, the relationship between figure and ground is important. Writers can apply these concepts to the choices they make about how and where to direct their reader's attention. Expert writers carefully consider the special ideas they want to highlight as their main focus of a text. They also consider the background and context needed to support

----

2. *See the work of Jim Burke, Gerald Graff, or Kelly Gallagher for examples of this usage.*

this focus. In contrast, novice writers often give excessive attention to minor details or neglect to spotlight major points.

In most texts, everything is not equally important. Indeed, it would tax reader's energy and focus were the writer to keep the volume at eleven for the duration of the text. As the twentieth-century Harvard economist John Kenneth Galbraith once said, "It is almost as important to know what is not serious as to know what is" (quoted in Goodman 2006). Papers that are just structured as a compilation of sources typically lack this important distinction between foreground and background. Readers should be able to discern what's important and what's less so.

IDENTIFYING THE FOREGROUND AND BACKGROUND

Directions to Students: Use the graphic organizer (Figure 7.16) to help determine your main focus for the text you are composing. List your main ideas in the tree (the foreground or focus of attention). Then list supporting ideas on the hillside under the clouds (the background). Consider the following questions as you decide what goes where:

- What special ideas are your main focus in this piece of writing?
- What other ideas provide helpful background, context, and support for your main focus?
- What are the main points you want your reader to see? What other ideas or concepts help support this understanding?
- What is the controlling idea in your composition?

Making Choices About Focus: Foreground and Background

FIGURE 7.16
Identifying the foreground and background helps students to see the predominant focus and supporting context of their argument.

Thinking about their ideas in terms of foreground and background can help students understand the relationships between different parts of the text.

Making Choices About Titles and Headlines

Encouraging students to consider the effects and functions of titles and headings is an additional way we can deepen their understanding of text structure. These text features, like all rhetorical moves, speak to specific audiences and purposes.

The Syfy Channel's comedic catastrophe movie *Sharknado* (2013) was originally pitched to potential cast members under a much less sensational title: *Dark Skies*. The reason? The title you choose to persuade reputable actors to work on your film is different from the title you use to attract television audiences. What draws in one audience could repel another.

Borrowing from design theory, writers can think about titles and headlines in terms of the user's experience. How do these structural features impact how readers interact with texts? The next two activities help students explore this question.

TITLE REWRITES

Directions to Students: How does your title shape your reader's experience? What does your title tell your reader to look for? How would an alternative title create an alternative reading experience? Discuss these questions with a partner. Then try writing a few alternative titles and see which ones you and your partner like best.

ANALYZING AND COMPARING HEADLINES

In news writing, headlines are often a paraphrase of the article. Yet the purpose of the headline (and who actually writes it) often changes according to the publication.

> Students who learn to "do school" by following rules are at a serious disadvantage in the myriad postsecondary settings where those rules no longer apply.

Directions to Students: Find an Associated Press article that appears in different publications under different headlines. What is the rhetorical purpose of the headline in each case? How can you tell? Share your thoughts through a quick-write or pairs conversation.

Conclusion: Moving Beyond Quick-Fix Formulas

I understand why teachers—myself included—sometimes make decisions about genre and structure for our students. There are times when we need to create an instructional focus or lighten the cognitive load. Or maybe we want to model the moves of expert writers. Many formulas and templates also offer instant payoffs; students' writing immediately looks better, as if it's undergone one of those miraculous makeovers we see on reality TV with their dramatic "before" and "after" shots. It seems like the writing problem is solved. No more zeros in the grade book. No more frustrated students. Proficient scores on state tests.

As a parent, I've also developed a visceral sense of the developmental differences between a 12-year-old and a 14-year-old and between a 14-year-old and a 16-year-old. Too much ambiguity and choice can be deeply unsettling to younger adolescents. Kids start to develop a mistrust of adults who consistently refuse to give clear answers.

But I want to argue that unless students know *why* their writing is effective in particular contexts (including in situations where they've used a formula), they won't be able to repurpose their learning for new situations. What's more, they aren't empowered to be critical thinkers, decision makers, and problem solvers because the problems and decisions have been taken out of their hands. Students need extended practice making choices and theoretical knowledge of how writing works to grow as independent thinkers and communicators.

In teaching writing for transfer, we're not just teaching for success on highly scaffolded school assignments. We're teaching for success in writing situations that are full of mystery and risk. And full of opportunities, too. Students deserve writing instruction that prepares them to take full advantage of those opportunities.

CHAPTER EIGHT

Revising Rhetorically

Revision is a mindset that writers use all the way through their writing.
—BARRY LANE

W e often speak of revision as "re-seeing"—that post-drafting perspective that allows us to view our writing from a different vantage point. Revising rhetorically means "re-seeing" our writing through key aspects of the rhetorical situation, including the audience, purpose, context, and genre. Instead of just using the lens of teacher approval, students who revise rhetorically see their writing through the various perspectives and practices of the discourse community they're trying to engage.

This has been a transformative idea for me. For many years in my life as a teacher, revision was a stage of the writing process more honored in the breach than the observance. I would tack some cursory peer response and revision activities on to the end of a unit mostly as a means of making my students' papers easier to grade (i.e., needing fewer "corrections"). After doing some low-level peer review, we'd work the OSCAR process of revision I'd learned myself as a student: Omit, Substitute, Combine, Add, and Rearrange. While these are indeed all things writers do during revision, the problem was my students didn't know what to omit, what to substitute, what to combine, add, or rearrange. They had no conditional knowledge of when these moves were relevant and desirable. So, when it came down to it, I largely made the choices for them. It became almost a game to see how many student questions I could answer on "revision day":

What should I add?

"Add some more examples!"

What do I omit?

"Omit repetitions!" (I'd fail to mention rhetorically effective repetitions.)

What am I supposed to substitute?

"Dead words! Swap out casual words for academic English."

This doesn't flow.

"Add some transitions!"

This sounds choppy.

"Combine those sentences!"

And, of course, students felt like they had to do something for each letter of OSCAR. That's how they knew when they were done revising—when they got to "R."

By telling students what to revise, I was increasing their dependence on me, not teaching for transfer of learning. I was trying to improve the writing instead of the writer.

I've since learned better. Now when students ask me those what-should-I-do questions, I say, "It depends," and toss the questions back to them: What are you trying to accomplish? What does your audience care about? What do you notice about the style and structure of other texts in this genre?

While the rhetorical approach isn't a magic bullet, I will say this: It's changed the conversation in my classroom about how we make choices as writers. Instead of a vague notion that revision involves cutting some things, adding some things, and changing some things, we can now talk about how to make strategic and selective communication choices in light of real situational contingencies. We can talk about the effects of those choices, including their impact on the writer's ethos and the kind of reader-writer relationships they create. A rhetorical approach makes clear the abundant choices we have as writers and the plentiful context clues that can tell us which choices are most likely to help us achieve our aims.

"It Depends": Developing Students' Conditional Knowledge

In *Revision Decisions: Talking through Sentences and Beyond*, Jeff Anderson and Deborah Dean talk about the importance of creativity and flexibility in acts of revision, and I couldn't agree more. Anderson and Dean's goal is to help students become "fluent writers brimming with possible decisions" who "can easily deal with today's changing writing landscape" (2014, 4). As Anderson and Dean note, revision is a messy, trial-and-error process rich with opportunities and options.

It's not enough to just show students what those options are. For students to make appropriate use of these options, they need conditional knowledge of the effects and functions of writer's choices. In other words, they need to know what those choices do under *specific conditions*. They also need to know that what works in one situation might not work in another. Conditional knowledge is knowing when and why to do something; it's a deep understanding of contingencies. At heart, it's *kairotic* knowledge—knowledge of "the opportune moment" and "what to say when."

To illustrate to students what I mean when I say, "It depends," I share the three pictures of floral bouquets shown in Figure 8.1.

FIGURE 8.1
"Good," "better," and "best" options

These images are based on photos you'll find on florists' websites. Since I have family members who live out of state, I'm well versed in the techniques online florists use to try to upsell their customers. Here's how it works: I choose one Mother's Day bouquet for my mom and then am suddenly shown a collection of three bouquets: my selection (the "good" bouquet), an arrangement with more flowers (the "better" bouquet), and then a lavish upgrade (the "best" bouquet). While I might bristle at the guilt ambush, the point is I have choices; there are different options for how I honor my mom on this special occasion, and the right one for me *depends* on my situation and goals. Do I need to save money? Or do I want to impress my mom with an extravagant gift? Will my mom be pleased if I go all out or would she prefer something more practical? I have to consider my purpose and audience.

Here's another example I share with my classes: How about three different ways to get to space? Companies such as Blue Origin, Space X, and Stratolaunch have all designed commercial spaceships intended to carry tourists into orbit (Figure 8.2). Some of these spacecraft blast off from a launchpad while others are towed by an airplane to an altitude of more than 40,000 feet before being released and firing their rockets. In a third approach, the spacecraft takes off from a conventional runway. Multiple different design solutions for the same problem. Which spacecraft design is "best" depends on your priorities: safety, comfort, simplicity, cost, range, capacity, reusability, and so on. The designs must be evaluated in context.

FIGURE 8.2
Good, better, best?

I also like these images for the lesson they tell about problem solving: There are lots of creative paths to the same goal. When we teach for transfer, we make it a priority to help our students see and assess the alternatives.

In writing, too, determining the "best" choice from a range of options is a matter of establishing your goals and priorities (along with those of your audience). The National Research Council identifies conditional knowledge as one of the requirements for successful transfer of learning, further noting that "understanding how and when to put knowledge to use—known as conditions of applicability—is an important characteristic of expertise" (*How People Learn* 2000, 236). I know students are starting to develop conditional knowledge when they can spin out for themselves some of the conditions on which a choice's effectiveness depends—like whether or not the audience already agrees with them, how sensitive the topic is, how much reader-writer trust has been established, or how formal the occasion is.

What is effective is in the eye of the beholder. The National Council of Teachers of English makes this point directly in its 2018 Position Statement on Understanding and Teaching Writing: "When writing reflects the expectations that audiences have for each of these elements [i.e., content, form, and style], it is considered good; when it does not, it is considered less than good . . ." Memorizing the traits of "good" writing becomes an obstacle to effective communication when that understanding conflicts with the values and practices of particular discourse communities.

Think about how the tips for "good" writing shown in Figure 8.3 could be reframed to promote transfer and conditional knowledge.

REVISION ADVICE	EXPANSIVE FRAMING: WHY IS THIS IMPORTANT? WHEN IS THIS ADVICE RELEVANT?
Add sensory details.	
Specify names of people and things.	
Eliminate "to be" verbs.	
Use active voice.	
Organize your ideas into paragraphs.	

FIGURE 8.3
Framing revision for transfer

The extent to which any piece of advice improves writing depends on what the writer's choices do in context and how readers value those particular moves. Using sensory language does not in itself constitute "good" writing. This judgment lies in the hands of readers. Expansive framing identifies the principles and conditions that make our advice to students meaningful.

Better yet, instead of giving student writers advice, try asking questions that activate rhetorical thinking. You'll find a list of these kinds of questions in the back of the book (see Appendix X). I know I've been too narrow and directive in my feedback to students if they say "I changed what you told me to change" when they submit their revisions.

A rhetorical approach to revision helps students understand that revising involves more than just fixing instructor "corrections" or completing a checklist. This approach recognizes that revision is a strategic, selective process. What writers choose to revise depends on the ultimate purpose of their writing. Not all potential improvements will be required by the rhetorical situation. Thus, the process of revising rhetorically can help students determine the essential characteristics of effective written communication in a specific context.

See the following quick-write prompt for developing conditional knowledge.

QUICK-WRITE PROMPT

Directions to Students: How do you know if a verb is weak? How do you know if a word is vague? Upon what conditions do these judgments depend? Respond to these questions in a four-minute quick-write.

> Effective revision decisions are situated in the context of students' writing.

Revision Starts with Reading

Reading strategies *are* writing strategies. I'm tempted to say just go read a book like Kelly Gallagher's *Deeper Reading* (2004), and have your students apply those strategies to their own writing, and you'll have revision covered. This is, in fact, one of the most important acts of transfer we work to facilitate—the transfer from reading to writing. Analytical reading strategies such as annotation and descriptive outlining are some of the best ways I know to improve students' writing abilities. In this next section, I share how to help students use the critical skills they develop through rhetorical reading to analyze their own drafts in preparation for making revision decisions.

This approach is really about improving students' reading skills—both their reading of texts and their reading of rhetorical situations—so we can improve their writing skills. When revision doesn't start with a deep reading of a text and its context, chances are what's being revised are just superficial features of writing that have been called out in a list of do's and don'ts.

By the way, this might be a good time to note that I permit students to revise and resubmit all their graded work in my classes. I don't know how I'd teach for growth if I didn't.

Rhetorical Analysis and Evaluation of a Draft

Figuring out when and why to make particular revision choices is a matter of reading the rhetorical situation. A good starting point is a rhetorical analysis of a draft. This requires the writer to assess the draft based on the purpose of the writing, the message of the argument, the needs of the audience (including genre expectations), and the ethos the writer adopts.

In my experience, the concept of audience is a particularly powerful lens for evaluating drafts because it so directly connects to purpose and occasion. Our purpose is what we want the audience to do, believe, or feel. The occasion is the event or circumstance that brings the audience and writer together and determines how they should act. Ultimately, everything depends on the audience because the audience is the only component in a rhetorical situation (besides the rhetor) that has a mind of its own. And it's going to use that mind to decide whether or not the rhetor is persuasive.

The following questions for rhetorical analysis come from the California State University's Expository Reading and Writing Curriculum (ERWC) Assignment Template.

Students can answer these in a quick-write or pairs conversation. Note the consistent focus on audience:

- What is the rhetorical situation? Who is my audience, and what is my argument?
- What types of evidence and appeals does this audience value most highly?
- How can I establish my own authority to address this issue? What credibility do I have with this audience?
- What are the most important factors contributing to either the success or failure of the argument?
- What is the most relevant feedback I have received about this audience and context?

These are the same questions I ask myself when I write for my job. For instance, if I've drafted a proposal to secure grant funding for a research project, I'm going to look closely at what grant evaluators say they want in the call for proposals. I'll also review the characteristics of winning proposals if any have been shared. And I'll share my draft proposal with the staff at our Grants and Contracts Office since they have expertise in this area. The revision decisions I ultimately make will be based on the factors that impact my chances of being awarded a grant.

Students who develop the ability to analyze their own writing rhetorically will be able to apply this valuable skill in a variety of real-life contexts.

PAPA SQUARE

In this activity adapted from Maxine Hairston (1986), students identify the **P**urpose, **A**rgument, **P**ersona, and **A**udience of a persuasive text, as well as its rhetorical methods and strategies. I like how a PAPA Square analysis highlights the dynamic components of a rhetorical situation, that is, the "set of related factors whose interaction creates and controls a discourse" (Grant-Davie 1997, 265).

The example PAPA Square in Figure 8.4 offers a rhetorical analysis of a student essay on F. Scott Fitzgerald's *The Great Gatsby*. The question at issue is the meaning of the novel. The choices the writer has made are in response to her understanding of the rhetorical situation, including the level of diction and syntax appropriate to academic writing and the kind of evidence her audience expects and values.

I often model a PAPA Square analysis for the whole class using one student's draft before asking students to complete a PAPA Square for their own or a peer's draft.

This can also be a good time to bring out a helpful equation we use for determining effective acts of communication:

Message/argument + means by which message is expressed + context/occasion = persuasion

PAPA Square:
Through a PAPA Square, students analyze the **purpose**, **argument**, **persona**, and **audience** of a text. Around the perimeter of the box, students will answer the following questions in response to their own writing: Who is my audience? What is the persona, or public image, that I create for myself through my language choices and tone? What is my thesis or argument? What is my purpose or desired outcome of my argument (i.e., what would I like my reader to do if he or she is persuaded by me?)? In the center of the PAPA Square, students will identify the stylistic devices and emotional, logical, and ethical appeals they use to persuade their audience. These may include types of evidence, figurative language, text structures (e.g., cause and effect), and tone.

Purpose:

Audience: **Argument:**

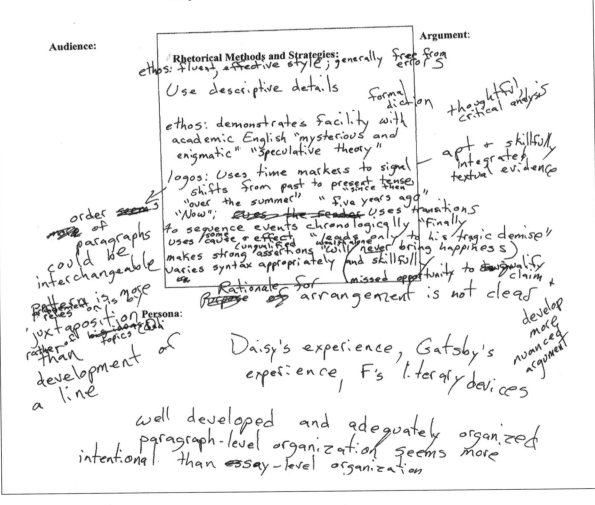

Rhetorical Methods and Strategies:

ethos: fluent, affective style; generally free from errors

Use descriptive details

formal diction

thoughtful critical analysis

ethos: demonstrates facility with academic English "mysterious and enigmatic" "speculative theory"

apt + skillfully integrated textual evidence

logos: Uses time markers to signal shifts from past to present tense; "over the summer"; "five years ago"; "since then" "Now"; ~~cues the reader~~ Uses transitions to sequence events chronologically "Finally" Uses cause + effect (unqualified, will alone) "leads only to his tragic demise" makes strong assertions "will never bring happiness) varies syntax appropriately and skillfully

order ~~seems~~ ~~more~~ of paragraphs could be interchangeable

Pattern is more ~~relies on~~ "juxtaposition rather of ~~independent~~ topics each than development of a line

~~Rationale~~ for ~~Purpose of~~ arrangement is not clear +

missed opportunity to ~~disqualify~~ qualify claim

develop more nuanced argument

Persona:

Daisy's experience, Gatsby's experience, F's literary devices

well developed and adequately organized paragraph-level organization seems more intentional than ~~essay~~ essay-level organization

FIGURE 8.4
PAPA Square analysis of a student essay

You might ask students to consider their own attempt at persuasion in light of their PAPA Square analysis and then apply this equation to their draft. Remind students that the means by which their message is expressed includes their choices about ethos, pathos, and logos and the effects of those choices. Do their strategies add up?

A rhetorical approach to revision considers the interactions among these related factors. We can make this point by having students draw arrows between the different components in the PAPA Square, showing the interactions between audience and purpose, purpose and persona, persona and audience, argument and purpose, and between the rhetorical context and the writer's strategies.

Reading a Draft Through the Audience's Eyes

Someday, our students are going to have to write texts that an unimpressed or resistant reader can just chuck aside without reading if they like. We *have* to read our students' writing whether we want to or not. It's our job. But eventually, our students will encounter writing situations where they are 100 percent responsible for keeping their readers' eyes on the page or screen. In classes where students are already writing for external audiences, that someday is today. Thinking about reader need and experience produces the conditional knowledge that helps students revise effectively.

This next activity asks students to think through how to keep their reader reading.

EVALUATING SUBJECT HEADINGS

What causes you to ignore an email in your inbox? Make a quick list in your head. Some of these same issues—irrelevant subject matter, inappropriate tone, unprofessional language, lack of credibility—can also cause readers of academic texts, including student essays, to disregard what writers have said. Writing rhetorically means writing with a heightened awareness of what might cause a reader to stop reading. I ask students, "Are there sections of your paper that are in danger of being 'unopened emails'?" "What messages, if any, might not get through?"

Thinking about the way we view subject headings in emails can help students understand how subject headings in an academic text are also opportunities to respond to audience need and interest while supporting the writer's purpose.

> *Directions to Students:* Add subject headings to the major sections of your essay that respond to your audience's needs and interests. What issues are important to your audience? What does your audience care about knowing? And what do you need to do to get your reader to stay with you for the whole of your argument? Then answer the following question in a quick-write: If these section headings were email subject lines, would any of these "emails" likely be ignored by your reader? Why or why not?

Seeing writing as communication can help students revise through the lens of the audience.

DESCRIPTIVE OUTLINING (REVISITED)

Descriptive outlining is one of those powerful multipurpose tools that help students as readers and writers. When applied to their own compositions, descriptive outlining shows students the logical progression of their ideas. This strategy helps students learn to look for patterns and for breaks in patterns, to notice changes in pace or force, and to understand the kind of experience they've created for their reader.

Here's a review of the basic procedure: After "chunking," or dividing their compositions into functional sections, students note what they are saying and doing in each paragraph or group of paragraphs. Each "says" statement is a paraphrase of that section's main points while the "does" statement is a description of the rhetorical function or effect of the section (i.e., the writer's moves) (see Chapter 7 for an example).

Composition scholar Kenneth A. Bruffee recommends using descriptive outlining in pairs or groups of three as part of the peer review process. For longer essays, he suggests students start by numbering the paragraphs in their essays. The numbering will help the peer reviewers to group clusters of related paragraphs into units. Students then exchange papers and write a descriptive outline of their partner's paper, explaining "how each cluster of paragraphs fits into the essay as a whole" (2007, 168). Bruffee offers peer reviewers additional guidelines for writing descriptive outlines:

1. What is the central point or proposition of the essay? What position does it take? Using your words or the essay's, state the essay's proposition in one sentence. [. . .]

2. Describe the essay's introduction. Where does it end? How many paragraphs are in it? What does it *do* to introduce the essay? What does it *say*?

3. Describe the essay's ending. Where does it begin? How many paragraphs are in it? What does it *do* to end the essay? What does it say?

4. Describe the essay's explanation or defense of its position. What does it *do* to explain or defend that position? What does it *say*?

5. What is the essay's overall plan? (2007, 168–169)

After students have written detailed descriptive outlines of their peers' essay, they can confer about the kind of experience they've created for their reader. Invite students to compare descriptive outlines and discuss whether or not the paragraphs say and do what the writer intended them to do. This kind of peer feedback is particularly important in a rhetorical approach because it helps writers gauge audience response. (By the way, if everyone's descriptive outline looks similar because they're all using the same formula, chances are instruction hasn't been framed for transfer.)

I find descriptive outlining is great for drilling down to the specifics of rhetorical choices—like how the rhetorical purpose of an essay's title is different from the rhetorical purpose of the essay as a whole. The title has a specific job to do. Or how an introduction does different work from a conclusion, which is why just repeating what's already been said in the introduction is probably not an effective closing.

Figure 8.5 shows the example of a descriptive outline of a student's essay on lying—an assignment I use in conjunction with my unit on Mark Haddon's novel *The Curious Incident of the Dog in the Night-Time.*

> The "does" statements in a descriptive outline answer the question, "What is the writer trying to accomplish here?"

What Descriptive Outlining Can Reveal

Descriptive outlining offers students important insights into how they should revise. In the example in Figure 8.5, for instance, the *does* statements reveal that most of the student's body paragraphs address questions of fact (What causes lying? How frequently do people lie?) while the introduction and conclusion address a question of quality (Are some lies justifiable?). The essay does not develop and support its stated thesis.

Like those purple tablets that dentists make kids chew to reveal the plaque on their teeth, descriptive outlining can expose problem areas. These include:

- Needless repetition
- Asking one question and answering another
- Overreliance on one type of source
- Formulaic organization
- Lack of integration of sources
- Missed opportunities (e.g., burying a key example or claim in a bloated, all-purpose paragraph)
- Disconnected or superfluous personal anecdotes
- Lack of rhetorical turns/progression (i.e., no "highlights" or "lowlights")
- Insufficient use of evidence

These signs of trouble, by the way, are not indicators of student deficits but rather opportunities for writers to practice the creative problem solving central to all academic work. All writing benefits from thoughtful evaluation and revision. All writing also benefits from encouragement. It's just as important for writers to know what works for an audience as to know what doesn't. Descriptive outlining gives teachers and students a way to talk about the effects of writers' moves from the perspective of reader understanding and experience.

Adapted from *Reading Rhetorically* by John C. Bean, Virgina A. Chappel, and Alice M. Gillam.

Descriptive Outlining

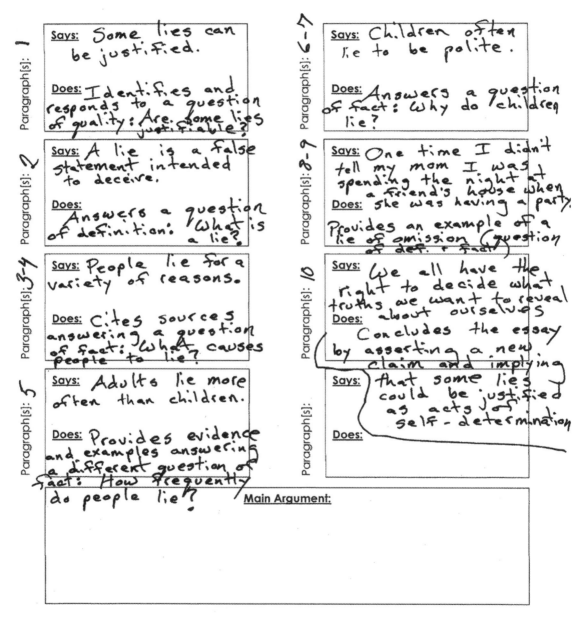

Paragraph[s]: 1

Says: Some lies can be justified.

Does: Identifies and responds to a question of quality: Are some lies justifiable?

Paragraph[s]: 2

Says: A lie is a false statement intended to deceive.

Does: Answers a question of definition: What is a lie?

Paragraph[s]: 3-4

Says: People lie for a variety of reasons.

Does: Cites sources answering a question of fact: What causes people to lie?

Paragraph[s]: 5

Says: Adults lie more often than children.

Does: Provides evidence and examples answering a different question of fact: How frequently do people lie?

Paragraph[s]: 6-7

Says: Children often lie to be polite.

Does: Answers a question of fact: Why do children lie?

Paragraph[s]: 8-9

Says: One time I didn't tell my mom I was spending the night at a friend's house when she was having a party.

Does: Provides an example of a lie of omission (question of def. + fact)

Paragraph[s]: 10

Says: We all have the right to decide what truths we want to reveal about ourselves

Does: Concludes the essay by asserting a new claim and implying that some lies could be justified as acts of self-determination

Paragraph[s]:

Says:

Does:

Main Argument:

FIGURE 8.5

Descriptive outline of a student essay (see Appendix T for a blank template)

DESCRIPTIVE PLOT OUTLINING: TELLING AN ARGUMENT STORY

If students have also learned how to do descriptive *plot* outlining in their work with literary texts, they can try telling the story of their argument. Charting an argument's dramatic arc helps students to see what they're doing to engage their readers' interest and keep their readers with them.

When my students are composing written arguments, I bring back out the plot chart we used when analyzing short stories and novels (Figure 8.6).

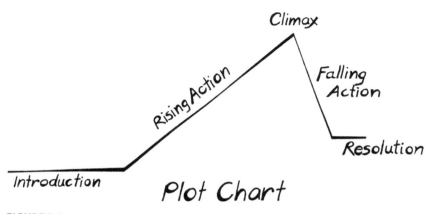

FIGURE 8.6
Plot chart

Then I ask students to think about the "plot" of their essay: What do they do to introduce the conflict, debate, and question at issue? What exposition or background do they provide? What's the inciting incident or exigence that launches the debate? How do they build interest and engage the reader's concerns through the rising action? How do they intensify the case they make? What's the most significant moment or turning point in their essay? When do they want this to happen? Where in the argument's development and arrangement should they place the most compelling evidence, dramatic data, or memorable anecdote? How will they provide a resolution or tying up of loose ends?

This kind of thinking leverages students' knowledge of narrative strategies and structures to enhance their argument writing.

> We can review what descriptive outlining does by asking students to write some descriptive statements for a shared reading and then use an interactive whiteboard, sentence strips and pocket chart, or sticky notes to display the statements to the class.

PIN THE DOUBT ON THE DRAFT

Playing the doubting game with a draft is another strategy that students can use to evaluate the effectiveness of their writing. Using Peter Elbow's (1986) model of against-the-grain reading that resists the authority of the text, students can practice questioning their own or a peer's claims and assumptions. For instance, in an essay on nerd identity and anti-nerd prejudice, one of my students wrote that "nerds are people, too." When we play the doubting game with a claim like this, we unpack the thinking behind the words: Does anyone say nerds aren't people? What do our sources say? Whose views are you engaging? What assumptions are you challenging? Do any of the readings you encountered make these assumptions?

Playing the doubting game with drafts can move students past everyone's-entitled-to-their-opinion thinking to situated, evidence-based reasoning.

Directions to Students:

STEP ONE: Create a set of ready-made "doubts" by writing the following questions on sticky notes: "How do you know?", "Do you have evidence for this claim?", "What do others say?", and "Are you sure about this?" (Figure 8.7).

STEP TWO: Now place these doubts by the least defensible assertions in your (or your partner's) essay draft. Remember, you are playing "the doubting game" with draft writing. In other words, you are deliberately being extra critical as a strategy for identifying weak logic.

FIGURE 8.7
Sticky notes for "Pin the Doubt on the Draft"

Better Writing Through Better Reading

In source-based writing assignments, revision decisions should be informed by how carefully the students have understood and analyzed the texts they're writing about. This is one of the conditions that determine success. Assessing students' analytical reading skills is thus another essential component of the feedback and revision process.

In academic settings, we typically read to write. But when it comes time for students to revise an academic paper, they often forget that reading constituted a good 50 percent or more of the effort they put into the assignment. They tend to concentrate on cleaning up the form of their paper without revisiting their response to their sources. Students tend to see revision as something that happens during the writing process, long after the reading process is over. Rare is the student who will crack open a book during revision and editing.

But when I evaluate student work, I often find that the area of greatest need is reading. I've worked with students who struggle with paraphrase and summary who say the problem with their essay draft is that they "just need to add more sources." I want to flip the switch to emphasize the importance of what we *do* with those sources. What matters is how we respond to what those sources are saying, not the quantity of sources we've cited.

Consequently, much of my feedback to students is on their reading and thinking rather than the form of their writing. Here, for instance, are my comments to a young woman who was writing a literary analysis of William Shakespeare's play *The Tempest*:

> All the bones of an excellent argument essay are here, Kaitlyn. You've tackled a sufficiently complex topic—the relationship between the imagery of the sea and Shakespeare's message about loss—and I'd like to see you achieve even more precision and sophistication in your opening lines.
>
> Take a look again:
>
> You write, "In *The Tempest* Shakespeare uses imagery and symbolism to show the relationship between the sea and loss to the reader. Images of drowning appear whenever characters undergo a change, a loss, or a recovery."
>
> The second sentence is quite interesting and moves the reader closer to understanding how drowning figures in Shakespeare's exploration of loss and recovery, but I'd like to know even more about the connection between the two. What is Shakespeare saying about loss and recovery? When and why does it happen and how do human beings deal with it? And what is it about the sea and drowning (e.g., what qualities/ characteristics/conditions) that gives us insight into this aspect of human experience?

Your argument gets more intriguing as your essay progresses (especially the idea of drowning knowledge/an old life—now we have figurative and literal meanings of drowning), but I'm not sure I fully understand your analysis. When you revise this, I recommend that you look at your most surprising or compelling examples and ask yourself again, "Why does Shakespeare do that? What does it all mean?"

This student also had some minor language issues that she could address, but just correcting a few spelling and grammatical errors wasn't going to significantly improve her essay. For that, she needed to revise her reading, as well as her writing.

I want my students to understand that revision starts by improving the quality of our reading and thinking. All of us tend to stop short in our early analysis. It can take several rounds of drafting and conferring to thoroughly examine the available evidence and unpack the implications of our findings. Close reading is hard work. Thinking is hard work. Textual analysis done well should produce the cognitive equivalent of brain freeze.

Reading Revisions

Instead of having students start their revisions by rewriting their drafts, I often have them begin by redoing their annotations. We call these reading revisions. The students use my comments on their papers to go back to the text and find all those opportunities for deeper analysis that they may have missed the first time. I also ask students to bring their annotations to their peer review workshops or writing conferences. We work together to see if we can get more out of the text.

It's at the revision stage that I push back on my students' thinking most vigorously (and thanks to Bill and Megan, my editor and reviewer, for doing the same to me). On the open floor of whole-class discussion or during the tenuous moments of early research and drafting, I'm very protective of my students' exploratory thinking, allowing them free reign to test out a variety of possible questions and answers. But once we move to revision, I shift from playing the believing game with their ideas to playing the doubting game. Now is when I remind students, "This is hard work, but you can do it, and I'll help."

ANALYZE THE SOURCES INSTEAD OF THE STUDENT'S WRITING

If I think my students need more help paraphrasing and analyzing the words of other writers, I sometimes skip over what my students have written and focus instead on what their sources have written. So I do a mini-close reading of a quotation they've cited. Especially if my students include a block quotation, they should expect me or another student to go in and highlight any of the good stuff they've missed. If we're going to give over four lines or more of a composition to another writer, it ought to be worth it.

Giving Feedback

I recognize that it's easy for writers to get discouraged. Sometimes instead of "good, better, best," we see our choices as "bad, worse, worst," especially if someone has told us everything that's wrong with our draft. That's why it's important that our students receive respectful feedback that keeps them moving forward as writers and thinkers. Students need to know that we're on their side—that we see the best in them and in their writing.

Giving feedback in terms of the reader-writer relationship (rather than the student-teacher relationship) puts us all on more equal footing and makes clear that we're participating in the same conversation and discourse community. Instead of giving students a list of rules to follow, I offer them some audience reactions to consider. This kind of reader-based feedback helps develop students' awareness of the rhetorical situation they're engaging.

> Without feedback that promotes rhetorical thinking, students will continue to depend on teacher instructions instead of activating their own decision-making process.

READER ANNOTATIONS

I write all over my students' papers when I give them feedback during in-class writing conferences because I want them to see what goes on in my reader's brain as I try to make sense of their text. I annotate, ask questions, underline important words, and talk back to them all in the hopes of developing their sensitivity to reader experience. I write check marks by their best bits to indicate those moments when I'm most impressed and persuaded. I don't use my teacher voice in these annotations; instead, I'm reacting as a colleague and audience member. My students receive the same kind of feedback that I give the members of my own writing group, a group of four women who try to meet monthly to share our work. (Please note: I don't do this with take-home grading—not enough time or context.)

Consequently, when I annotate students' drafts, I don't tell them what to do. I tell them what I understand and what I need help understanding. For instance, one of my students started a paragraph with the following sentence: "In this next paragraph, I will address my second topic." Instead of giving a teacher directive like "use a different transition" or "state your main idea," I wrote on her paper, "What are your options for transitions? What connections are you trying to make?", putting the choice back on her and paying respect to her autonomy as a writer.

Laila's exemplary analysis of *The Absolutely True Diary of a Part-Time Indian* (see Figure 8.8) gave me abundant opportunities to let her know what she was doing well. My annotations mark those moments when I'm especially moved by her language or intrigued by her thinking, especially her ability to analyze the effects and functions of Sherman Alexie's choices.

> We foster rhetorical agency when we react to students' writing as readers.

In *The Absolutely True Diary of a Part-Time Indian*, Sherman Alexie places the tragedies of the main character, Junior, in direct juxtaposition with his lighthearted tone. This side-by-side comparison allows the reader to learn the truth about how marginalized Junior's life has been, as well as experience the optimism that is the heart of his survival.

Junior begins the novel with an anecdote about how he was born with too much cerebral spinal fluid inside of his skull, forcing him to undergo surgery at six months old that was predicted to have one of two outcomes: his death, or brain damage so severe he would "live the rest of [his] life as a vegetable" (8). Though the content of his anecdote is tragic, his language is full of jokes; he makes fun of himself for being born with a deformity, "But weirdo me, I was born with too much grease inside my skull…" (8), of the deformity itself, "…like my brain was a giant French fry" (8), and of the physical problems resulting from his brain damage, "…I ended up having forty-two teeth… Ten teeth past human" (8-9). In further describing his physical form, he describes his eyes as "so lopsided" (9), being so skinny he'd "turn sideways and disappear (9), and having a head so big "that little Indian skulls orbited around it" (9). He also informs the reader that he had a stutter and a lisp, "Or maybe I should say… a st-st-st-st-stutter and a lishthththp" (9), and that "Everybody on the rez calls [him] a retard about twice a day" (9)

While the anecdote tells the reader that Junior's life has been tragic since he was born, his silly attitude towards his brain damage, and the permanent effects of it, sets the tone for the rest of the book: one that lets the reader know that Junior prefers to laugh at his hardships as opposed to feel pity for himself. His humor is used as a tactic to downplay the severity of his tragedies, making them seem less invasive and impacting on his life.

[Handwritten annotations: "precise focus on the purpose and effect of Alexie's choices"; "right → this is an interesting and important contrast"; "That's the tension"; "yes!"; "This is a compelling reading of the novel"; "I like how you are describing what Alexie is saying and doing"; "These examples let your reader appreciate the same edgy humor you describe in your analysis"; "significant"; "good word-- I'd want to qualify this statement, too. Alexie doesn't spare his readers the pain of understanding his experiences."; "anything else?"; "clear articulation of how these choices impact meaning"]

FIGURE 8.8
Reader annotations for student essay on *The Absolutely True Diary of a Part-Time Indian*

KEY WORD BANKS

One of the more unusual forms of feedback I offer my students during the revision process is a variant of the key word bank activity I use when I teach research projects (see Chapter 5). This activity serves as a form of paraphrase of a student's argument. Like descriptive outlining, it's a way to mirror back to writers what we hear them saying.

It works like this: As I read a student's paper, I take note of key terms and concepts that are central to their main idea, listing these words in clusters of related items (similar to List, Group, Label). I write these lists on the back of the student's paper or in a comment section if I'm reviewing work electronically. I continue adding to the key word bank as I read the entire paper, contributing my own suggestions for synonyms if I think the student needs more language to describe their big ideas. Since the words are typically terms or ideas that recur *throughout* the paper, my clusters don't usually match the student's paragraph organization (nor should they). Figure 8.9 shows what it looks like.

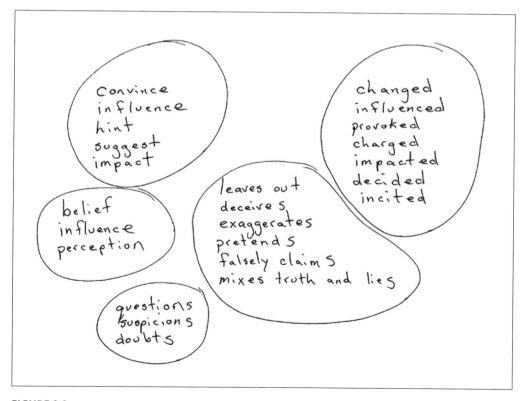

FIGURE 8.9

Key word bank for a student essay on William Shakespeare's *Othello*

When I confer with students, I ask if my key word bank captures the main focus of their essay. If not, we work together to find the ideas that will give their writing greater cohesion. Finding students' key words is one of the ways I try to read students' work supportively. I want students to know that I'm seeing interesting trends in their thinking—that there's good potential in what they've written. Feedback should help writers find a way forward, not dishearten them.

> In a rhetorical approach, we take our reader feedback seriously because we care about making our writing work.

Making Choices About Arrangement

I'm happiest as a teacher when my students are engaged in meaningful, interactive problem solving. The following stand-up, hands-on activity makes me giddy with teacher joy. Much thanks to my colleague Nelson Graff for suggesting this additional use of Hilda Taba's excellent List, Group, Label strategy (1967) to evaluate the organization of essay drafts. In this case, List, Group, Label acts as a powerful tool for helping students see ways they can improve the logical arrangement of their ideas (see Figure 8.10).

HEADING LIST, GROUP, LABEL

Directions to Students: Use the List, Group, Label process to evaluate the effectiveness of your organization. Follow the steps below.

STEP ONE: Number the paragraphs in your draft in the margin of your essay.

STEP TWO: Draw a line between functional sections of your draft (sections can include multiple paragraphs).

STEP THREE: Note what each section is saying and doing (you can use a descriptive outlining template or annotate your draft).

STEP FOUR: Add headings to each of your major sections that orient your reader to the content and purpose of this section.

STEP FIVE: Write your headings on individual sticky notes.

STEP SIX: Post your sticky notes on the wall of the classroom.

STEP SEVEN: Use List, Group, Label to organize your headings into groups that make sense to you. Then, arrange your groups of sticky notes into an order that will make sense to your reader.

STEP EIGHT: Compare your List, Group, Label to the actual order of sections in your draft.

STEP NINE: Make changes to the arrangement of paragraphs in your draft that improve that logical progression of your ideas.

I conclude this activity by having students stand by their List, Group, Label and explain the changes they plan to make to the rest of the class. This one's an easy win.

FIGURE 8.10
Making choices about arrangement using List, Group, Label

SHORT STORY OR ESSAY MASH-UP

When you have the luxury of time, try having your students spin out paragraph-level options for their compositions by writing different versions of a short story or essay and then creating mash-ups with the various alternatives. Warning: Your students won't like the extra work. Reassure them that this will be worth the effort and give them time in class to write the different versions.

> *Directions to Students:* Write three versions of your essay or short story. Play around with your composing options by mixing and matching different sections from the alternative versions. Then choose the best intro, best central moment, and best conclusion. Incorporate the other chunks of your draft as you see fit.

A variation of this is to have students just write three different introductions for a composition (give them about 45 minutes to do this). Then have students label each intro as "good," "better," or "best."

Making Choices About Language: Good, Better, Best Revisited

One of my students was struggling to find the best word while writing a paper on Arundhati Roy's novel *The God of Small Things*. Gina wanted a word to describe the small details Roy allows to fill the narrative during accounts of trauma, like when the little girl Sophie Mol drowns in a river and Roy focuses on a baby bat at Sophie's funeral. The word Gina chose to describe this effect was "fluff." "Fluff" was a good word to represent what Roy was doing, but I thought Gina could find an even better word. So I circled the word "fluff" on Gina's draft during our writing conference and wrote, "What are your other word choices?" She and I then spun out an array of additional options: trivial, mundane, humble, unassuming, everyday, ordinary, insignificant, simple, little. Gina ultimately landed on the phrase "the simple things" which ended up playing an important conceptual role in her argument. Finding the best words to describe a particular moment or effect is an exercise in critical analysis that can help students take their writing to the next level.

The activities in this next section help students evaluate their options for meaning making.

CHOICE POEMS

Poet and writing teacher Natalie Goldberg offers a helpful tip to writers who find themselves struggling for the right word: "Don't cross out" (2016, 8). Instead of forcing yourself to make a choice while you're still drafting, Goldberg recommends writing down all your options at this stage and then going back and choosing the best word later, after you have a better sense of the writing as a whole. This sage advice has kept me from getting bogged down during the composing process countless times, for which I am deeply thankful. But Goldberg has also earned my gratitude as a teacher because her writing tip makes visible a fact of composition my students don't always see clearly—that writers have choices. A big part of our work as writers is to spin out the full array of our meaning-making options and then select the best words, sentences, content, style, and arrangement based on our genre, audience, and purpose. Reading and writing rhetorically means we take these options seriously; we understand that a single choice can have a profound impact on our meaning.

To help make this point, I share the poem "The Girlfriends" by Diana Garcia (2000). Because of its sexual content, I'd recommend using this poem with older students. Garcia's poem is particularly powerful because it exemplifies the power of a writer's meaning-making options in action, and it is explicitly a poem about how the choices we make shape our personal stories. I then ask students to write their own "Choice Poem" following Garcia's model.

"The Girlfriends" by Diana Garcia

Rosie/I
got pregnant.
Her/my
lover swore it wasn't
his/their
fault. It was
cinco de mayo/16 de septiembre
and I/we/she/he/they
broke loose.

Loose hips whipping
through cumbias
ankling through rancheras
hips grinding
through night-long sets
of lovemaking, the intensity
of a rolling tent revival.
Rosie/I had a
miscarriage/baby
Rosie/I thought
I/she
was lucky.

Directions to Students: Write a "Choice Poem" showing some of the meaning-making options you have as a writer. Indicate your selection of word choices by dividing the options with a forward slash (/), as in the following example:

> "and I/we/she/he/they
> broke loose."

Consider options that change the meaning of your poem significantly—for instance, a choice between words with positive and negative connotations or a choice between prepositions or pronouns that alter the point of view. You may write your "Choice Poem" on any topic you like. Poems should be twenty lines or longer and include at least five lines containing a set of language choices.

It will be up to your reader to construct various interpretations of your poem based on the options you provide. Think of this as a choose-your-own-meaning poem!

My students have responded brilliantly to this task. See the samples that follow.

"Sunshine"

I feel loved/silenced.

My parents were always/never around.

I am happy/alone.

I read stories about people like me

feeling strong/oppressed.

These stories reflect the feelings in my soul.

I feel affirmed/broken.

What can I do in this world?

I am at a crossroads of happiness/uncertainty.

Which way do I go? I need a sign!

My best friend is getting married/divorced.

My sister just started college/got fired.

My husband loves/hates his career.

I am just graduating/can't afford school.

I feel proud/ashamed of my life.

What do I do now?

I have so many/no choices.

I must look up—to the sunshine.

The sunshine will lead me to where I need to go.

Sunshine can't be bad, can it?

Sunshine, lead me to happiness/light/love/freedom.

"Choice Poem"

I/He/The child

cried at the sky

a wail as

pronounced/quiet

as the stars themselves

in the

black/illuminated/desolate

sea above.

Liberated/Lonely

from the brief respite,

that death brought.

My/his/its

heart

opened/closed/fragmented/beating

for fear of the unknown.

I/He/The child,

weary/broken/resolute

for the journey ahead.

I/He/The Child

prays/wishes/dreams

for/of

forgiveness, despite

opportunity/tragedy

bestowed.

Students who have written choice poems can transfer their heightened awareness of a writer's options to their revision work. A student searching for the right word to describe those special details in *The God of Small Things*, for instance, might write "fluff/trivial/little/small" in their draft and wait to make their final selection until after they've had time to consider the implications of each option.

Making Choices About What to Keep and What to Cut

Students need help developing conditional knowledge of what to omit during revision. I've never forgotten an anecdote George Burns tells about his wife, Gracie Allen, in his loving memoir of their life together. Always the picture of perfect taste, the impeccably dressed Gracie apparently made it a rule to always remove one small item—a pin or scarf—before leaving the house, so she would never be over-accessorized. This seems to me like a good approach to writing, as well. Sometimes we need to take something off our reader's plate, so that the special moments we've created can shine. A section revealed by descriptive outlining as doing less important work for the writer might be a good accessory to leave at home. Or those leftover headings from List, Group, Label that didn't fit anywhere: These are good candidates for omission. Effective writing balances concision with complexity.

FINDING QUOTE-WORTHY MATERIAL

To help students see what to keep and what to cut, I ask them to identify "quote-worthy" material—those sound bites they'd want to see quoted. These moments are definite keepers.

Directions to Students:

STEP ONE: Imagine your essay is being published in a magazine or scholarly journal. The editor has asked you, the writer, to highlight key phrases or sentences that best capture the spirit of your piece. These should be your best bits, the "sound bites" you'd want quoted by your readers. Look for your most elegant and insightful language. See if you have any especially short and powerful sentences that you'd like readers to notice and remember. What you choose to highlight, the editor tells you, will be featured in bold window quotes when your essay is published. These phrases or sentences will also be used on the publication's website to entice readers to read your essay.

STEP TWO: Debrief with a partner, reflecting on what you noticed. Use the following questions to guide your conversation:

Where did you find your best bits? Were any of your most quote-worthy sentences or phrases topic sentences? Were any concluding sentences? Was it a challenge to find those special moments in your essay? Could you revise your essay to include a few concise and compelling sound bites?

Highlighting quote-worthy lines can also reveal dead zones—passages of an essay without quote-worthy material. These are probably the same sections a writer would want to leave out of an oral presentation. If your students notice dead zones, ask them if there's anything they can do to add some pith to these problem areas (for instance, telling a story) or if they'd be better off leaving these out.

THE READ-ALOUD TEST: LOVE IT OR LEAVE IT

Ralph Waldo Emerson writes ([1841]1883), "When skating over thin ice, our safety is in our speed." I've skated over plenty of thin ice in my writing over the years, but I'm learning that if I feel I'm on shaky ground, my audience probably does, too. Plagued with a deadline, I submit what I have and hope for the best. *Maybe nobody will notice this section is weaker than the rest of my paper*, I rationalize. But I find that when I present at conferences, I skip over the weakest parts of my writing anyway. Now I tell students, "If you don't want to read those sentences again, chances are nobody else does either."

Reading their work aloud can cue students to the sections a reader may want to skip. Do they get bogged down in a long block quote? Or stumble through a convoluted explanation? I advise students to omit the stuff readers tend to skip. By the way, I tremble at the way I'm opening myself up here to readers' justifiable accusations that I haven't followed my own advice ("But you've left lots of stuff in this book that I skipped right over!").

CUTTING ROOM FLOOR

If you write as slowly as I do, it can be painful to have to trim a paragraph of writing that took you an hour or more to compose. That's why for each of my writing projects, I create a file called my "cutting room floor" in which I paste deleted material. It takes the sting out of cutting words that I otherwise might not have the heart to delete. I can tell myself, "At least I still have those sentences. Maybe I can use them for something else." This practice helps me be more discriminating during revision while avoiding the "Penelope syndrome" of recklessly undoing a day's labor because none of it is good enough.

Saving my scraps gives me more material to work with should I need to rethink my rethinking. Consider these words of wisdom from a famous teacher:

> I find that often students who struggle with an assignment are inclined
> to abandon the struggle and begin again. This practice unnerves me,
> because it's like playing roulette with one's work. What assurance does
> one have that the next spin of the wheel will be successful? Important
> learning occurs when a struggle is examined and analyzed, diagnosed, and
> a prescription offered. Ergo, make it work. (2007, 16)

Sounds like one of your favorite writing instructors, right? Maybe Peter Elbow or Kelly Gallagher? Nope. It's Tim Gunn, of *Project Runway* fame, and he's talking about clothing design, not writing, but his observations apply to all acts of composing. We make it work by working the process.

The Sweat Behind the Sparkle

No matter how big the mess they've made, students need reassurance that they can clean it up. There's no place for flat-out rejection in a teaching for transfer approach; all writing should be treated as "revise and resubmit" because all writing is an opportunity for students to develop persistence, flexibility, and problem-solving skills. In moments of difficulty, students need to trust their ability to work the problem.

Our students could learn a lot about the role of hard work in the revision process from Christopher Lehman, an artist and illustrator whose whimsical images have appeared in *The New Yorker*. In an interview for NPR, Lehman described the sweat behind the sparkle ("How Does Christopher Lehman Make Art Look Effortless? With a Lot of Work"; Oct. 31, 2016):

> The bolt of inspiration is what the reader is supposed to feel when they look at the drawing. What creates that moment is 100 very boring, unsexy steps—you know, move the line a little further to the left; draw a dog instead of a cat; . . . draw a chair instead of a table.

Lehman rejects the notion of raw talent producing art. Instead, he says, it's effort, time, and "friction" that ultimately create a finished work of art. "It's all about sitting down and the time you spend at your desk," Lehman says.

I remember the day I proudly shared my draft of the final chapter of my dissertation with my advisor and asked what I needed to do to wrap things up. Expecting a quick punch list before I could put the project to bed, I was instead taken aback when my advisor looked at me wryly and said, "I don't think you're as far along as you think you are." He was so right.

Revision can take longer—and be more painful—than drafting. The payoff is in our growth as writers.

> Encouraging students to resubmit revised work supports their growth as writers and rhetorical thinkers.

Reflecting on Learning

Reflection strengthens our faith in our ability to improve. When we teach for transfer, the practice of reflecting on learning holds a special place in our classrooms. Like research, revision is a process of trial and error. Failure is a powerful teacher, but it takes a reflective mindset to bounce back from our mistakes. Metacognitive prompts like those below call attention to the empowering choices students have as learners and communicators. Invite students to respond to a few of these prompts in a pairs conversation, quick-write, blog, or voice memo before submitting their work.

- What language choices did you make? What organizational choices did you make? Why?
- What other organizational options did you consider?
- What worked? What didn't? What might you do differently next time?
- What kind of feedback did you receive?
- How effectively do you think you accomplished your purpose? Did you reach your target audience?
- How did you deal with any difficulties or obstacles you encountered?
- What's the most important thing you learned?
- What questions do you still have?

These kinds of reflective questions remind students that they have control over process and product.

Ultimately, we know our students have developed transferrable skills and knowledge for revising their work when they can articulate their own theory of revision. What principles or beliefs about effective writing guide their decision-making process? How do they know what to revise when? How do they know whether a revision decision makes their writing better? Students who can answer these questions have the deep and enduring learning that will help them adapt to the literacy tasks of tomorrow.

Conclusion: Caring Enough to Get It Right

Future-ready students understand that writing is a way of doing real work in the world. Beyond the realm of grades and credits, the test of writing's effectiveness is whether or not it "works" in a given situation. Teaching students to write and revise rhetorically empowers them to make choices based on conditional knowledge, deciding for themselves what to say when and measuring the success of their writing "by the degree to which it accomplishes worthy social aims" (Crosswhite 1996, 3). All students deserve to have their words and ideas taken seriously. And all students can express themselves in language that is intellectually and aesthetically compelling.

One final thought: Think about how much harder you try to "get it right" when you're writing from the heart. Nothing drives us to revise more carefully than genuinely caring about our message, purpose, and audience. In *After the End: Teaching and Learning Creative Revision*, the wonderful Barry Lane says that good argument writing "begins in the gut" (2016, 158). This is the thought I want to leave you with for now. I'll meet you in the book's conclusion to explain more.

Conclusion: *A Few Final Words . . .*

One thing I want to keep doing is writing about myself because there is just so much to tell.

—EXCERPT FROM A STUDENT REFLECTION

Throughout this book, I've repeatedly stressed the importance of teaching writing for transfer and agency. I've argued that rhetorical thinking is the key to transfer because it prepares students to independently adapt and apply their literacy learning in new situations. But once again I need to be honest here: You don't have to teach this way. Students can pass high-stakes tests using formulas. They can graduate from high school as dependent learners. I've never heard of a teacher receiving a negative performance evaluation for prescriptivism or bounded framing. And, frankly, many students will thank you for giving them a list of rules, paragraph templates, and step-by-step instructions so that they know exactly what to do to earn an A.

But if you're concerned about your students' life after school, then transfer matters. And if you're concerned about the quality of public discourse, the well-being of our communities, and our collective capacity for problem solving, then teaching for transfer—with its attention to the mindsets and principles cultivated by our approach—matters.

This approach demands more of teachers and students. I wouldn't spend this much time writing about how to move students beyond their surface understandings or their dependence on scaffolds if these were things that just naturally happened. But we don't get to depth, complexity, and independence without productive struggle. And it's hard to sustain a struggle without support. So I keep pursuing a goal that I must admit sometimes feels pretty aspirational. My students aren't always OK with the extra space I give them to do their own thinking. Sometimes that long view of learning I ask them to keep their eye on just seems too far down the road. There are days when they just want to earn their points and not think about underlying principles and future applications.

Yet other times that long view is exactly the perspective we need to infuse our work with a sense of passion and purpose. And the more that students see their education as preparation for the kind of contributions they want to make, the less perfunctory and compliant their academic work becomes. Students stop "doing school" and start learning for transfer.

I want to offer this reassurance too: Students will experience less frustration in the long run if they don't have to undergo the radical reorientation toward rhetorical thinking required by college and workplace literacy tasks. The hard work we put in now to transform how our students think about written communication will produce numerous future benefits. Students who are confident rhetorical problem solvers can go into any situation knowing they have the knowledge needed to figure out how to effectively communicate in that context.

Our students deserve writing instruction that develops the practices and dispositions that lead to informed, effective, and ethical responses to twenty-first-century problems. And we all deserve a world where writing and reading start with genuinely caring about what people have to say.

So I'd like to go back to Barry Lane for the final words:

> We as teachers . . . can empower writers, or we can force them into compliance. We can invite them to write for authentic audiences and purposes, or we can make them play the game of school. We can, in short, raise their voices or stifle them. (2016, 272)

By teaching writing rhetorically, we empower students to raise their own voices and make their own choices as writers and learners.

Appendix Contents

Providing Expansive Framing

Additional Aspects of Learning That Can Be Framed

	SETTING	PLACES	PARTICIPANTS	TIME
Expansive Framing	Ask student to specify other settings in which the topic(s) have, are, or will be likely to come up in their lives.	Refer to other places—their home, school, doctor's office, etc.—in which they can use what they're learning.	Treat learning as involving the whole class, the school, the discourse community, plus the students' families, friends, teachers, and anyone else connected to the learning.	Use present progressive verbs ("you're figuring out"). Refer to other times, both inside and outside of the lesson.
Bounded Framing	Do not ask student to specify other settings in which the topic has, is, or will be likely to come up in their lives.	Do not make references to other places outside of the room.	Treat learning as involving only the students and teacher in a particular class.	Use simple past with completion verbs ("we're finished with that now"). Make no references to times other than the lesson just completed.

Source: Adapted from "How Does Expansive Framing Promote Transfer?" by Randi A. Engle, Diane P. Lam, Xenia S. Meyer, and Sarah E. Nix (2012).

Practicing Rhetorical Problem Solving: Choosing a New Logo for an Animal Shelter

1. **The Scenario**

   Imagine you are part of a group of volunteers at an animal shelter that has been tasked with helping to choose a new logo for the shelter. The design company has already presented several options to the shelter's executive director, and now she wants your group to recommend the design that best capture's the shelter's image.

   You must submit your written recommendation to the executive director via email.

2. **The Request**

   Dear Volunteer,

   We need your help! We've been working with a designer to create a new logo for the Animal Friends Rescue Shelter. We've enjoyed a positive image in our community for many years and feel confident that our "brand" is strong. The animals in our care are adopted quickly, we receive generous support from donors, and our number of volunteers continues to grow—although we'd like to see even more young people get involved.

   Our current logo, however, does not match our brand or how the community feels about us. When the logo was created forty years ago, we were a very different organization. The logo we have now is outdated and confusing. We need a logo that represents who we are now and that works with today's technologies, including an app we're developing for the shelter. The new logo will also appear on volunteers' uniforms and in advertisements for pet adoptions.

   To help us in selecting the new design, we've identified three key ideas we want the logo to convey: safety, compassion, and dependability. Please keep these words in mind as you review the options. Discuss the different designs as a group, and please submit your recommendation to me via email.

   Thank you for all you do for the animals!

   Sincerely,

   Mataya Whitfield

   Executive Director

   Animal Friends Rescue Shelter

3. **The Specifics**

   The new logo will be used for all of the following:

   - The app for the animal shelter

   - Volunteers' uniforms

   - Brand merchandise (mugs, pens, T-shirts, etc.)

   - The shelter's website

   - Advertisements for pet adoptions

   - Volunteer recruiting efforts

4. **The Audience**

What you need to know:

- The executive director of the animal shelter thinks the current logo is confusing and outdated.
- The shelter can only accept cats, dogs, rabbits, and other small household pets. The executive director doesn't like having to turn away people who bring in wild animals or exotic pets.
- The executive director would like to recruit more young people as volunteers.

5. **Considering Your Task and Your Rhetorical Situation**

- What does the organization want the logo to do?
- What content or message does the logo need to present?
- What are the audience's needs?
- What are the genre features of a business email?
- What makes a recommendation persuasive?

6. **Your Role in the Rhetorical Situation**

Remember that as a volunteer, you will be wearing the new logo on your uniform. Consider how your role as a volunteer might shape your letter to the executive director of the animal shelter.

7. **The Designs: Choose One**

8. **The Recommendation**

In your group, write an email to the executive director recommending the logo design you think best captures the animal shelter's brand and that works best for the shelter's purposes. Keep in mind how the logo will be used by the shelter and the messages the executive director wishes to convey. Support your recommendation with reasons and examples. As you compose your email to the executive director, carefully consider your audience, purpose, and genre.

Appendix C

Collaborative Rhetorical Problem Solving

Working together on rhetorical problems builds community and communication skills. This activity invites students to respond to a scenario in small groups. In addition to the description of the scenario, groups will also need a large index card for this activity.

Scenario

Directions to Students: Imagine you are college students who have just been awarded scholarships to study abroad for a year in a country of your choice. How exciting! This is your dream come true. But there's a catch: the scholarships require that you find a professor at the host institution who agrees to be your mentor. You'll have to contact potential mentors on your own, without any help from the scholarship organization. Oh, and this will be a cold contact. You'll be writing to people you've never met and who have never heard of the scholarship you've just won.

Your task is to draft an email introducing yourself, explaining the award, and asking the professor to consider being your mentor. In your group, help each other brainstorm possible ways to respond to this rhetorical situation.

STEP ONE: Analyze the rhetorical situation as a group. What's the rhetorical problem? What are your audience, purpose, occasion, and genre? What resources could help with this task? What research, if any, do you need to do? What constraints do you face? What are the risks and benefits of sending an email (versus a direct message or making a phone call)?

STEP TWO: As a group, work together to draft the opening line of this email. Write this sentence on the index card provided. Keep in mind you're writing to a busy person who receives lots of emails. Include a subject line that will motivate this person to open and read your email.

STEP THREE: On the back of your index card, explain what you had to do to write this opening line. What was your thinking and composing process? Why did you choose that subject line?

STEP FOUR: Choose a spokesperson from your group to share your opening sentence, subject line, and thought process with the class.

You can conclude this activity by inviting spokespeople to share their opening lines and their process for composing them.

Appendix D

Planning Tool for Taking Rhetorical Action

1. What's the need or problem? (exigence)	**2.** What do you want to know about it? (question)
3. What do you want to do about it? (purpose)	**4.** Why is now the right time to act? (*kairos*)

Appendix E

Planning Tool for Socratic Seminar

What's the need or problem?	What do you want to know about it?
(exigence)	(questions)
What have others already done to address this need or problem?	What do the people involved care about?
(reading selections)	(pathos)

Appendix F

Checklist for Listening to a Socratic Seminar

This checklist works for the inner/outer circles model of a Socratic seminar. Students in the outer circle use the checklist to record the communication practices and habits of mind they observe among the discussion participants in the inner circle.

Directions to Students in the Outer Circle: As you listen to the Socratic seminar, keep track of what students do during the discussion. Place a check mark by the communication practices and habits of mind you observe. Consider the extent to which each one can help you make informed and responsive contributions to academic conversations.

___ Assume the best intentions

___ Postpone judgment

___ Ask questions that move the conversation forward

___ Build on others' ideas

___ Identify needs and opportunities

___ Make connections to the readings

___ Explain the urgency of an issue

___ Explore the context

___ Paraphrase or summarize others' viewpoints

___ Listen empathically

___ Consider the evidence

___ Respond to the cares and concerns of others

___ Demonstrate curiosity

___ Clarify definitions

___ Find common ground

___ Offer a personal response

___ Bring assumptions into the open

___ Be open to new ideas

___ Promote equality and inclusion

___ Allow time for others to respond

Appendix G

Essay: Writing a Reading-Based Argument Prompt

Read the passage carefully. For many years now, writing prompts in ELA classes across the country have opened with this key direction. Gone are the days when a typical essay assignment asked students to respond to a topic rather than engage with a text. The writing tasks students are most likely to encounter today acknowledge that the ability to read critically and closely is at least as important as the ability to write clean academic prose.

But creating a successful reading-based writing prompt isn't easy. What kinds of texts should we use for the reading passage? How long should the passage be? Should we choose an excerpt from a published work or write the passage ourselves? What directions should we give? The answers to these questions can vary depending on the purpose and format of the assessment—like whether the essay will be timed or a process piece, is part of a thematic unit or a stand-alone task, or will be used as a diagnostic or summative tool. Often, we want open-ended questions that allow students to conduct their own inquiry and choose their own conversation to join. But sometimes we need to convene the conversation ourselves, especially when we want to assess specific skills, like reading comprehension.

My friend and colleague Robby Ching, a consultant with the California State University's Chancellor's Office, developed the following guidelines to help teachers create reading-based prompts:

1. Find an engaging topic that relates to the experiences of all students.

2. Write a prompt that makes a debatable claim and offers evidence as support. For on-demand essays, limit the reading passage to 100–200 words. Try to start with an argument you've found in print and then modify it as needed. Blogs, letters to the editor, and op-ed pieces are good candidates for argument prompt writing. Acknowledge the original author if the passage is only slightly altered.

3. Evaluate the prompt and have colleagues evaluate it. Sometimes a prompt looks great on paper but utterly fails to generate the kind of thinking and writing we want our students to produce. The only way to know if a prompt is successful is to field test it.

Successful reading-based argument prompts stimulate analytic thought and engagement. They show what writers are capable of achieving when they genuinely care about an issue. The reading passages in these prompts make provocative claims that invite critique but cannot be easily dismissed. Some prompts do this by offering a reasonable description of a problem capped off by a modest proposal worthy of Jonathan Swift. Others might make compelling claims based on faulty assumptions. The trick in prompt writing is not to tip the scales too heavily in one direction.

The good prompts also don't script the response for students. An overly structured prompt—for example, one that has three major divisions or examples—can discourage students from generating their own content or inventing their own organizational structure. Students might think a five-paragraph essay is called for if they see three main points in the directions, thereby missing their opportunity to showcase their own creativity. We want prompts that give students different directions they can go.

It helps to offer students some tantalizing bait—in other words, an exigence, or sense of urgent need that motivates them to write. I've learned from books like Claude M. Steele's *Whistling Vivaldi* (2011) that I need to be mindful about the intensity of the exigencies I ask students to contend with, at least when it comes to high-stakes academic assessments. The right amount of mad helps us to do our best work; the wrong amount can cause us to choke. When I create writing tasks for students, I need to help them identify exigences that will showcase their best thinking.

The following prompt is one I wrote with these guidelines in mind. While authentic texts are best, a teacher-written passage addressing a current issue can be helpful for pinpointing specific competencies. Using this prompt as a diagnostic tool tells me what other kinds of preparation students might need. Often, it's additional help with summary and negotiating meaning, in which case, I might redouble our efforts with the believing game and dialogue.

Here's the prompt:

> Humans are hard at work trying to develop ever more sophisticated and serviceable forms of artificial intelligence. We already have voice-operated technology that can play our favorite music, turn off the lights, wash our clothes, lock our houses, tell us the forecast, order our groceries, and vacuum our floors. We even have "smart" toilets now that flush on command. Soon, we'll be able to order our cars around, too.
>
> But in our frantic quest to find new applications for artificial intelligence, have we considered what we're teaching our children about good manners and personal responsibility? Today's kids and their parents spend more and more time bossing their digital assistants around. There's no "please" or "thank you," just an imperious command: "Alexa, turn on the sprinklers!" What does this teach children about the idea of service? About polite communication? Self-reliance? Ordering a human-sounding device around opens a Pandora's box of social ills: entitlement, laziness, dependence, rudeness, ingratitude. "Smart" technology is anything but smart; it's creating a dangerous desire for human-like servants who don't have to be treated with human respect. For this reason, we should prohibit the use of artificial intelligence in household appliances.
>
> **—Hal Greenleaf**

Explain the argument that Greenleaf makes and discuss the extent to which you agree or disagree with his reasoning and conclusion. Remember that you are writing for an academic audience and setting.

The custom-made prompt allows me to see how students handle shifts in other writers' arguments. In this case, the passage leaps from a question of quality to a question of policy. Students who don't address the final policy recommendation in their response—with its complex implications (and dodgy reasoning)—haven't yet fully explained the writer's argument.

This is important data that will help me plan my next moves as a teacher.

I've learned from experience that prompts that relate to students' backgrounds and interests set students up for success. They allow students to draw on what they know—for example, technology, interpersonal communication, families, education—while also inviting them to consider new perspectives and nuances. When my students responded to this prompt as part of my start-of-the-semester diagnostic assessment, they came up with a variety of reasonable responses, a sign that the prompt was working well. Note the diversity of thinking in the following claims:

- "Technology has always been about reducing the need for manual labor, not increasing it. The digital age needs knowledge workers, not manual laborers."

- "It's not about the machines; it's about what humans learn from the way they use their machines."

- "People understand that a device like Alexa is no more human than the first cars were horses. A machine is not a living thing. It doesn't have feelings."

While the prompt admittedly does include three questions that could lead students to write a five-paragraph essay, this is a bit of a trap since the questions don't directly engage the final policy recommendation. For this, students have to develop their own approach.

Students who are newer to argumentation often substitute an easier task for a harder one—in this case, either just writing a "technology is bad/good" essay, or answering my questions about service, manners, and self-reliance. And that's what I'm looking for. I want to know what kind of help students need explaining the arguments of others, so that they are prepared to enter conversations in a responsive and responsible manner. Teacher-generated prompts are scaffolds on the road to independence. The ultimate goal is for students to be able to identify and respond to questions at issue in conversations that matter to them.

One of the benefits of argumentation, notes writing scholar Annette T. Rottentberg, is that it "teaches students to read and listen with more than ordinary care" (*The Structure of Argument* 1994, v). When we ask students to "read the passage carefully" in preparation for writing an argument essay, we are asking them to do more than just be sure they follow all the directions. We are asking them to read with an awareness of reasoning, evidence, context, and point of view; to understand not only what the text *says* but also what it *does*; to uncover and analyze a writer's assumptions; to evaluate a writer's conclusions—to read, in other words, with an *extraordinary* degree of care.

Sample Student Diagnostic Essay

Diagnostic Essay

In the paragraph we are given the author, Hal Greenleaf's perspective on "today's smart technology. In the passage he shows his audience how this "smart" technology isn't as smart as we think they are. His overall view on smart technology is that it shouldn't be further enhanced into our lives considering that it changes human kind.

Hal Greenleaf explains to us that our parents never had this type of technology and so the way they raised us would be different to the way we raise future generations. "There's no 'please' or 'thank you,' just an imperious command" significantly shows us that future generations would not have any respect to their peers if they aren't taught or aware that good manners develops to a good person full of respect. Even today's parents has taken a liking into the smart technology. "kids and their parents spend more and more time bossing their digital assistants" which shows us that not only ikids are affected but parents as well. This technology should give a helping hand not become a lifeless maid. At this point theres no respect or good manners with "Alexa turn on the sprinklers!".

The author also gives reason that smart technology is making us lazy. Having new technology be created gives human kind a better chance to get more lazy in even the most simplest task. "That can play our favorite song, turn off the lights, water our plants, lock our houses, tell us the forecast, order our food, and vacuum our floors" is all the task that is already taken over by smart technology; things we could've done ourselves. Society is creating these smart technology and making it possible for us to become lazy. Soon we won't have to do anything ourselves. Everything will soon have a robot doing our work. "We even have 'smart' toilets now that flush on command... Soon we'll be able to order our cars around too" which is showing that this society is trying to make profit and make us lazy as well. Soon we will become the characters in the movie Wall-E. In this that all we do is sit and become fat; never having to leave our spot even if it's to go outside.

I do strongly agree with the author because I see it myself as well. Where my sisters won't leave the room and spend all day on their technology. As to when I was a kid I wouldn't want to go inside being to happy being outdoors. My sisters never wanting to clean, while I'm out making sure even our yard is spotless. Not only my siblings though, this includes my parents. Spending all their time on their phones instead of going to the park to walk the dogs. My father hardly even pays attentions; always bumping into walls because he can't take his eyes off the phone.

Overall, Hal Greenleaf does make a very strong point in prohibitting the uses of artificial intelligence in household appliances because sooner or later we can see a new generation filled with an image of "rude, ingratitude, entitlement, laziness, and dependence."

Conversation Planning Notes

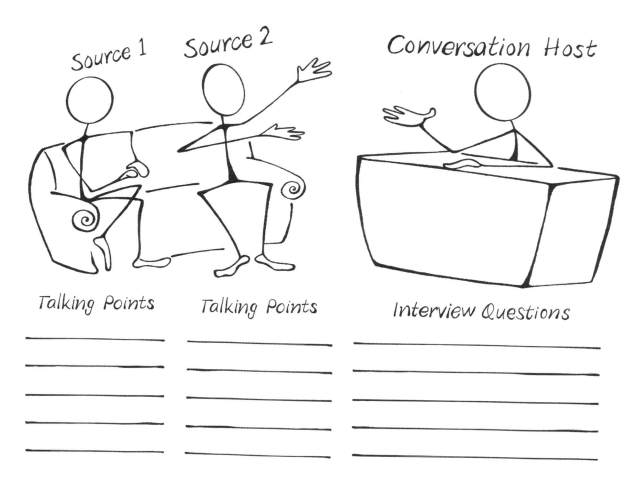

Source 1   Source 2   Conversation Host

Talking Points   Talking Points   Interview Questions

Appendix F

Charting Claims Across Multiple Texts

Adapted from the California State University's Expository Reading and Writing Curriculum.

Directions to Students: As you read about the issue, keep track of the claims different writers make and how these claims relate to the views of other writers. Annotate each text, noting the author, genre, main ideas, and key examples. Then use the chart below to compare the texts.

TITLE AND AUTHOR	GENRE	QUESTION AT ISSUE	KEY CLAIMS	EXAMPLES AND/OR QUOTATIONS

Appendix K

The Design Process

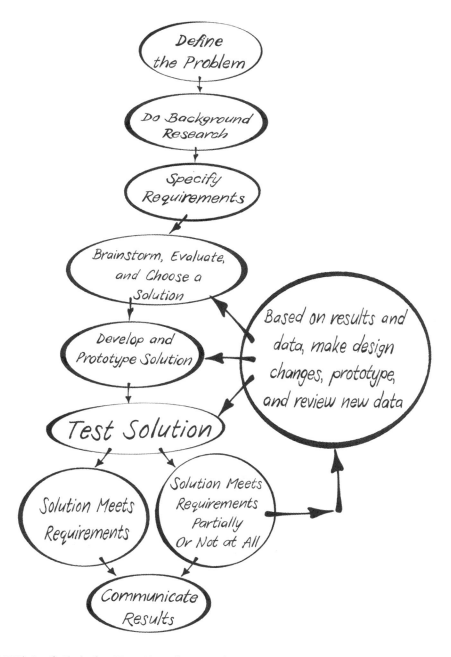

Appendix L

Four Square Reasoning

Data: What is your evidence?	**Claim:** What does the evidence suggest?
Warrant: Why do you think this? A key premise of this claim is _____ . This claim relies on the foundational assumption that _____ .	**Backing:** Where does this way of thinking come from?

Quick-write: How do you expect your audience to react to your claim? Will they accept it? Challenge it? Explain your response.

Claim Analysis and Evaluation

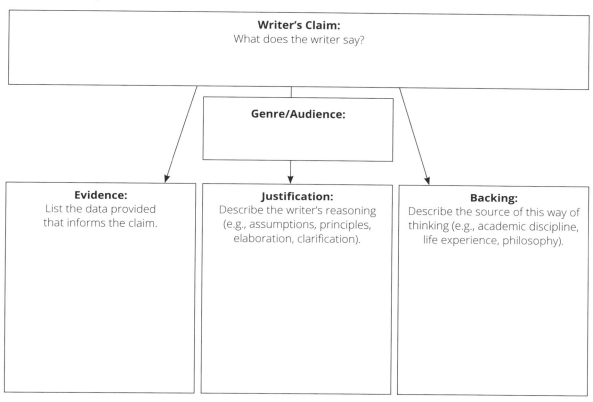

Writer's Claim:
What does the writer say?

Genre/Audience:

Evidence:
List the data provided that informs the claim.

Justification:
Describe the writer's reasoning (e.g., assumptions, principles, elaboration, clarification).

Backing:
Describe the source of this way of thinking (e.g., academic discipline, life experience, philosophy).

Degree of Certainty:
Rate the degree of "truth" or certainty the writer establishes for the claim on a scale of 1–5.

1	2	3	4	5
highly doubtful		possible		highly certain

Quick-write: How convincing is this claim? To what extent does the writer draw on reasonable and sufficient support for the claim? To what extent is the claim warranted or justified? Is the line of reasoning appropriate to the genre and audience? Explain.

What I Know I Really Know, What I Sort of Know, What I Know I Need to Know

Directions to Students: Use the three-column chart below to assess the degree of confidence you have in the argument you are making. Which claims do you strongly believe to be valid (what you really know)? Which claims are a little fuzzy or doubtful (what you sort of know)? What gaps do you see in your knowledge (what you need to know)? Consider views, sources, or perspectives you haven't yet engaged for this last column.

WHAT I KNOW I REALLY KNOW	WHAT I SORT OF KNOW	WHAT I KNOW I NEED TO KNOW

From *Writing Rhetorically*. Portsmouth, NH. Stenhouse. Adapted from *Making the Journey*, Second Edition. © 2000 by Leila Christenbury.

Claim and Backing T-Chart

Directions to Students: In the left column, write a claim from your essay draft. Then back up your claim in the right column, explaining how you know what you know. In other words, what life experience, academic training, or belief system informs your way of thinking?

CLAIM	I KNOW THIS BECAUSE . . .

Making Choices About Genre and Structure: Self-Assessment

Directions to Students: Some of the choices writers must make about form and style involve specific features of genre and text structure. Take a look at the following table and think about how often you get to make your own decisions about these options. Choose the frequency rate that best describes your experience.

Frequently = F   Sometimes = S   Rarely = R

GENRE CHOICES		STRUCTURE CHOICES	
Genre or form		Text structure (e.g., cause and effect, frame)	
Types of sentences		Beginnings/introductions	
Use or avoidance of figurative language		Inductive or deductive reasoning	
Formatting conventions		Transitions	
Documentation style (if required)		Twists or shifts	
Types of evidence/examples		Use or avoidance of narrative	
Medium		Endings/conclusions	
Level of diction		Repetition	
Other stylistic devices		Organization	

Making Decisions About Audience and Genre

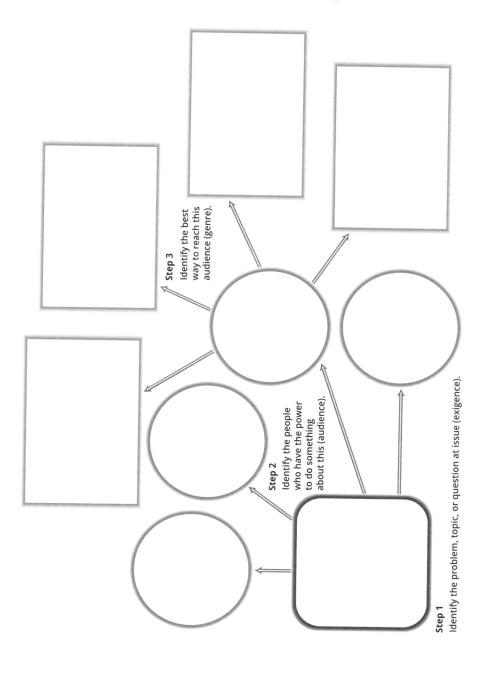

Step 3
Identify the best way to reach this audience (genre).

Step 2
Identify the people who have the power to do something about this (audience).

Step 1
Identify the problem, topic, or question at issue (exigence).

Appendix R

Genre Analysis

Genre Name: _____

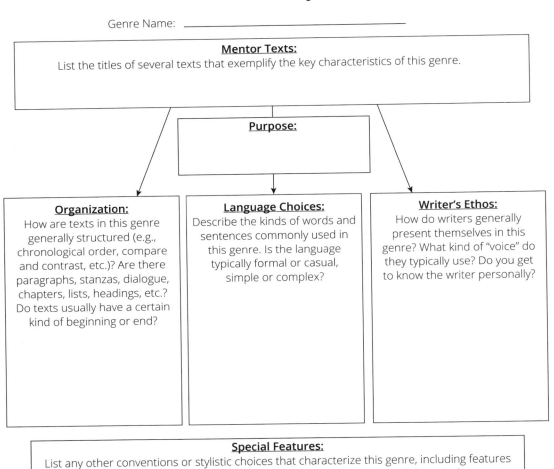

Mentor Texts:
List the titles of several texts that exemplify the key characteristics of this genre.

Purpose:

Organization:
How are texts in this genre generally structured (e.g., chronological order, compare and contrast, etc.)? Are there paragraphs, stanzas, dialogue, chapters, lists, headings, etc.? Do texts usually have a certain kind of beginning or end?

Language Choices:
Describe the kinds of words and sentences commonly used in this genre. Is the language typically formal or casual, simple or complex?

Writer's Ethos:
How do writers generally present themselves in this genre? What kind of "voice" do they typically use? Do you get to know the writer personally?

Special Features:
List any other conventions or stylistic choices that characterize this genre, including features like documentation style (e.g., MLA), figurative language, pictures, and rhetorical moves.

Context and Audience: In what situations is this type of writing typically used? Who typically reads this genre?

Genre Analysis

Genre Name: <u>Informative</u>

Mentor Texts:
List the titles of several texts that exemplify the key characteristics of this genre.

~~B Impressive~~ Pro Elkay EZ H2O

Purpose:

To describe the features of a product

Organization:
How are texts in this genre generally structured (e.g., chronological order, compare and contrast, etc.)? Are there paragraphs, stanzas, dialogue, chapters, lists, headings, etc.? Do texts usually have a certain kind of beginning or end?

- small paragraphs
- descriptive
- headings
- ~~compare an~~

Language Choices:
Describe the kinds of words and sentences commonly used in this genre. Is the language typically formal or casual, simple or complex?

- simple language
"ambient", "arise", "enhancements"

Writer's Ethos:
How do writers generally present themselves in this genre? What kind of "voice" do they typically use? Do you get to know the writer personally?

since writing is just to describe a product, you are not able to get to know the writer

Special Features:
List any other conventions or stylistic choices that characterize this genre, including features like documentation style (e.g., MLA), figurative language, pictures, and rhetorical moves.

Bullet points used to list features of product. Pictures are also included for readers to see how it actually looks

Context and Audience: In what situations is this type of writing typically used? Who typically reads this genre?
- used for ~~sales~~ selling/brochures
- Readers are interested customers

Appendix T

Adapted from *Reading Rhetorically* by John C. Bean, Virgina A. Chappell, and Alice M. Gillam.

Descriptive Outlining

Paragraph[s]:

Says:

Does:

Paragraph[s]:

Says:

Does:

Paragraph[s]:

Says:

Does:

Paragraph[s]:

Says:

Does:

Paragraph[s]:

Says:

Does:

Paragraph[s]:

Says:

Does:

Paragraph[s]:

Says:

Does:

Paragraph[s]:

Says:

Does:

Main Argument:

Appendix U

Rubric for Assessing Rhetorical Decision Making

Adapted from the California State University's Expository Reading and Writing Curriculum.

6   A "6" response demonstrates exceptional achievement. It develops a sophisticated line of reasoning appropriate to the genre and context using inquiry-based argumentation. Evidence is significant and credible. The writer's choices are strategic and impactful, effectively and compellingly conveying the writer's message to the intended audience. An exceptional response attends to audience needs, interests, and expectations and communicates its central ideas to the audience through an engaging and appropriate form and style. It also demonstrates mature control over language choices and a sophisticated understanding of the issue. Design choices (including use of genre features) expertly focus the audience's attention on key claims or messages. The text(s) produced make(s) a meaningful contribution to the conversation by offering new or deeper understandings of the issue and/or by promoting significant responses to the issue.

5   A "5" response demonstrates commendable achievement. It grounds its claims in evidence and develops a line of reasoning appropriate to the genre and context using inquiry-based argumentation. The writer's choices are skillful and informed, effectively conveying the writer's message to the intended audience. While a commendable response attends to audience needs, interests, and expectations, it may be less responsive and nuanced than a "6" response. It nevertheless still communicates its central ideas to the audience through an appropriate form and style. The response also demonstrates control over language choices and a strong understanding of the issue. Design choices focus the audience's attention on key claims or messages. The text(s) produced contribute(s) to the conversation by offering new or deeper understandings of the issue and/or by promoting productive responses to the issue.

4   A "4" response demonstrates adequate achievement. It uses evidence to develop an inquiry-based argument appropriate to the genre and context. The writer's choices are generally appropriate for the audience and purpose. This response may show less attention to or awareness of audience needs, interests, and expectations. It communicates its ideas to the audience through a generally appropriate form and style, although it may occasionally lapse into rhetorical choices not suited to the rhetorical situation. It also demonstrates adequate control over language choices and an adequate (or occasionally superficial) understanding of the issue. Design choices may not consistently help focus the audience's attention on key claims or messages. The text(s) produced join(s) the conversation by offering additional information or understandings and/or by calling for an appropriate response to the issue.

3   A "3" response demonstrates limited achievement. The writer may have neglected to respond to important aspects of the task. While the response may include some evidence, the evidence may not be clearly connected to the writer's claims. Evidence may also be insufficient and/or inappropriate to the genre and audience. The central message may also be unclear or underdeveloped. The audience's cares and concerns may receive only minimal attention. The writing may demonstrate occasional lack of control over language choices.

2   A "2" response represents an inadequate response to the task. In addition to not meeting all requirements, this response may also demonstrate a clear disregard for the rhetorical situation. It may neglect to target an intended audience or identify a clear purpose. The message may be unfocused and confusing, and claims may be unsupported and unconvincing. Choices about genre may likewise show little to no consideration for the rhetorical situation. The writing may demonstrate consistent lack of control over language choices.

1   A "1" response shows little to no evidence of achievement. It compounds the issues represented by a score of "2" through a response to the task that is notably incomplete and/or inappropriate.

Appendix V

DIY Submission Checklist

Directions to Students: After studying a collection of mentor texts in the genre you'll be writing in, create your own submission checklist for your composition. This kind of DIY style guide is a good way to make sure you are responding to the demands of a rhetorical situation. See the sample submission checklist from the *Journal of Adolescent and Adult Literacy* (JAAL) below.

JAAL Submission Checklist

Abstract and Keywords: Please re-visit stages 1 and 2 of your submission information in the system. In stage 1, verify that your Abstract is up to date. In stage 2, verify that you have selected Extended Keywords to help make your paper more searchable on the ILA website (www.reading.org) and Wiley Online Library.

Sidebars: Does your Article include the three Required Sidebars?

- Teaser Text
- Take Action!
- More to Explore

Sidebars are only required for Articles, not Departments, Reviews, Commentaries, or Literacy Lenses.

For more information on Sidebars, please visit JAAL's Author Guidelines: http://onlinelibrary.wiley .com/journal/10.1002/%28ISSN%291936-2706/homepage/ForAuthors.html

Short Paragraphs: Please look for opportunities to shorten paragraphs for better readability in the journal's multicolumn format. Extremely short paragraphs of just a few sentences are fine and are in fact preferred—keep in mind that a paragraph that runs 3 or 4 lines long in a Word document will run 8 or 10 lines long in the journal layout!

Organizational and Visual Appeal: Make every effort to include subheadings (up to 3 levels of subheads can be accommodated in RT), bulleted and numbered lists, figures and tables, or other visual elements in the text to increase readability and visual interest.

References: Ensure that your references are correct and complete and that they adhere to the **APA 6th edition** reference structures. **NOTE: References will not be fact checked in copy editing; it is the author's responsibility to verify the accuracy of all references and their corresponding citations.**

Ensure that references include complete author initials with no space between initials, ampersand for multiauthored works, year, full titles of books including edition/volume, page numbers for book chapters, month for presentations, volume and issue number for journal articles, etc. Ensure that authors for a single source are listed in correct order.

Literature titles should be pulled out into a separate reference list (e.g., Literature Cited). **NOTE: Literature that is mentioned but not actually cited does not need a parenthetical citation or inclusion in a reference list. Only if it matters which published edition of the book was used are parenthetical citations and reference entries needed.**

Figures and Tables: Tables should be embedded at the end of the manuscript text. Figures should be submitted as separate, original image files (e.g., jpg, pdf, tif, eps) with a resolution of 300 dpi or higher. Please do not embed images in a Word file, because that process degrades the quality of the image. We'll get the best print reproduction if we work with the original image file.

Supplementary Material: Authors are welcome to submit online-only supplementary material with their paper. Supplementary Material must be important, ancillary information that is relevant to the parent article but that does not or cannot appear in the printed edition of the journal (e.g., audio or video files). All Supplementary Material must be cited in the text.

See http://authorservices.wiley.com/bauthor/suppinfo.asp for more details.

Title Page: Please fill out and upload a Title Page for your article, using the below template.

Title

Authors

Author blurbs (one for each author):

[Author Name] is a/an [professional title] at [professional affiliation], [City, State, Country]; email [email address].

Submission Type: [Article, Department, Review, Commentary]

Permissions: Have all necessary permissions been secured and submitted to the editorial office with your files? If you are not sure something in your article needs permissions, please write to the editorial office and ask: jaaleditorial@wiley.com.

Making Choices About Focus: Foreground and Background

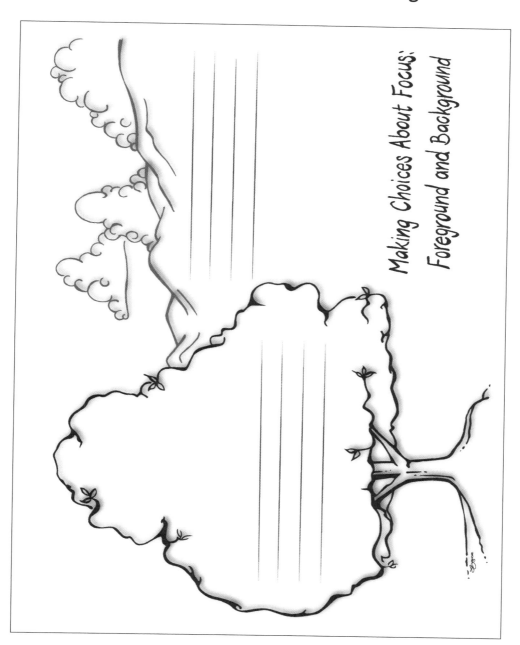

Appendix X

Questions for Fostering Rhetorical Thinking

Questions About Audience

Does your reader need this context?

Does your reader need an explanation of this term?

What does your reader need to know about this source?

Questions About Organization

What are your choices for transitions here?

What are your organizational choices for this section?

What are the focus and function of this section?

How do your organizational choices help your reader to follow your line of reasoning?

Questions About Claims and Evidence

Where do you see this?

What is the basis for this generalization?

How do you know?

Questions About Exigence

What's at stake?

Why is this issue timely and important?

Who cares about this issue? Why?

Questions About Process

What did you do?

How would you describe your writing process? How do you make choices as you write?

How do you know when to use a particular strategy?

How can you use this strategy in other areas of your life?

What did you learn? How did you learn it?

Writing Prompts on Nerd Identity: New Pride or Old Prejudice?

Directions: Respond to ONE of the prompts below in a well-developed, multiparagraph essay.

Question at Issue: Is "nerd" identity a source of pride or a target of prejudice? Or both?

Prompt 1:

Read the passage carefully. Then write an essay in which you explain the author's argument and discuss the ways in which you agree or disagree with her views. Support your position, providing reasons and examples from the sources you've read. You may also choose to include personal observations and experiences as appropriate. Organize your essay carefully.

In the 21st century, nerd is the word and geek is chic. Gone are the days when an interest in computers made kids different from their peers, when brainy students were left on the sidelines of athletic fields and school dances. Gone, too, are the days when a love of fantasy fiction meant social death. The new millennium has instead seen nerdiness achieve a place of unprecedented coolness. From Hollywood to Milan, from New York to Silicon Valley, nerd power is celebrated in a variety of industries and forms. Girl geeks wear $200 nerdy glasses from Dolce and Gabbana. Nerds of color rock comic book conventions. Children play with Computer Engineer Barbie. The "Geek Squad" are the heroes of home tech support. "Nerdcore hip hop" and "geeksta rap" are becoming mainstream music genres. The best-selling books of the century are about a glasses-wearing wizard who is best friends with a bookworm. Even President Obama was honored as "Nerd-in-Chief." After decades of social exclusion, smart kids of all ethnicities and genders can now enjoy equal popularity with jocks and cheerleaders. Antinerd prejudice—and its narrow definition of who's a nerd—is at last a thing of the past.

—Maria Jimenez

Prompt 2:

The following excerpt is adapted from *Nerds: How Dorks, Dweebs, Techies, and Trekkies Can Save America* (2011) by psychologist David Anderegg. Read the passage carefully. Then write an essay in which you explain the author's argument and discuss the ways in which you agree or disagree with his views. Support your position, providing reasons and examples from the sources you've read. You may also choose to include personal observations and experiences as appropriate. Organize your essay carefully.

[. . .] nerd and geek stereotypes persist when other stereotypes are fading. Adults do not condone racial stereotypes, and when kids use them, they usually run into a heap of trouble from the adults in charge. But adults allow, and give voice to, antinerd prejudices all the time. It is simply amazing to encounter the number of adults who reify this stereotype in front of their kids by deriding their schoolmates as nerds and geeks. It is a completely acceptable stereotype in most social circles. Even people who bear all the visible stigmas of nerdiness will go out of their way to assert that they are "really" not nerds rather than to assert that "nerd" is not a useful or socially acceptable way to talk about people. This systematic disparagement of "nerds" in our culture is bad for our children and even worse for our country. In order to prepare rising generations to compete in the global marketplace, we need to rethink how we think about "nerds."

—**adapted from David Anderegg**

References

Adler-Kassner, Linda, and Elizabeth Wardle, eds. 2015. *Naming What We Know: Threshold Concepts of Writing Studies*. Boulder: University Press of Colorado.

Allen, Janet. *Words, Words, Words*. 1999. Portsmouth, NH: Stenhouse.

Anderegg, David. 2011. *Nerds: How Dorks, Dweebs, Techies, and Trekkies Can Save America and Why They Might Be Our Last Hope*. London: Penguin Books.

Anderson, Jeff, and Deborah Dean. 2014. *Revision Decisions: Talking Through Sentences and Beyond*. Portsmouth, NH: Stenhouse.

Andrews, Larry. 2006. *Language Exploration and Awareness: A Resource Book for Teachers*. 3rd ed. Mahwah, NJ: Lawrence Erlbaum Associates.

Applebee, Arthur N., and Judith A. Langer. 2013. *Writing Instruction That Works: Proven Methods for Middle and High School Classrooms*. Berkeley, CA: National Writing Project; New York: Teachers College Press.

Aristotle. *Rhetoric*. 1984. Translated by W. Rhys Roberts. New York: McGraw-Hill.

Association of American Colleges and Universities. 2009. "Integrative and Applied Learning VALUE Rubric." https://www.aacu.org/value/rubrics/integrative-learning.

Bakken, Gordon Morris, and Brenda Farrington. 1999. *Learning California History: Essential Skills for the Survey Course and Beyond*. Wheeling, IL: Harlan Davidson.

Bazerman, Charles. 1995. *The Informed Writer: Using Sources in the Disciplines*. 5th ed. Boston: Houghton Mifflin.

———. 2013. *A Rhetoric of Literate Action: Literate Action Volume 1*. The WAC Clearinghouse; Parlor Press. https://doi.org/10.37514/PER-B.2013.0513.

Bean, John C. 2001. *Engaging Ideas: The Professor's Guide to Integrating Writing, Critical Thinking, and Active Learning in the Classroom*. San Francisco: Jossey-Bass.

Bean, J. C., Chappell, V. A., and Gillam, A. M. 2014. *Reading Rhetorically*. 4th ed. Upper Saddle River, NJ: Pearson.

Beaufort, Anne. 1999. *Writing in the Real World: Making the Transition from School to Work*. New York: Teachers College Press.

———. 2007. *College Writing and Beyond*. Logan, Utah: Utah State University Press.

Benner, Patricia. 1982. "From Novice to Expert." *American Journal of Nursing* 82(3): 402–407. www.jstor.org/stable/3462928.

Best of Enemies. 2015. Directed by Robert Gordon and Morgan Neville.

Bitzer, Lloyd F. (1968) 1999. "The Rhetorical Situation." In *Contemporary Rhetorical Theory: A Reader*, ed. John Louis Lucaites, Celeste Michelle Condit, and Sally Caudill. New York: Guilford.

Blau, Sheridan. "The Problem and Promise of Close Reading." National Council of Teachers of English (NCTE) Annual Convention. November 17, 2017. St. Louis, MO.

Booth, Wayne C. 1974. *The Rhetoric of Irony*. Chicago: The University of Chicago Press.

Booth, Wayne C., Gregory G. Colomb, and Joseph M. Williams. 1995. *The Craft of Research*. Chicago: University of Chicago Press.

Bruffee, Kenneth A. 2007. *A Short Course in Writing: Composition, Collaborative Learning, and Constructive Reading*. 4th ed. New York: Pearson Longman.

Bucholtz, Mary. 1999. "Why Be Normal?: Language and Identity Practices in a Community of Nerd Girls." *Language in Society* 28(2): 203–223. www.jstor.org/stable/4168925.

———. 2001. "The Whiteness of Nerds: Superstandard English and Racial Markedness." *Journal of Linguistic Anthropology* 11(1): 84–100.

Burke, Jim. 2018. *The Six Academic Writing Assignments: Designing the User's Journey*. Portsmouth, NH: Heinemann.

Bush, George W. 2016. *Remarks by George W. Bush at an Interfaith Memorial Service for the Victims of the Dallas Police Shooting at the Morton H. Meyerson Symphony Center in Dallas, Texas, on July 12, 2016.* https://time.com/4403510/george-w-bush-speech-dallas-shooting-memorial-service/.

California State University, Task Force on Expository Reading and Writing. 2013. *Expository Reading and Writing Curriculum.* 2nd ed. Long Beach, CA: California State University.

———. 2019. *Expository Reading and Writing Curriculum.* 3rd ed. Long Beach, CA: California State University.

Charon, Rita. 2004. "Narrative and Medicine." *New England Journal of Medicine* 350(9): 862–864. www.nejm.org/doi/full/10.1056/NEJMp038249.

Christenbury, Leila. 2000. *Making the Journey: Being and Becoming a Teacher of English Language Arts.* 2nd ed. Portsmouth, NH: Heinemann.

Coates, Ta-Nehisi. 2017. *We Were Eight Years in Power: An American Tragedy.* New York: One World.

Corbett, Edward P. J., and Robert J. Connors.1999. *Classical Rhetoric for the Modern Student.* 4th ed. New York: Oxford University Press.

Corbett, Edward P. J., and Rosa A. Eberly. 2000. *The Elements of Reasoning.* 2nd ed. Boston: Allyn and Bacon.

Council of Writing Program Administrators (CWPA), National Council of Teachers of English (NCTE), and National Writing Project (NWP). 2011. *Framework for Success in Postsecondary Writing.* Berkeley, CA: National Writing Project.

Crocco, Margaret, Anne-Lise Halvorsen, Rebecca Jacobsen, and Avner Segall. 2018. "Less Arguing, More Listening: Improving Civility in Classrooms." *Phi Delta Kappan* 99(5). https://kappanonline.org/crocco-less-arguing-listening-improving-civility-classrooms/.

Cross, Tracy L. 2005. "Nerds and Geeks: Society's Evolving Stereotypes of Our Students with Gifts and Talents." *Gifted Child Today* 28(4): 26–27, 65.

Crosswhite, James. 1996. *The Rhetoric of Reason: Writing and the Attractions of Argument.* Madison: University of Wisconsin Press.

———. 2013. *Deep Rhetoric: Philosophy, Reason, Violence, Justice, Wisdom.* Chicago: University of Chicago Press.

Crowley, Sharon, and Debra Hawhee. 2009. *Ancient Rhetorics for Contemporary Students.* 4th ed. New York: Pearson Longman.

Davenport, Christian. 2016. "Elon Musk Says Rocket Explosion Is the Most 'Difficult and Complex' Failure SpaceX Has Ever Had." *The Washington Post,* September 9.

Dean, Deborah. 2008. *Genre Theory: Teaching, Writing, and Being.* Urbana, IL: National Council of Teachers of English.

DiAngelo, Robin. 2018. *White Fragility: Why It's So Hard for White People to Talk About Racism.* Boston: Beacon Press.

Diaz, Junot. 2008. *The Brief Wondrous Life of Oscar Wao.* New York: Riverhead Books.

Downs, Douglas, and Elizabeth Wardle. 2007. "Teaching About Writing, Righting Misconceptions: (Re)envisioning 'First-Year Composition' as 'Introduction to Writing Studies.'" *College Composition and Communication* 58(4): 552–584.

Duffy, John, and Patrick Clauss. 2016. "A Brief Essay on the Troubling Distinction Made in the Common Core State Standards for Writing Between Argument and Persuasion," March 23.

Edlund, John. 2018. "Pathos as Inquiry and Strategy." *Teaching Text Rhetorically* (blog). January 12. https://textrhet.com/2018/01/12/pathos-as-inquiry-and-strategy/.

Elbow, Peter. 1986. *Embracing Contraries: Explorations in Learning and Teaching.* New York: Oxford University Press.

Elon Statement on Writing Transfer. 2013. Accessed October 19, 2019. https://www.centerforengagedlearning.org/elon-statement-on-writing-transfer/.

Emerson, Ralph Waldo. [1841] 1883. "Prudence." *Essays.* Boston: Houghton, Mifflin, and Company.

Engle, Randi A., Diane P. Lam, Xenia S. Meyer, and Sarah E. Nix. 2012, "How Does Expansive Framing Promote Transfer? Several Proposed Explanations and a Research Agenda for

Investigating Them." *Educational Psychologist* 47(3): 215–231. doi:10.1080/00461520.2012 .695678.

Fisher, Douglas, Nancy Frey, and John Hattie. 2016. *Visible Learning for Literacy: Implementing Practices that Work Best to Accelerate Student Learning.* Thousand Oaks, CA: Corwin.

Fletcher, Jennifer. 2015. *Teaching Arguments: Rhetorical Comprehension, Critique, and Response.* Portland, ME: Stenhouse.

Flower, Linda. 1979. "Writer-Based Prose: A Cognitive Basis for Problems in Writing." *College English* 41(1): 19–37. www.jstor.org/stable/376357.

———. 1989. "Rhetorical Problem Solving: Cognition and Professional Writing." In *Writing in the Business Professions*, ed. Myra Kogen. Urbana, Il: National Council of Teachers of English.

———. 2008. *Community Literacy and the Rhetoric of Public Engagement.* Carbondale, IL: Southern Illinois University Press.

Friedrich, Linda, Rachel Bear, and Tom Fox. 2018. "For the Sake of Argument: An Approach to Teaching Evidence-Based Writing." Washington, DC: American Federation of Teachers. https://www .aft.org/ae/spring2018/friedrich_bear_fox.

Gage, John T. 2001. *The Shape of Reason.* New York: Pearson.

Gallagher, Kelly. 2004. *Deeper Reading: Comprehending Challenging Texts.* Portland, ME: Stenhouse.

Garcia, Diana. 2000. "The Girlfriends." In *When Living Was a Labor Camp.* Tucson, AZ: University of Arizona Press.

Gibson, Angela. 2017. "MLA Style Workshop." National Council of Teachers of English Annual Convention, St. Louis, MO.

Goodman, Andy. 2006. *Why Bad Presentations Happen to Good Causes.* Los Angeles, CA: Cause Communications.

Goldberg, Natalie. 2016. *Writing Down the Bones.* Berkeley, CA: Shambhala.

Graff, Gerald. 2003. *Clueless in Academe: How Schooling Obscures the Life of the Mind.* New Haven, CT: Yale University Press.

Graff, Gerald, and Cathy Birkenstein. 2014. *They Say, I Say. The Moves that Matter in Academic Writing, High School Edition.* New York: W. W. Norton.

Graff, Nelson. 2010. "Teaching Rhetorical Analysis to Promote Transfer of Learning: This Strategy Has the Potential to Help Students Develop the Rhetorical Awareness and Meta-Knowledge About Writing That Can Help Them Transfer Their Learning About Writing to New Contexts and Tasks." *Journal of Adolescent and Adult Literacy* 53(5): 376–385.

Grant-Davie, Keith. 1997. "Rhetorical Situations and Their Constituents." *Rhetoric Review* 15(2): 264–279.

Graves, Donald. 1983. *Writing: Teachers and Children at Work.* Portsmouth, NH: Heinemann.

Gunn, Tim, with Kate Moloney. 2007. *A Guide to Quality, Taste and Style.* New York: Abrams Image.

Haddon, Mark. 2003. *The Curious Incident of the Dog in the Night-Time.* New York: Vintage.

Hairston, Maxine. 1986. *Contemporary Composition.* Florence, KY: Cengage.

Hammond, Zaretta. 2015. *Culturally Responsive Teaching and the Brain: Promoting Authentic Engagement and Rigor Among Culturally and Linguistically Diverse Students.* Thousand Oaks, CA: Corwin.

Hart Research Associates. 2015. *Falling Short? College Learning and Career Success.* Washington, DC: Association of American Colleges and Universities.

Haskell, Robert E. 2001. *Transfer of Learning: Cognition, Instruction, and Reasoning.* San Diego, CA: Academic Press.

Hillocks, George, Jr. 1995. *Teaching Writing as Reflective Practice.* New York: Teachers College Press.

Historical Thinking Project. https://historicalthinking.ca/.

Hoggan, James, with Grania Litwin. 2016. *I'm Right and You're an Idiot: The Toxic State of Public Discourse and How to Clean It Up.* Gabriola Island, BC, Canada: New Society Publishers.

Horvath, Liza. 2018. "Trumping Powers." https://www .montereyherald.com/2018/04/14/liza-horvath -senior-advocate-trumping-powers/.

Intersegmental Committee of Academic Senates (ICAS). 2002. *Academic Literacy: A Statement of Competencies Expected of Students Entering California's Public Colleges and Universities*. Sacramento: ICAS.

James, Missy, and Alan P. Merickel. 2005. *Reading Literature and Writing Argument*. 2nd ed. Upper Saddle River, NJ: Pearson.

Johns, Ann M. 2008. "Genre Awareness for the Novice Academic Student: An On-Going Quest." *Language Teaching* 41(2): 237–252.

Kinney, David A. 1993. "From Nerds to Normals: The Recovery of Identity among Adolescents from Middle School to High School." *Sociology of Education* 66(1): 21–40. www.jstor.org/stable/2112783.

Kissel, Brian. 2017. *When Writers Drive the Workshop*. Portsmouth, NH: Stenhouse.

Knisley, Lucy. 2010. "Live Nerd Girls." Comic strip.

Lam, Andrew. 2012. "Waste More, Want More." New America Media, *NewAmericaMedia.org*.

Lane, Barry. 2016. *After the End: Teaching and Learning Creative Revision*. 2nd ed. Portsmouth, NH: Heinemann.

Lindemann, Ericka. 2001. *A Rhetoric for Writing Teachers*. 4th ed. New York: Oxford University Press.

Makau, Josina M., and Debian L. Marty. 2001. *Cooperative Argumentation*. Long Grove, IL: Waveland Press.

———. 2013. *Dialogue and Deliberation*. Long Grove, IL: Waveland Press.

McCann, Thomas M. 2014. *Transforming Talk into Text: Argument Writing, Inquiry, and Discussion, Grades 6–12*. New York: Teachers College Press.

Meyer, Jan H.F and Ray Land. 2006. *Overcoming Barriers to Student Understanding: Threshold Concepts and Troublesome Knowledge*. London: Routledge.

Miller, Carolyn R. 1984. "Genre as Social Action." *Quarterly Journal of Speech* 70(2): 151–167.

Miller, Donalyn. 2014. *Reading in the Wild*. San Francisco: Jossey-Bass.

Minor, Cornelius. 2018. *We Got This: Equity, Access, and the Quest to Be Who Our Students Need Us to Be*. Portsmouth, NH: Heinemann.

———. n.d. Interview for the blog *Literacy Junkie*. https://www.literacyjunkie.com/coffee-break/2018/4/19/coffee-break-part-2-with-cornelius-minor.

Mirra, Nicole. 2018. *Educating for Empathy: Literacy Learning and Civic Engagement*. New York: Teachers College Press.

Modern Language Association. 2016. *MLA Handbook*. 8th ed. New York: MLA.

Moore, Jessie L., and Randall Bass, eds. 2017. *Understanding Writing Transfer: Implications for Transformative Student Learning in Higher Education*. Sterling, VA: Stylus Publishing.

Monterey County Herald. 2018. "Trump." May 8.

National Council of Teachers of English (NCTE). 2016. *Position Statement on Professional Knowledge for the Teaching of Writing*. Urbana, IL: NCTE.

———. 2017. *Resolution on Contemporary Discourse and the English Language Arts Classroom*. Urbana, IL: NCTE. https://ncte.org/statement/contemporary-discourse/.

———. 2018. *Position Statement on Understanding and Teaching Writing: Guiding Principles*. Urbana, IL: NCTE.

National Governors Association (NGA) and the Council of Chief State School Officers (CCSSO). (2010). *Common Core State Standards for English Language Arts & Literacy in History/Social Studies, Science, and Technological Subjects*. Washington, DC: Authors. www.corestandards.org/read-the-standards.

National Research Council (NRC). 2000. *How People Learn: Brain, Mind, Experience, and School*. Washington, DC: National Academy Press.

———. 2012. *Education for Life and Work: Developing Transferrable Knowledge and Skills in the 21st Century*. Washington, DC: National Academy Press.

Newkirk, Thomas. 2009. *Holding on to Good Ideas in a Time of Bad Ones*. Portsmouth, NH: Heinemann.

———. 2014. *Minds Made for Stories*. Portsmouth, NH: Heinemann.

Noden, Harry. 2011. *Image Grammar*. Portsmouth, NH: Heinemann.

Nowacek, Rebecca S. 2011. *Agents of Integration: Understanding Transfer as a Rhetorical Act.* Carbondale: Southern Illinois University Press.

NPR. 2015. "On the Cold, Dead Fringes of The Solar System, Pluto Looks Shockingly Lively." *Morning Edition*, July 17.

Nugent, Benjamin. 2012. "Who's a Nerd, Anyway?" *New York Times Magazine* (online). First published July 29, 2007.

Obama, Barak. 2016. *Remarks by the President at Memorial Service for Fallen Dallas Police Officers.* https://obamawhitehouse.archives.gov/the-press -office/2016/07/12/remarks-president-memorial -service-fallen-dallas-police-officers.

Ong, Walter. 1981. *Fighting for Life: Contest, Sexuality, and Consciousness.* Ithaca, NY: Cornell University Press.

Panetta, Leon E. 2001. "The Price of 'Spin' versus the 'Truth.'" *Monterey County Herald*, September 9.

Perkins, David N. 2014. *Future Wise: Educating Our Children for a Changing World.* San Francisco: Jossey-Bass.

Perkins, David N., and Gavriel Salomon. 2012. "Knowledge to Go: A Motivational and Dispositional View of Transfer." *Educational Psychologist* 47(3): 248–258.

Rabinowitz, Peter J. 1987. *Before Reading: Narrative Conventions and the Politics of Interpretation.* Columbus: Ohio State University Press.

Readence, John E., Thomas W. Bean, and R. Scott Baldwin. 2004. *Content Area Literacy: An Integrated Approach.* Dubuque, IA: Kendall Hunt.

Reid, E. Shelley. 2011. "Ten Ways to Think About Writing: Metaphoric Musings for College Students." In *Writing Spaces: Readings on Writing Series,* vol. 2, ed. by Charles Lowe and Pavel Zemlianski. writingspaces.org/reid--ten-ways-to-think.

Rieke, Richard D., Malcolm O. Sillars, and Tarla Rai Peterson. 2005. *Argumentation and Critical Decision Making.* 6th ed. New York: Pearson.

Rottentberg, Annette T. 1994. *The Structure of Argument.* Boston: Bedford Books of St. Martin's Press.

Savini, Catherine. 2011. "Looking for Trouble: Finding Your Way into a Writing Assignment." *Writing Spaces: Readings on Writing* 2 https://wac.colostate .edu/books/writingspaces2/savini--looking-for -trouble.pdf.

Schick, Kurt, and Laura Schubert. 2014. *So What? The Writer's Argument.* New York: Oxford UP.

Seixas, Peter, and Tom Morton. 2012. *The Big Six: Historical Thinking Concepts.* Toronto: Nelson.

Serwer, Adam. 2009. "What Color Is Your Superhero?" *Washington Post*, March 8.

Simon, Leslie. 2011. *Girl Geeks Unite: Why Fangirls, Bookworms, Indie Chicks, and Other Misfits Will Inherit the Earth.* New York: HarperCollins.

Slomp, David, Rita Leask, Taylor Burke, Kacie Neamtu, Lindsey Hagen, Jaimie Van Ham, Keith Miller, and Sean Dupuis. "Scaffolding for Independence: Writing-as-Problem-Solving Pedagogy." *English Journal* 108.2 (2018): 84–94.

Smith, Michael W., and Jon-Philip Imbrenda. 2018. *Developing Writers of Argument: Tools and Rules That Sharpen Student Reasoning.* Kindle Edition. Thousand Oaks, CA: Corwin.

Soto, Gary. 1999. *Nerdlandia.* New York: Penguin.

Stanford News. 2017. "Loss of Protections for Marine Sanctuaries Could Threaten Oceanic Environment and Fisheries, Stanford Experts Say." November 9. https://news.stanford.edu/2017/11/09/ocean -sanctuaries-face-possible-loss-protection/.

Steele, Claude M. 2011. *Whistling Vivaldi: How Stereotypes Affect Us and What We Can Do.* London: W. W. Norton.

Taba, Hilda. 1967. *Teachers' Handbook for Elementary Social Studies.* Reading, MA: Addison-Wesley.

Takacs, David. 2003. "How Does Your Positionality Impact Your Epistemology?" 19(1): 27–38.

Tannen, Deborah. 1990. *You Just Don't Understand: Women and Men in Conversation.* New York: Ballantine.

———. 1996. "Researching Gender-Related Patterns in Classroom Discourse." *TESOL Quarterly* 30(2): 341–344.

———. 1999. *The Argument Culture: Stopping America's War of Words*. New York: Ballantine.

Toulmin, Stephen E. (1958) 2003. *The Uses of Argument*. Updated ed. New York: Cambridge University Press.

Trut, Lyudmila, and Lee Alan Dugatkin. 2017. "How to Turn a Fox into a Dog: A Bold Experiment Tests Ideas about Domestication." *Scientific American*, May.

VanderMey, Randall et al. 2014. *The College Writer: A Guide to Thinking, Writing, and Researching*. Independence, KY: Cengage.

Wardle, Elizabeth. 2009. "'Mutt Genres' and the Goal of FYC: Can We Help Students Write the Genres of the University?" *College Composition and Communication* (60)4: 765–789.

Warner, John. 2018. *Why They Can't Write: Killing the Five-Paragraph Essay and Other Necessities*. Baltimore, MD: Johns Hopkins University Press.

Weaver, Constance. 1996. *Teaching Grammar in Context*. Portsmouth, NH: Heinemann.

White, Tim et al. 2017. "Assessing the Effectiveness of a Large Marine Protected Area for Reef Shark Conservation." *Biological Conservation* 207: 64–71.

Yancey, Kathleen Blake, Liane Robertson, and Kara Taczak. 2014. *Writing Across Contexts: Transfer, Composition, and Sites of Writing*. Boulder, CO: Utah State University Press.

Yankelovich, Daniel. 1999. *The Magic of Dialogue: Transforming Conflict into Cooperation*. New York: Touchstone.

Young, Vershawn Ashanti. 2019. Call for Proposals for the Conference on College Composition and Communication (CCCC).

———. *Your Average Nigga: Performing Race, Literacy, and Masculinity*. Detroit, MI: Wayne State University Press.

Young, Vershawn Ashanti, Rusty Barret, Y'Shanda Young-Rivera, and Kim Brian Lovejoy. 2018. *Other People's English: Code-Meshing, Code-Switching, and African American Literacy*. Parlor Press.

Zimmerman, Ann. 2010. "Revenge of the Nerds: How Barbie Got Her Geek On." *Wall Street Journal*, April 9.

Zwiers, Jeff, and Marie Crawford. 2011. *Academic Conversations: Classroom Talk that Fosters Critical Thinking and Content Understanding*. Portland, ME: Stenhouse.

Index

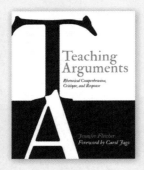
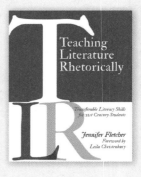